MANAGING CHINA'S MODERNIZATION

PERSPECTIVES ON DIPLOMACY, POLITICS, EDUCATION AND ETHNICITY

MANAGING CHINA'S MODERNIZATION

PERSPECTIVES ON DIPLOMACY, POLITICS, EDUCATION AND ETHNICITY

Edwin Pak-wah Leung

HOMA & SEKEY BOOKS

Paramus, New Jersey

FIRST EDITION

Library of Congress Cataloging-in-Publication Data

Leung, Pak-Wah, 1950-
Managing China's modernization : perspectives on diplomacy, politics, education and ethnicity / Edwin Pak-wah Leung. -- 1st ed.
p. cm.
Includes index.
ISBN 978-1-931907-74-3 (hardcover)
1. China--History--20th century. 2. China--History--19th century. 3. China--Foreign relations--19th century. 4. China--Politics and government--20th century. 5. Chinese students--United States--History. 6. China--Ethnic relations--History--20th century. 7. National characteristics, Chinese. I. Title.
DS774.5.L485 2011
951.05--dc22

2010043793

Published by Homa & Sekey Books
3rd Floor, North Tower
Mack-Cali Center III
140 E. Ridgewood Ave.
Paramus, NJ 07652

Tel: 201-261-8810, 800-870-HOMA
Fax: 201-261-8890; 201-384-6055
Email: info@homabooks.com
Website: www.homabooks.com

Printed in U.S.A.
1 3 5 7 9 10 8 6 4 2

Contents

PART III Education and Modernization

PART IV Ethnicity and National Integration

PART V Book Reviews

About the Author
Dr. Edwin Pak-wah Leung

Dr. Edwin Pak-wah Leung came to the U.S. from Hong Kong for graduate studies in 1972 on scholarships from the University of California and the U.S. State Department. He has been teaching at Seton Hall University since 1978 and is currently Professor and Chairman of the Department of Asian Studies. He has published over 20 books and is an internationally known scholar. He is particularly interested in promoting Asian Studies among American people so that they can have a better understanding of the Asian people and their culture. He has been serving as an intellectual bridge between the Chinese Americans and the mainstream Americans, as well as between China and America, through his public lectures and writings. He travels widely in America and the world to lecture. He is an international and cultural ambassador among peoples.

For over three decades, Dr. Leung has been very active in serving the Asian American communities in New Jersey and the Greater New York areas. He served as President of the American Chinese Professionals Association, President of the U.S.-China Foundation for Medical Science and Technology, Founding Chair of the New Jersey Chinese Cultural Studies Foundation, President of the Livingston Chinese Association, Principal of the Livingston Chinese School, President of the New Jersey Alliance for Learning and Preserving the History of World War II in Asia, and had been on the planning committee for the New Jersey state-wide Chinese Festival. Currently, he is serving for the second time as Chair of the New Jersey Chinese Cultural Studies Foundation.

Dr. Leung's services are unique because he has been able to utilize his professional knowledge and ability to better serve the Asian American communities. For example, as Co-director of the Bilingual Education Teacher Training Program at Seton Hall University, he was able to secure federal funding to train a large number of Asian American bilingual teachers for local school districts in an effort to help educate new immigrant students from Asia. He has also recently created a graduate program to train Chinese language teachers for the American schools.

Professor Leung has climbed the academic ladder with a very impressive record of accomplishments. Appointed as Assistant Professor by Seton Hall University at the age of 27, he was promoted to Associate Professor with tenure in 1984 with unanimous approval by various internal and external evaluation committees. In 1992, he was promoted to Full Professor, again with unanimous approvals by all committees involved, at a relatively young age of 41. He has published over 20 books (one of which won the CHOICE Outstanding Academic Book in 1992), 70 academic articles, and over 200 other articles. He has also presented papers at numerous academic and public meetings.

Professor Leung is also an internationally known scholar. He has had professional affiliations with the following academic institutions: Princeton University, Columbia University, University of California at Berkeley and Los Angeles, University of Michigan,

University of Hong Kong, The Chinese University of Hong Kong, The Hong Kong Polytechnic University, Wuhan University, Zhejiang University, Peking University, and University of Tokyo. While excelling in his professional career, Dr. Leung has never forgotten about his services to the Asian American communities. He has served with a deep sense of commitment and dedication.

Dr. Leung has done so much in terms of his professional achievements, as well as his services to the Asian American and global communities. He is not only devoted but also persistent, and has been honored for his contributions by many organizations. For example, he received the Asian American Achievement Award (AAAA) from the New Jersey state-wide Asian American Ethnic Council (1996), and the Asian American Leadership Award from Bergen Community College (2001). He also received awards from: The U.S.-China Foundation for Medical Science and Technology (1998); Livingston Chinese School (1999); American Chinese Professionals Association (1999 & 2004); New Jersey Chinese Cultural Studies Foundation (2000); Yale University (2001); and Seton Hall University (1989, 1994, 1999, 2004). In 2007, he was awarded the nationally prestigious Ellis Island Medal of Honor—the same award that six U.S. Presidents have also received.

Laudation for Professor Edwin Pak-wah Leung Chairman, Department of Asian Studies Seton Hall University

Pronounced in South Orange, New Jersey
on
November 7, 2003
and
Delivered by Dr. Molly Smith,
Dean of College of Arts and Sciences

The Department of Asian Studies at Seton Hall University was established to enhance understandings between the West and the East and to make Asian cultures, histories, languages, and politics the objects of scholarly reflection. Today, too, faculty and friends of the Department are convinced that these goals are of ever-increasing importance as Asian nations and territories expand their cultural and political influence and economic might internationally.

This evening's gathering of friends and junior and senior colleagues to honor Edwin Pak-wah Leung during his twenty-fifth anniversary year at Seton Hall University is only in small part because he is the Chairman of the Department of Asian Studies at an important juncture in its forty-five year history. Primarily, we celebrate this milestone anniversary because Professor Leung is a scholar of international standing and an eminent representative of the Seton Hall community who has devoted his active professional life to the study of Asia, to nurturing generations of students of the field, and to the promotion of good will between Western and Asian peoples.

Professor Leung was born in Hong Kong in 1950, and was graduated from The Chinese University of Hong Kong in 1972. In 1974, he received an MA degree from the University of California, Santa Barbara, and in 1978, he completed his doctorate in History, also at the University of California. He was appointed to the position of Assistant Professor at Seton Hall University in 1978, received his appointment to Associate Professor with tenure in 1984, and was promoted to Full Professor in 1992. In 2003, he was elected Chairman of the Department of Asian Studies.

Professor Leung, who directs the Department of Asian Studies Graduate Program, has taught a wide breadth of courses, including Asian Politics, Contemporary Chinese Politics, China in World Affairs, Contemporary China, China and the United States, the History of Modern Asia, American Foreign Policy in Asia, and International Politics in the Far East. His published works during the 1980s and 1990s include six authored texts and five edited and co-edited books, covering a wide range of topics, from practical information about studying in American universities and scholarship and financial aid for students, to international business and trade, edited papers on China's war with Japan, and modern transitions in Chinese diplomacy. His edited volume, *Historical Dictionary of Revolutionary China, 1839-1976*, won one of the CHOICE awards for an Outstanding Academic Book of 1992. Two recent publications include an authored volume, *Historical Dictionary of the Chinese Civil War,* and an edited work, *Political Leaders of Modern China.*

Professor Leung has been honored with numerous awards. Among them are seven Faculty Merit Awards at Seton Hall and the 1996 Outstanding Professional Achievement Award of the New Jersey Asian American Ethnic Council. His services to regional Asian American communities and his profound dedication to helping their members are seemingly inexhaustible and widely acknowledged. His receipt of one of the outstanding Asian Leadership Awards from Bergen Community College in 2001 is further evidence of the deep appreciation felt in the broad community for his selfless service to others.

During the short time since his election as Chairman of the Department of Asian Studies, Professor Leung has dedicated himself to enhancing undergraduate and graduate programs and to mapping the Department's way forward. Meanwhile, his contributions to important organizations beyond Seton Hall have not diminished. He currently is assisting a division of the State of New Jersey to evaluate Asia-centered academic programs in the public school system.

Professor Leung's published works, conference participation, public presentations, and service in important capacities at Seton Hall and beyond have made a valued contribution to the advancement of better understandings between peoples of Western and Eastern cultures. As an academician, Department Chairman, and member of the Asian-American community, his mission continues, focused on building enduring bridges between the Department of Asian Studies and the wider Seton Hall community, among junior and senior scholars of Asian Studies internationally, among Americans of varying cultures and ethnicities, and among Pacific rim nations.

For all these reasons, we join together this evening to honor Professor Edwin Pak-wah Leung and to celebrate the silver anniversary of his faculty membership and his many important contributions to Seton Hall University.

Preface

As China is re-emerging to world-power status in the 21st century after over a century of foreign aggressions and internal struggles, the study of its modern history is becoming more and more important and necessary in helping us to better understand China's paths to modernization. Such an understanding in turn would help to shed light on where China is heading in the future. This book attempts to provide such perspectives by exploring different aspects of modern China's developmental experience. Collectively, these perspectives will enable the readers of this book to gain a more comprehensive and in-depth understanding of China today.

This book is divided into the following four themes: (1) diplomacy and territorial integrity; (2) politics and leadership; (3) education and modernization; and (4) ethnicity and national integration. Each of these themes deals with an important aspect regarding China's management of its modernization. The pieces included in this book are selected from many of my academic articles written over the span of three decades. Research was conducted off and on in many countries, particularly in China (including Taiwan and Hong Kong), Japan, and the United States.

Since much of the research was carried out over a three-decade period, I am therefore naturally indebted to many individuals who have provided much advice and support during my research process. To Professors Immanuel C.Y. Hsu, Alexander De-Conde, Kwang-ching Liu, Teh-chao Wang, Ting-i Lee who served as my academic mentors. To Professors Barry B. Blakeley, John Young, Frank Podgorski, and Gilbert Mattos who were my inspiring colleagues at Seton Hall University in New Jersey. To my mother Lee Shui, wife Vera, and son Immanuel who have given me their unfailing patience, love, and support. And of course to all my students over the years for their support of me in my teaching. To all of them I want to express my heartfelt appreciation. Needless to say, any shortcomings of the book are entirely mine.

Edwin Pak-wah Leung, Ph.D.
Professor and Chairman
Department of Asian Studies
Seton Hall University,
South Orange, New Jersey
U.S.A.
May 4, 2010

PART I

DIPLOMACY AND TERRITORIAL INTEGRITY

1

The Quasi-War in East Asia: Japan's Expedition to Taiwan, 1874

The year 1868 witnessed Meiji Japan embarking upon the road to modernization. This island country was formally opened by the United States in 1854. By the time of the Meiji Restoration, it had not only ended the Tokugawa feudal society that had existed for more than two and a half centuries, but also unleashed the forces that quickly transformed Japan into a modern society.

The Restoration brought to power a dozen or two young reformers who, as quickly as their power mounted, swept away much of the feudal structure, not only political, but also social and economic. Upon seizing power, the new regime committed itself on the one hand to restoring the ancient imperial political institutions and, on the other hand, to establishing a modern administration. The first step was the centralization of political authority.

The news of the Restoration was brought to Ryukyu through the Satsuma-han, which had just returned its feudal territorial rights, including the surrender of suzerainty over the Ryukyu Islands by its daimyo, to Emperor Meiji. In 1872, the Meiji government, although substituting the prefectures *(ken)* for the *han* jurisdictions in Japan proper, abolished the Chuzan Kingdom and established a special Ryukyu-han under the jurisdiction of the Foreign Ministry *(Gaimusho)*.[1]

Taking advantage of the official visit of Ryukyuan Prince Ie (Shang Chien) and Ginowan Oyakata (Hsiang Yu-hang) to Japan in September 1872, Emperor Meiji issued an edict proclaiming the incorporation of the former kingdom of Ryukyu into Japan as an integral part of the empire:

> We have here succeeded to the Imperial Throne of a line unbroken for ages eternal, and now reign over all the land. Ryukyu, situated to the south, has the same race, habits and language, and has always been loyal to Satsuma. We appreciate this loyalty, here raise you to the peerage and appoint you king of Ryukyu-han. You, Sho Tai, take responsibility in the administration of *han,* and assist us eternally.[2]

Subsequently, the king of the Chuzan Kingdom, Sho Tai, was given the symbolic title of a peer *(kazoku)* in the Japanese empire. Although it was not announced to the Chinese, Japan had unilaterally incorporated the Ryukyu Islands into the empire in October of 1872. At the same time, to forestall foreign objections, Japan notified the governments of the United States, France, and the Netherlands that the treaties they had concluded with the kingdom of Ryukyu would henceforth be honored by the government of Japan.[3]

But the odd existence of a feudal domain within the Meiji modern empire immediately invited criticism from many quarters of Japanese society against this governmental decision. Newspapers and journals in the capital, for example, found in the Ryukyu problem a new issue with which to harass and embarrass the administration. They called into question the government's right to reprimand the Ryukyuans and asked the government to produce a treaty or formal agreement by which Ryukyu was bound to accept Tokyo's demands. The *Hochi Shimbun,* on the other hand, advised the government to abandon the Ryukyu Islands entirely.[4]

The Meiji government, however, had determined to integrate Ryukyu into the empire, despite its awareness of China's suzerainty over the tributary states. That the jurisdiction of the Ryukyu domain was placed under the Foreign Ministry was a clear indication of the Japanese intention to solve Ryukyu's dual-subordination problem with China through diplomatic means. The Japanese government first would challenge the Chinese suzerainty in Ryukyu and then legitimate its claim by stating that it had already exercised sovereignty over Ryukyu. Only by taking these steps could Japan claim that the Ryukyuan people were indisputably Japanese subjects. The Formosan incident, which will be discussed in the following pages, provided an opportunity for the Japanese to challenge the deteriorating Manchu Confucian universal empire.

I. The Sino-Japanese Friendship Treaty of 1871

Official Sino-Japanese relations had been held in abeyance for the three hundred years preceding 1871. For a time during the Ming period Japan had also paid tribute to China, when the Japanese shogun, Ashikaga Yoshimitsu, accepted the tributary status in order to enrich his coffers from trade. However, nationalistic Japanese statesmen found such relations humiliating, and discontinued the practice after the middle of the sixteenth century, thus ending official contact with the mainland.

The year 1871 marked a new change in Sino-Japanese diplomatic relations. Soon after the newly created Japanese Foreign Ministry came into being in 1870, Yanagihara Sakimitsu was sent by his government to Peking to seek a commercial treaty similar to China's treaties with Western nations. He was instructed, in particular, to secure the most-favored-nation clause in the treaty. Although his mission was viewed by the ultra-conservative elements in the Chinese government as opportunistic and ill-timed, it was warmly received by the more pragmatic and progressive leaders, like Li Hung-chang, newly appointed governor-general of Chihli and superintendent of trade of the Northern Ports. Li felt that:

> Japan, which was not a dependency of China, was totally different from Korea, Ryukyu, and Annam. That she had come to request trade without first seeking support from any Western power showed her independence and good will. If China refused her this time, her friendship would be lost and she might even seek Western intervention on her behalf, in which case it would be difficult for China to refuse again. An antagonized Japan could be an even greater source of trouble than the Western nations because of her geographical proximity. It was therefore in China's interest to treat Japan on a friendly and equal basis and send commissioners to Japan who could look after the Chinese there, watch the movements of the Japanese government, and cultivate harmonious relations between the two states.[5]

Li Hung-chang toyed with the idea of a possible Sino-Japanese 'alliance' in the wake of Western encroachments in Asia. His suggestion to 'cultivate harmonious relations' with China's ex-tributary state was not made out of a love for Japan, but out of a cold realization of the need to strengthen China's position in order to ward off the Western threat.[6] Li was also aware that 'an antagonized Japan could be an even greater source of trouble than the Western nations because of her geographical proximity!'[7]

With this attitude in mind, the Yanagihara mission was well received. In fact, to show Chinese good will, a Sino-Japanese treaty with eighteen articles and a trade regulation of thirty-three articles were finally signed in 1871 by Li and Yanagihara's successor, Date Munenari. Among other things, the treaty provided for the exchange of envoys and counsels and the rendering of good-offices to each other should a third party intimidate or threaten either of the contracting parties.

Article I of the Treaty was an important provision: 'In all that regards the territorial possessions of either country the two governments shall treat each other with proper courtesy, without the slightest infringement or encroachment on the other side.'[8] China took it for granted that the term 'territorial possessions' was meant to include those tributary states around China's frontiers. But this Chinese assumption was not to be shared by the Japanese. This ambiguity was not realized until the controversies over Taiwan and Ryukyu arose in 1873 and over Korea in 1876.

By careful negotiation, however, Li Hung-chang purposely excluded the most-favored-nation clause in the Treaty and prohibited sword-carrying by the Japanese in the Chinese ports. Due to the *Wako* (Japanese pirate) disturbances along the China coast in the sixteenth-century, he thought it wise to prohibit the stay of the Japanese ex-*samurai* in China.

Sword-carrying had for long been a custom of the Japanese *samurai* warriors. The modernization of Japan, nonetheless, had its disruptive influences on this vested-interest group. Uprooted by the transformation, they demanded new outlets for their energies. Many of them had indeed played an important and constructive role in the building of the new Japan. Others, however, trying to find satisfaction in the ventures of foreign expansion, became modern Japan's advocates of an aggressive expansionist policy.

The conquest of Korea, for instance, was first conceived and advocated by a group of *samurai* under the leadership of Saigo Takamori, the leader of the *samurai* of Satsuma where feudal forces had been strongest and therefore social discontent most acute. In 1872, under his promotion, the idea of the conquest of Korea *(Seikan-ron)* had gained substantial support among government leaders. However, in 1873, due to a change of leadership, this plan failed to draw continued governmental support. This led not only to the resignation from office of expansion-minded officials like Saigo and Soejima Taneomi, but also to local disturbances such as the one in the Saga region.[9] To consolidate its hold, as well as to pacify its more assertive elements, the Japanese government could not but shift its attention once again toward foreign horizons. It was then that Taiwan entered the picture.

II. The Ryukyu Shipwreck Incident in 1871

Due to the exclusion of Tokyo's much desired most-favored-nation clause, the Japanese government was not satisfied with the initial arrangement of the 1871 Treaty. As a result, Date Munenari, signer of the Treaty, was immediately expelled from the government. Yanagihara was ordered to try again to revise the treaty. His second mission was unsuccessful and his attitude adversely affected the formerly sympathetic Li Hung-chang. While making no progress in his official mission, Yanagihara's stay in China was quite fruitful on another score. Besides his close observation of the Chinese political situation, he gained information that proved to be of the utmost importance to future Sino-Japanese relations. Reading through the *Peking Gazette* of May 11, 1872, he learned from Fukien Governor-General Ho Ching's memorial of the fate of two groups of Ryukyuan people who had been shipwrecked on the coast of Taiwan during the previous winter. He lost no time in reporting this incident to his government from Tientsin on May 19.[10]

The Ryukyu shipwreck incident of 1871 has been a subject of much study among scholars: Tabohashi Kiyoshi, Yamanaka Sho, Kinjo Seitoku, Hanabusa Nagamichi, Shozi Mantaro, Hsu Shih-chien, Sophia Yen, among others.'[11] These scholars agree that the Japanese government sent an expeditionary force to Taiwan in 1874 to punish the aborigines who had killed fifty-four shipwrecked Ryukyuans in 1871. Consequently, Japan was able to claim retroactively that the Ryukyuan castaways were Japanese subjects. The rationale behind this maneuver hinged upon international law which provides the right of a sovereign government to protect its nationals.

While most of these scholars have stressed the Japanese design to lay sovereign claim over Ryukyu, few have sufficiently dealt with the problem of legality in defining Ryukyu's political status in the 1874 Treaty of settlement between China and Japan. Furthermore, none of them have observed that the Japanese Formosan expedition was not mono-causal; that is, besides the Ryukyuans, there were other victims of Japanese citizenship who had also been maltreated by Taiwan aborigines before 1874. Yet, this incident became the immediate factor leading to the Meiji government's decision for retaliation. The entire episode, therefore, needs reinvestigation.

To begin with, it should be noted that the accidental wrecking of Ryukyuan ships on Chinese shores was a recurring incident. Table 1 gives us a general idea of the number of such incidents.[12] It reveals that the total number of Ryukyu ships wrecked along the Chinese coast from 1701 to 1876 numbered 278. On Taiwanese shores in particular, the number reached more than fifty. Clearly, the 1871 Ryukyuan shipwreck was but one among many similar incidents. Most of the time, the Chinese government provided the shipwrecked victims with liberal relief. The massacre of shipwrecked victims by Taiwan aborigines had happened before, but Ryukyu had never made any complaints.[13]

In late 1871, two groups of Ryukyuan people were shipwrecked on the coast of Taiwan. One group, consisting of forty-six crew members, had landed on the southeastern coast of Taiwan where their ship was hit by strong winds and sunk. They were given food and clothing and conducted, first of all, to the Feng-shan magistrate's office and subsequently to Taiwan-fu for repatriation.

TABLE 1

Ryukyuan Ships Wrecked on Chinese Shores, 1701-1876

Place of Wreckage	Number of Ships
Chekiang coast	114
Taiwan coast	53
Fukien coast	38
Kiangsu coast	31
Shangtung coast	11
Kwangtung coast	10
Fengt'ien (Manchuria) coast	1
Korea	7
Annam (Vietnam)	2
Luzon	2
unknown	9
Total	**278**

Around the same time, another group with sixty-nine crew members, ran into a violent storm to the north of the island. Three members of the crew were drowned, while the remaining sixty-six members were able to make shore on December 18, 1871. Unfortunately, however, the luckless sailors landed in an area populated by the Vojyan (or *Mulan, Botan)* and Kusukus *(Kao-shih-fu)* tribes of the Taiwan aborigines. After capturing their sailors, the head-hunters subjected them to a shocking slaughter.[14] Of the sixty-six crew members, fifty-four were killed, while the remaining twelve managed to take refuge in the house of a local Chinese settler named Yang Yu-wang. With his help they succeeded in escaping from the slaughter. On January 1, 1872, they were escorted to the Magistrate's office in Fengshan. Two survivors, Shang Tse-fu and Chung Te-hsiu, wrote on the same day to Taiwan-tao Hsia Hsien-lun, expressing their thanks to Yang Yu-wang and asking the Chinese official to send them to Foochow for eventual return to Ryukyu.[15] In gratitude for the rescue of his people, Sho Tai sent money to reward the Chinese officials. He also sent an official to investigate the incident, and the matter seemed to have been closed.[16]

Upon receiving the report of these events from Taiwan, officials in Fukien and in Peking expressed their wish for a thorough investigation into the matter so as to 'warn the violent and pacify the docile.' Unaware of its possible repercussions, however, no other action was taken and the whole matter was soon buried in the files of the Chinese government.[17]

III. Japan's Response and Charles W. LeGendre's Involvement

The news concerning the massacre of the Ryukyu sailors must have fired the imagination of the Japanese government. At a time when a new outlet was needed to satisfy the expansionist elements in Japan, the incident of the Ryukyu sailors was undoubtedly a god-sent opportunity. From the Japanese point of view, the rather vague and anomalous political status of the Ryukyu Islands, provided an exploitable opportunity. Thus early in 1872, upon learning of the incident, the officials in Kagoshima, capital of the former Satsuma-han, immediately pleaded with the Japanese government for formal action. This plea was soon echoed by the voices of many expansion-minded officials, like Saigo Takamori and Soejima Taneomi, in the central government.

As mentioned earlier, Ryukyu had never made any complaints over the maltreatment of her people by the Taiwan aborigines. In view of this fact, one is inclined to exercise some skepticism as to the reasons why Yanagihara Sakimitsu told the Tsungli Yamen in 1874 that the Ryukyuan government had submitted a petition to subdue the Formosan savages and that Japan's subsequent response to sending troops to Taiwan was made in compliance with Ryukyu's petition.[18] It is probably due to this claim of Japan that many Western-language accounts report that the Ryukyuan king, on learning of the massacre of his people by the Taiwan aborigines, petitioned Tokyo for protection, thus voluntarily placing his kingdom 'under the wing [of Japan].'[19]

Consideration of the Chinese statements on the shipwrecked Ryukyuans fosters doubt as to whether this singular action by the Ryukyuan government actually occurred. A Japanese official document entitled 'Ryukyu shishin raicho ni kansuru kogai josho' (A memorandum summarizing the background of the presence of the Ryukyuan ministers in court (in 1872)) helps answer the above question.[20] This record reveals that the so-called petition from Ryukyu is actually non-existent—the report of the 1871 Formosa shipwreck incident to the Japanese government was not made by the king of Ryukyu, but by the Japanese representatives in the Ryukyuan capital of Shuri.

In January 1872, Japan sent two officials, Ijichi Sadaka and Narahara Kogoro, from the Kagoshima Prefecture (formally the Satsuma-han) to Shuri to discuss the adjustment of administrative relations between the Ryukyu court and the new Meiji government. In August of the preceding year, a new system of prefectures replaced the feudal divisions of Japan. Since Ryukyu was originally subordinate to Satsuma-han, arrangements had to be made to meet the new situation.[21]

While discussions between the Japanese and the Ryukyuan officials were held, the twelve survivors of the 1871 Formosa incident returned to Naha in June. Upon learning of the incident, the two Japanese representatives summoned two of the survivors, who were local officials in the Miyako Island, inquired about the case, and made a detailed report.[22] On July 14, Ijichi and Narahara returned to Kagoshima and submitted to Oyama Tsunayoshi, governor of the Kagoshima Prefecture, an account of their negotiations with the Ryukyu government as well as the Formosa incident. Apparently considering the latter a very important matter, Oyama soon sent Ijichi to Tokyo to present his recommendation on how to handle the Formosa case. Ijichi left Kagoshima on July 28, and arrived at Tokyo on August 12. He personally informed the Foreign Ministry about the Formosa incident and Governor Oyama's recommendation. According to the official *Nihon gaiko bunsho* (Diplomatic documents of Japan) and the *Ryukyu shobun* (The Disposition of Ryukyu), Oyama recommended a punitive expedition to Taiwan, and his recommendation was supported by Saigo Takamori, Itagaki Taisuke, Soejima Taneomi, and other Japanese leaders.[23]

Extant records show that Ryukyu never submitted a formal request to Tokyo for Japanese military protection. The *Narahara Kogoro shokan* (letters of Narahara Kogoro) contains a rare document which shows that Tsuhako Oyakata, a Ryukyuan noble and envoy in Tokyo, informed the Japanese government of the 1871 shipwreck incident.[24] In this letter to Home Minister Okubo Toshimichi, the Ryukyuan representative neither made any complaints over the maltreatment of his people by the Taiwan aborigines, not did he submit an official petition to Japan for military help to redress the shipwrecked Ryukyuan. Furthermore, the letter was written in July 1874 (no specific day provided), long after the Japanese invasion of Taiwan had taken place (in April 1874).

The foregoing details indicate that the 1871 incident was brought to the attention of the Japanese government entirely by the Kagoshima officials and Yanagihara. The Japanese Formosan expedition, in this sense, was a singular action undertaken by the Japanese themselves; it was not launched at the request of the Ryukyuans.

In late 1872, when Japan notified the governments of the United States, France, and the Netherlands that jurisdiction of the Ryukyu kingdom had been transferred to the Japanese Foreign Ministry, the United States State Department reacted sensitively. The American minister in Tokyo, Charles E. De Long, on October

22 asked the foreign minister of Japan about the status of the American *compact* concluded by Commodore Perry with Ryukyu in 1854.[25] Soejima Taneomi assured De Long that the United States need not worry: Japan would observe this *compact.*[26] De Long went further with his inquiries and sought confirmation of the news concerning the wrecking of a Ryukyu junk and the murder of its crew on the Formosan coast.[27] Soejima confirmed the news, but in turn wanted information about the abortive American expedition which had been undertaken by Rear Admiral H. H. Bell and General Charles W. LeGendre in the summer of 1867, shortly after the American bark, *Rover,* was wrecked off the coast of Taiwan and her American crew massacred by the aborigines of the island. Japan looked to the American expedition as a precedent justifying a punitive expedition of her own against Taiwan.[28]

LeGendre was brought to the attention of Soejima by De Long who informed the Japanese government of LeGendre's qualifications and of the values of Formosa.[29] Moreover, De Long suggested the advisability of an immediate retaliatory expedition and direct negotiations with the aborigines.

LeGendre lost no time in preparing his memorandums on Formosa and outlining strategies for future negotiations with the Chinese. He particularly stressed the necessity for Japan to possess the land [Taiwan] without leaving it in Westerners' hands.' He urged that the Chinese government would find it more 'convenient' to have a country like Japan there rather than a Western power, which he assumed would be inevitable if Japan should overlook this opportunity. However, at times he referred to the aboriginal part of Formosa, and on other occasions, to the entire island.[30] He was an outspoken advocate of Japanese expansion to prevent the British and Russians from threatening Japan's position in Asia. Certainly the Formosa question and the proper recognition of Japan's claims to sovereignty in the Ryukyu Islands had become to him, and others, an 'affair of honor' that had to be resolved.[31]

LeGendre was offered the position of counsellor to the proposed mission (led by Soejima himself) to China, with the prospect of further advancement in the Japanese service; and he accepted this offer, resigning as American consul on December 12, 1872.[32] The employment of LeGendre as an advisor to the Japanese was condemned by American Secretary of State Hamilton Fish and the Grant administration, as contrary to American law and practice.[33] The American minister in Peking, Frederick F. Low, felt that the employment of LeGendre by the Japanese was unfortunate and a bad precedent.

On December 12—the same day LeGendre resigned his American office—Emperor Meiji issued an edict announcing the appointment of Soejima as Minister Plenipotentiary and Ambassador Extraordinary to China. The alleged purpose was to exchange the ratifications of the 1871 treaty, as well as to offer congratulations to the Chinese Emperor T'ung-chih upon his *de facto* accession to the throne and his marriage.[34] But according to LeGendre, a third purpose of the mission was to negotiate the Formosa–Ryukyu situation.[35] LeGendre tutored the Japanese officials for several months, preparing them for the mission. It was not until March 11, 1873, that Soejima, together with Yanagihara, Interpreter Tei Ei-nei (or Cheng Yung-ning in Chinese, a descendant of the Ming loyalist Koxinga), and LeGendre finally left Yokohama for China.[36]

IV. Soejima Taneomi's Mission to China, 1873

The mission reached Tientsin on April 20 and was received by Li Hung-chang four days later. At this time there was a strong feeling of friendship between China and Japan, augmented by a Japanese decision to return Chinese coolies who had been liberated from a Peruvian ship that had taken shelter in Japanese waters.[37] Under the spirit of cordiality, the instruments of ratification were subsequently exchanged on April 30. During his brief stay in Tientsin, Soejima and Li Hung-chang also conferred on a wide range of topics of joint concern, but the problem of Taiwan-Ryukyu was cautiously avoided by Soejima. According to one historian, the Japanese foreign minister 'clearly wished to avoid opening negotiations [with Chinese officials] on the Ryukyu-Formosa issue.' Although he considered Japanese possession of the Ryukyu Islands non-negotiable, he was 'fully aware that the Chinese still laid claims to suzerainty over that island kingdom.'[38]

On June 21, Soejima sent Yanagihara and Tei Ei-nei to the Tsungli Yamen to discuss the Formosa-Ryukyu as well as the Korea issues. By doing so, he was able to avoid getting personally involved. Mao Ch'an-hsi and Tung Hsun were the two Yamen ministers to receive Yanagihara, and this brief interview was the only official exchange of views on these issues that Soejima deemed so important. The interview is all the more significant and controversial because, on the basis of assurances that Soejima said were given by the Chinese in this interview, the Japanese actually launched a punitive expedition against aboriginal Formosa in April 1874. In addition, when that action took place, the Chinese government flatly denied that it either had been informed of, or had given its consent to, any Japanese military operations on Formosa. The contradiction between Soejima's claims and the Chinese counterclaims, and the resultant controversy, have provoked considerable historical commentary.

As far as the Ryukyu problem was concerned, the Yanagihara-Yamen interview on June 21 has remained a matter of dispute, partly because the Tsungli Yamen ministers apparently failed to make a written record of the discussion.[39] In the absence of official Chinese records, it is necessary to rely on Japanese sources alone, particularly those by Soejima himself and Interpreter Tei Eineі's *Soejima taishi teki Shin gairyaku* (A summary of Ambassador Soejima's Mission to Ch'ing China) (1875).[40]

The interview began with Yanagihara making a brief inquiry about the status of Korea and Macao. He then brought up the Formosa-Ryukyu issue, stating that after the Chinese had taken over Formosa from the Dutch, they ruled only half of the island and that the ungoverned aboriginal inhabitants of the eastern side (actually the southeastern section) had murdered 'Japanese subjects' in the winter of 1871.[41]

The Yamen ministers replied that they had heard only of a massacre of Ryukyuans, not of Japanese, and quickly noted that Ryukyu was under Chinese suzerainty. According to Mao and Tung, Ryukyu had been a tributary state to the Middle Kingdom for hundreds of years, and the relationship between the two had been a cordial one. They added that the governor-general of Fukien, Ho Ching, had rescued the survivors of the massacre and returned them safely to Ryukyu.

Yanagihara countered that Ryukyu had always belonged to Japan, that there was not a single person on the islands who was not a Japanese subject, and that these people were entitled to the protection of the Japanese government. He then asked why the Chinese had done nothing to punish the guilty aborigines or to govern them. The Chinese replied that there were two kinds of aborigines on Taiwan: those who were governed by the local Chinese, and those 'raw barbarians' who were beyond Chinese cultural influence. The Chinese government had not chastised these aborigines 'because they were beyond the reach of our [the Chinese] government and customs.' They added, however, that they had received an official report on the incident from the governor-general of Fukien who had rescued the Ryukyuan survivors, and that they would answer Yanagihara's query after consulting that report.

Yanagihara quickly rejected the suggestion of further negotiations, stating that he was already familiar with the report, which had been published in the *Peking Gazette*, and that Soejima was hastily preparing for his departure from Peking and could not wait for any further response. He then terminated the discussion, thus ending the first Sino-Japanese debate over the political status of the Ryukyu Islands.

In his memoir, Soejima recorded that he had satisfactorily ascertained that the Chinese government had not opposed Japan's claims to sovereignty over the Ryukyu Islands, disclaimed any jurisdiction over aboriginal Formosa and had not opposed—or, in effect, had consented to—Japan's sending an expedition against the aborigines.[42] These claims were extremely tenuous, if not completely unfounded, for a careful reading of the Yanagihara-Yamen discussion reveals that both parties laid claim to the Ryukyu Islands and that the Chinese did not consent to a Japanese military operation against the Formosan aborigines. Nonetheless, Soejima was apparently persuaded, and would later insist, that he had, on the basis of this interview, established adequate grounds for Japan's freedom of action in these areas.

The question why Soejima had failed to obtain a written agreement explicitly setting forth China's sanction for a Japanese expedition to Formosa would later be raised by other Japanese leaders as well as historians. Certainly, Soejima was an astute diplomat and knew that, for matters as important as these, verbal assurances—even if clearly made—could hardly be accepted as reliable guarantees.[43]

But, in fact, it would scarcely have been possible for Soejima to secure such a written agreement. Soejima clearly wished to avoid opening formal negotiations on the Formosa-Ryukyu issue. As he later explained in his memoir: 'On the issue of China's sovereignty over aboriginal Formosa, I knew that, if I were to conduct formal negotiations, it would take several years to reach an agreement, because of the usual tergiversation of Chinese officials.[44] This explanation is valid only in a limited sense; it would have been more accurate to say that the Chinese would never have given formal recognition to Japan's claims to sovereignty over Ryukyu. This was an essential premise to Soejima's argument for Japan's right to launch an expedition against the Formosan aborigines.

Therefore, it was the prospect of interminable and inconclusive debate on this Ryukyu question, as well as on the jurisdiction of China over the aboriginal Formosa, that accounts for Soejima's avoidance of open negotiations and for his failure to obtain, or even attempt to obtain, a formal written agreement from the Chinese.

V. The Oda Shipwreck Incident and the Formosan Expedition

In 1874, Japan decided to send an expeditionary force to Taiwan to chastise the aborigines. Several factors contributed to this action, but the immediate factor was the Oda shipwreck incident of 1873. The Meiji government did not send its troops to Taiwan *solely* to redress the Ryukyuan grievances. A careful reading of the *Nihon gaiko bunsho: Meiji nenkan tsuiho* (Diplomatic Documents of Japan: Supplements to the Meiji period), and many other official and unofficial documents, confirms this view.[45] A book published by the Japanese government in 1893, shortly before the outbreak of the

Sino-Japanese war of 1894-95, contains an interesting report of the Formosan expedition:

> In the winter of 1872 [*sic*], some inhabitants of Loochoo [Ryukyu] were cast away on the eastern coast of Formosa, and murdered by the natives, and in the following year some shipwrecked sailors from the province of Bitchu [Oda] experienced the same fate. Soyeshima Taneomi was sent by the Government as Plenipotentiary to Peking to complain these outrages against Japanese subjects, but the Chinese government made no satisfactory reply and declined to acknowledge their responsibility for the acts of the natives of Formosa. The Japanese Government was thus compelled to take into its own hands the task of exacting reparation. In April 1874, Lieutenant-General Saigo Tsugumichi was appointed to the command of a punitory expedition to Formosa.[46]

From this official description, it is plain that the Japanese government decided to send troops to Taiwan not only to protect the Ryukyuans, but also to redress some Japanese subjects who had been shipwrecked on the Taiwan coast and were maltreated by the aborigines there.

On March 8, 1873, sometime before the Japanese cabinet crisis over the *Seikan-ron,* a Japanese ship from Oda Province of the Bitchu Prefecture (it was incorporated into the Okayama Prefecture on December 10, 1875)[47] was cast ashore on Taiwan and was attacked by the aborigines on the eastern coast. Four Japanese subjects (Sato Rihachi and others) had their property plundered and barely escaped alive after almost indescribable hardship. When the news of this maltreatment was reported to the Japanese government, plans were made for a punitive expedition to Taiwan in the name of retaliation against the outrage done to the Japanese subjects.[48]

On February 6, 1874, Home Minister Okubo Toshimichi and Finance Minister Okuma Shigenobu formally presented their statement on the 'Matter of Aboriginal Territory in Taiwan' to the Council of State, calling for expeditionary action against Taiwan.[49] While the Council deliberated on the question of the expedition to Taiwan, the disgruntled ex-*samurai* elements had already caused disturbances in the Saga area. This was undoubtedly an uprising staged in protest against the government's stand on the Korea issue. But, at the same time, it was also a shot in the arm for the expansionists. The Taiwan plot began to figure even more prominently in the minds of the officials as a convenient design to appease and to divert the rebels. What followed was a series of official acts toward the realization of this goal.

On February 25, a notification of the Japanese First Minister of State, Sanjo Sanetomi, announced that fifty-four Ryukyuans and four men of Oda had been maltreated in Formosa, and stressed the necessity of preventing a recurrence of similar outrages. Lieutenant-General Saigo Tsugumichi was nominated commander of an expedition for that purpose. The notification reads in full as follows:

> In the eleventh month of the fourth year of Meiji fifty-four Ryukyuans, who were cast ashore in the savage part of Formosa, were murdered by the natives, and in the third month of the sixth year of Meiji *four men of the Oda Province* were cast ashore there, and treated in a brutal manner. These affairs were made the sub-

> ject of representation to the government of China by our Ambassador Plenipotentiary.
>
> Now Formosa not being far from Japan, it is probable that there will be other cases from time to time of Japanese being cast ashore there, and considering the progress which is gradually being made in navigation, it may be expected that our people will in the future visit that country.
>
> Under such circumstances, the repetition of similar outrages is greatly to be apprehended, and His Majesty Emperor Meiji has therefore at this time appointed Saigo Tsugumichi, General of the Second Rank, Commander of an expedition to that island. It will be his duty, first to call to account and deal with the persons guilty of outrages on our subjects; and secondly, to take such steps as will insure the safety of our people's navigation in the future.[50]

On April 4, the Japanese government also announced the establishment of the Bureau for Aboriginal Affairs of Taiwan, and Okuma was appointed to direct it. In the meantime, expeditionary forces were prepared by Lieutenant-General Saigo Tsugumichi. In order to secure a diplomatic front, Tokyo also decided to appoint Yanagihara Sakimitsu, now an old China hand, to head a mission to China. The order of appointment, dated April 8, 1874, explicitly alleged that the Taiwan aborigines had maltreated the Oda castaways.[51]

Before the actual departure of the Japanese forces, however, foreign envoys in Tokyo such as the British Minister Sir Harry S. Parkes and the new American Minister, John A. Bingham, who replaced Charles E. De Long in the Fall of 1873, all began to express their doubts about the legitimacy of the projected Japanese action. Similar reservations were subsequently made by diplomatic representatives from Russia, Italy and Spain. Fearful of intervention from these Powers, the Japanese made a last effort to stop the forces from leaving Nagasaki. But Saigo refused to follow the cabinet order on the grounds that he himself had been instructed directly by the Emperor to carry out the expedition. He advised that in case of any difficulty the Japanese government should consider him a pirate to avoid assuming officially any international responsibility. He successfully ignored the last minute decision of the Japanese government, thus setting a precedent of disobedience.[52]

VI. The Peace Settlement of 1874 and the Ryukyu Question

The news of the Japanese invasion of Taiwan reached Thomas F. Wade, the British minister in Peking, on April 10. He, in turn, brought the news to the attention of the Tsungli Yamen on April 18. On May 4, the Yamen received the news from Fukien that Japanese warships had entered the harbor of Amoy in the latter part of April.

Realizing that the invasion was now a reality, Prince Kung, head of the Tsungli Yamen, responded officially. In his memorial to the throne, he reported on the conversation which had taken place the year before between the Yamen ministers (Mao Ch'an-hsi and Tung Hsun) and Yanagihara on the status of Taiwan and Ryukyu. He then recommended that a high-ranking official, well versed in foreign affairs, be dispatched to Taiwan to look into the situation. He also notified the Japanese Foreign Ministry of his disagreement and demanded an explanation of the Japanese military action.[53] In the mind of the Chinese, there was little doubt that Japan's action was a violation of the 1871 Sino-Japanese Treaty which required respect for each other's 'territorial possessions.'

Since an early reply from Tokyo was not forthcoming, the situation went from bad to worse. As a result, Shen Pao-chen, the high official in charge of shipbuilding, was appointed to the post of Special Imperial Commissioner in charge of military and diplomatic affairs in Taiwan. The governor-general and other officials of Fukien were instructed to cooperate fully with him, and P'an Wei, the provincial treasurer of Fukien, was appointed as an assistant to Shen.[54]

At the time when formal confrontation was to begin, both sides seemed to have had second thoughts. For China, this was a time when the revolts in Yunnan and Kansu were just ending and a large army was required for the pacification of the Sinkiang disturbances. Whether China could allow a second front in Taiwan was therefore very much in doubt.[55]

Moreover, the situation in Indochina was also deteriorating. By establishing its protectorate over Indochina in 1874, the French had come nearer than ever to the Chinese border. A Sino-Japanese war at this time would expose the vulnerability of China in such border areas. With these things in mind, it was natural for the Chinese government to opt, albeit secretly, for a waiting policy.

Meanwhile, the Japanese government was informed in its latest report that the Western powers had become increasingly sympathetic to the Chinese cause. Okubo, who had recommended the military action in order to allay internal dissent and discontent, and who was unable to restrain Saigo Tsugumichi when the pressure of the foreign envoys forced him to back down, felt the pressure of time. On May 15 he stated that he would accept responsibility for the consequences which would arise from his failure to halt the Saigo expedition. On July 13 he personally appealed to the Council of State to appoint him as a negotiator to Peking. And on August I he was appointed by an imperial edict to be a Minister Plenipotentiary and Ambassador Extraordinary to supersede Yanagihara in the negotiations.[56]

Okubo reached Peking on August 27, and immediately entered upon important negotiations. During the long process of negotiation, he found that the Chinese ministers were tough negotiators. For students of Sino-Japanese relations of this period, it is both interesting and pertinent to ask what had sustained China in adopting this seemingly hard line *vis-a-vis* Japan which contributed to these long-drawn-out negotiations.

The domestic scene of Japan must have been an important influence on the Chinese decision-makers. In Shen Pao-chen's letter to Li Hung-chang, he pointed out that Okubo was obviously under pressure from Tokyo to strike a quick bargain with China. For this reason he advised the government to bide its time. In Li Hung-chang's communication to the Tsungli Yamen, he, too, characterized the Japanese attitude as 'intimidation' which should not, in his view, disrupt China's effort to bide her time.[57] In short, they believed that China could wait while Japan could not, and it was in China's best interests to do so.

But this concealed optimism on the part of the Chinese government was not to be shared by all the foreign representatives in China. The British Minister, Thomas F. Wade, and the French Minister, Louis de Geogroy, approached the matter quite differently. Thinking of their own interests, the deadlock could develop into a war between China and Japan, and to them Japan was something to be feared. Should a war end with a Japanese victory, their interest in Taiwan and other ports of China would inevitably be prejudiced by an expanded Japanese power. In case of a Chinese victory, the pride of a victorious China would be so inflated as to create many problems for the West. Caught on the horns of such a dilemma, they took steps to avert a Sino-Japanese conflict. What followed, therefore, was a series of unsolicited offers rendered by Wade and de Geogroy to both of the feuding parties in the Taiwan crisis. An agreement between Japan and China with reference to the Island of Formosa was finally signed on October 31, 1874; the Ryukyu Islands, however, were not mentioned in the Treaty.[58]

As far as Ryukyu's sovereignty is concerned, it is debatable whether or not China, by signing this agreement, had 'accepted that the Japanese contention that the Lew Chews [Ryukyuans] were Japanese subjects was correct.'[59] One historian has remarked that 'the phraseology of the first article clearly affirmed the Japanese right to protect "her subjects," which was a clear recognition that the inhabitants of the Lew Chews [Ryukyus] were subjects of Japan.'[60] The question stands: Was the Treaty really a 'clear recognition' that the Ryukyuans were Japanese subjects? More specifically, had Okubo and the Yamen ministers intended to find a solution to the Ryukyu problem during the course of their negotiations? It is highly unlikely that either side, at least in 1874, had intended to clarify the ambiguous political status of the Ryukyu Islands at the risk of directly opposing the other.

With the benefit of historical hindsight, two points emerge in support of this view. First, China during the second half of the 1870s still strongly maintained her claim over the Ryukyu Islands. Secondly, if the case of the Ryukyu problem was legally solved by the 1874 Treaty, the decision of Japan in 1880 to send Shishido Tamaki to China for further negotiations on the same issue becomes incomprehensible. The fact that Japan in 1880 sent her representative to China to discuss the issue clearly indicates that the dispute had not been legally closed in 1874. The three articles of the 1874 Treaty speak for themselves:

1. The proceedings of Japan on this occasion having originally been taken for the rightful object of protecting her people, China does not regard them as wrongful.
2. China shall pay consolation money to the families of the distressed (or shipwrecked) people who were injured on the former occasion, and as she wishes to retain for her own use the roads, houses and other works constructed by Japan at the said place, China first agrees to pay for the same under arrangements set forth in a separate document.
3. The whole of the correspondence relating to this question which has passed between the two nations will be withdrawn and cancelled by both parties, and discussion thereon will cease forever. As to the savage tribes of the said locality China ought, of course, to take measures for keeping them under proper control, in order

> that navigators may be forever protected, and not again exposed to outrage or wrong.[61]

When comparing the articles of the treaty in both Chinese and Japanese texts, one cannot find any specific—in fact, not even one single—mention of Ryukyu in the context. But many historians, probably due to their lack of knowledge about the 1873 Oda shipwreck incident and its influence on the Meiji policy-makers, have rashly concluded that, in the words of Chow Jen-hwa, 'By the implication of the first article in which China agreed to pay compensation for damage done to the "Japanese subjects," China had tacitly renounced her claim over Ryukyu and yielded to the Japanese claim which she had earlier disputed.'[62] This argument, widely shared by Japanese scholars, contends, first, that since China in the 1874 Treaty recognized Japan's action in Taiwan as 'righteous,' she was thus implicitly giving up her suzerainty over Ryukyu. Secondly, by agreeing to pay the handsome sum of money to compensate the shipwrecked Ryukyuans of 1871, China had explicitly abandoned her responsibility, and thus her sovereign right, over the Ryukyuan people.

Nevertheless, as discussed earlier, the immediate factor leading to the Japanese Formosan expedition was not the Ryukyu shipwreck incident of 1871, but the Oda incident of 1873. China had long considered the case of the shipwrecked Ryukyuans settled by the Chinese and Ryukyuan governments. In the Chinese mind, the term of the maltreated 'Japanese subjects' in the 1874 Treaty referred only to the Japanese of the Oda Province, not to the Ryukyuans.

The distinction mentioned above is not just an academic one. Contemporary Chinese were reportedly annoyed by the later Japanese 'distortion' of the 1874 Treaty. For example, Wang T'ao wrote an article: 'Liu-ch'iu hsiang-kuei Jih-pen pien' (Does Ryukyu belong to Japan? A Clarification), charging that since the Japanese first used the Oda shipwreck incident as an excuse to send an expeditionary force to Taiwan, the Treaty stating Japan's right to protect her subjects was therefore naturally referring to the Oda Japanese.[63] As the Treaty had provided no agreement on the political status of Ryukyu, Wang argued, how could one say that the Ryukyuan people were Japanese subjects?

Wang T'ao also wrote 'Liu-ch'iu ch'ao-kung kao' (A Study of Ryukyu's tribute presentation) and many newspaper editorials to prove the point that the Sino- Ryukyuan tributary relationship was indisputable. His arguments were typical of the general view among the Chinese people. Li Hung-chang himself, who was responsible for signing the 1874 Treaty, made a similar comment in 1879:

> At the time when Japan was annexing Ryukyu into the Okinawa Prefecture (in April 1879), other nations criticized that it was entirely due to China's concessions and weakness in settling the Formosan incident of 1874. It appears to be so; but it is not true. In the year 1874, Chinese officials of high and low were questioning the Japanese that Ryukyu had been China's dependency, the maltreatment of Ryukyuan shipwreckers was therefore China's internal affair, and that China would consider punishing the Taiwan aborigines accordingly. What has this to do with the Japanese?[64]

To be sure, the Japanese 'distortion' of the 1874 Treaty arose from the ambiguities of the treaty itself. Moreover, these ambiguities were tailored by the Meiji government in Japan's favor upon the advice of Gustave Boissonade—Okubo's trusted French legal advisor—in March 1875. But in 1874, Okubo Toshimichi himself, while in Peking, was unaware of the possible implication that China, by recognizing the Japanese Formosan expedition as 'righteous' and by paying the consolation money to Japan, was to recognize Japan's sovereignty over Ryukyu. He made a frank confession on December 15, 1874, that the treaty he had just signed with China had *NO* legal basis for Japan's sovereign claim over Ryukyu.[65]

Earlier, in a letter to his friend Kuroda Kiyotaka, written on October 30—a day before the signing of the 1874 Sino-Japanese Treaty, Okubo had suggested that a good sum of the relief money be paid to those who displayed valor in battle. The remaining four hundred thousand taels should be returned to China to be spent in Taiwan for the administration of the area inhabited by the aborigines and for the protection of navigators against future outrages.[66] Although his proposal was not acted upon, it indicates that Okubo did not consider the payment of consolation money an indication of China's agreement to abandon her suzerainty over the Ryukyu Islands. What concerned the Japanese home minister at this point was not the Ryukyu problem, but a quick conclusion of the Formosan expedition. In fact, during the course of negotiations with the Chinese officials, Okubo, like Soejima, deliberately avoided raising the Ryukyu issue in their discussions.[67]

Okubo's outward semblance of affecting a sense of humanity by remitting the relief money was not the real reason behind his gesture; rather, it was based upon political considerations. By this unprecedented move, he hoped to dispel China's suspicion toward Japan, at the same time revealing to the world Japan's magnanimity.[68] He was anxious to reach *a rapprochement* with China, a country with which Japan would have to cooperate if her future prosperity were to be assured.[69] Okubo's expression of good will towards China, conveyed in the course of his November 3 talk with Li Hung-chang in Tientsin, was not mere formality, but a genuine declaration of his feelings.[70] This undoubtedly impressed upon Li Japan's desire for a closer relationship with China. Li Hung-chang was receptive, yet equally aware of the rapidly rising power of Japan and its threat to China's security. But Li feared the Western maritime powers more; Li initially directed his schemes for self-strengthening against the West, not Japan. It was logical for him to think of Japan as a possible 'ally' to ward off the Western threat, since China and Japan were geographically closer and culturally similar. Throughout the 1870s, Li Hung-chang was relatively tolerant of Japanese expansionism until 1879 when Ryukyu was annexed against China's will, and he was shocked into the realization that a Sino-Japanese 'alliance' would be impossible.

Since the treaty did not identify the victims, it was ambiguous as to who was to receive the compensation, and controversy arose. The Chinese later maintained that the consolation money should go to the shipwrecked Oda Japanese, not to the Ryukyuans. The *Shishido Tamaki kankei bunsho* (The Shishido Tamaki Papers, now deposited in the National Diet Library at Tokyo) contains valuable information about this Chinese statement. In a visit to Japan's Foreign Minister Terashima Munenori in Tokyo on January 13, 1880, Sir Harry S. Parkes, the British minister in Japan, repeatedly stressed the Chinese contention that the one hundred thousand taels were to compensate the shipwrecked Oda Japanese, and not the Ryukyuans.[71] The Chinese expressed doubts as to the validity of Japan's interpretation because no clear statement regarding Ryukyu had been made in the 1874 Treaty.

The Sino-Japanese dispute arose from Ryukyu's dual-subordination to both China and Japan. One of the major reasons for the Japanese Formosan venture, as has been discussed, was to redress the maltreatment of shipwrecked Ryukyuan and Oda castaways, on the grounds that these people were Japanese subjects. But in the settlement of October 31, 1874 between China and Japan, the Kingdom of Ryukyu was not once mentioned specifically in the Treaty, while both China and Japan still maintained their claims over the islands. The Treaty, however, stated that Japan had acted justly in Taiwan, whereby the Japanese *later* took for granted that China had indirectly given up her suzerainty over the Ryukyuans, while China still considered the tributary status of the kingdom unchanged. Thus the question, which was colored by the mixed Japanese motives of territorial expansion and frontier security, and the Chinese determination to preserve the *status quo*, remained an acute issue during the following years.

Abbreviations

CD Despatches from U.S. Ministers to China, 1843-1900. Department of State, National Archives, M92, 131 rolls, in microfilm.

CLCC Ch'ing-tai Liu-ch'iu chi-lu chi-chi (Selected collection of Ryukyu mission journals of the Ch'ing period) (Taipei, 1971).

CTSM *Tung-chih Chia-hsu Jih-ping ch'in-Tai shih-mo* (A complete account on the Japanese Formosan Expedition of 1874) (Taipei, 1959).

IWSM *Ch'ou-pan I-wu shih-mo* (The complete account of the Management of barbarian affairs) (Peking, 1930).

:TK Tao-kuang period

:HF Hsien-feng period

:TC T'ung-chih period

JD Despatches from U.S. Ministers to Japan, 1855-1906. Department of State, National Archives, M13, 82 rolls, *in* microfilm.

JI Diplomatic Instructions of the Department of State, 1801-1906, Japan. Department of State, National Archives, M77, no. 104-108, in microfilm.

KK Kiyosawa Kiyoshi, *Gaiseika toshite no Okubo Toshimichi* (Okubo Toshimichi as a diplomat) (Tokyo, 1942).

LWCK *Li-wen-chung-kung ch'uan-chi* (Complete works of Li Hung-chang) (Shanghai, 1921).

:IS *I-shu han-kao*

:PL *P'eng-liao han-kao*

:TK *Tsou-kao*

NGB *Nihon gaiko bunsho* (including *Dai-Nihon gaiko bunsho)* (Diplomatic Papers of Japan) (Tokyo, 1937-40, 1949-)

NGB:TH *Nihon gaiko bunsho: Meiji nenkan tsuiho* (Diplomatic Papers of Japan: supplement to the Meiji period) (Tokyo, 1964).

OKS *Okinawan-ken shi* (History of the Okinawa Prefecture), 25 vols (Naha, 1966-).

OTB *Okubo Toshimichi bunsho* (The Okubo Toshimichi Papers), 10 vols (Tokyo, 1967-69).

RS Matsuda Michiyuki, *Ryukyu shobun* (The Disposition of Ryukyu), 3 vols (1878); reprinted in *Meiji bunka shiryo sosho* IV (Tokyo, 1962).

SP Shishido Tamaki kankei bunsho (The Shishido Tamaki Papers, unpublished materials on and relating to the Ryukyu dispute). Located in the Kensei Shiryo Shitsu, National Diet Library, Tokyo.

TCK *Tai-wan sheng tung-chih kao* (A Draft gazetteer of the Taiwan Province) (Taipei, 1960).

Notes

1. For details, see: Gaimusho, *Ryukyu huhan jiryaku* (Ryukyu feudal province digest) (2 vols, 1873); Kobayashi Kyokei (comp.), *Ryukyu-han shi* (History of the Ryukyu domain) (2 vols, 1874).
2. NGB, V. no. 177, enclosure; *Sanjo Sanetomi Ko nenfu* (Biographical chronicle of Sanjo Sanetomi) (Tokyo, 1969), 27: 7b—10a.

3. NGB:TH, I, 227.
4. *Shimbun shusei Meiji hennen ski* (A chronological history of Meiji Japan based on materials from newspapers) (15 vols, Tokyo, 1965).
5. IWSM:TC, 77:35.
6. See my article in Chinese: Liang Po-hua, 'Yang-wu yun-tung shih-ch'i Man-ch'ing wai-chiao cheng-ts'e chuan-pien ti shen-chueh' (Diplomatic change in China during the Self-Strengthening Movement period), *Shih-ch'ao* 7 (October 1971), 7-24.
7. See note 5.
8. NGB:TH, I:142; IWSM:TC, 96:27-32.
9. See, for example, Sonoda Hiyoshi, *Eto Shimpei to Saga no ran* (Eto Shimpei and the Saga Rebellion) (Tokyo, 1974), *passim.*
10. OKS, II:110.
11. Tabohashi Kiyoshi, 'Ryukyu hanmin bangai jiken ni kansuru kosatsu' (An investigation of the outrage suffered by the natives of Ryukyu at the hands of the aborigines in Taiwan) in *Ichimura Hakushi koki kinen Toyoshi ronso* (Fuzambo, 1933), 663-88; Yamanaka Sho, 'Miyako tomin no Taiwan sogai' (Victims of the Miyako Islanders in Taiwan in 1871), *Nanto 3* (September 1944), 136-73; Kinjo Seitoku, 'Taiwan jiken (1871-74 nen) ni tsuite no ichi kosatsu—Ryukyu shobun no kiten to shite' (A study of the Japanese Formosan Expedition and its relations to the disposition of Ryukyu), *Okinawa rekishi kenkyu I* (October 1965), 33-49; Hanabusa Nagamichi, 'Sen happiyaku nanaju yo nen Taiwan bansha jiken' (Japanese Expedition against Formosan aborigines in 1874), Keio Gijuku Daigaku, *Hogaku kenkyu* 24.9/10 (September-October 1951), 51-79; Shozi Mantaro, trans. by Hsueh Yu, 'I-pa ch'i-ssu nien Jih-pen chu-shih T'ai-wan yu Li Shan-te' (Charles LeGendre and the Japanese Formosan Expedition of 1874), *Tai-wan yin-hang chi-k'an* 10.3 (March 1959), 135-49; and Sophia Yen, *Taiwan in China's Foreign Relations, 1836-1874* (Hamden, Conn., 1965).
12. Ch'en Ta-tuan, 'Sino-Ryukyuan Relations in the 19th century' (Ph.D. dissertation, Indiana University, 1963), 104.
13. *Ibid.*
14. Shozi Mantaro (see note 11), 135-49.
15. Ino Yoshinori, *Taiwan bansei shi* (An account of the rule over the Taiwan aborigines) (Taipei, 1973), 593.
16. Chow Jen-hwa, 'The Taiwan Incident and the Diplomatic and Consular Missions in Japan,' *Nanyang University journal* VI (1972), 73, quoting Li

Heh-nien to Yamen, May 30, 1873; Yamen to Li, June 6,1873 (Chinese Foreign Ministry Archives, *Chung-Jih hsiu-hao t'iao-yueh).*

17. TCK, III: 171-4.
18. *Tai-wan tui-wai kuan-hsi shih-liao* (Historical materials on Taiwan's foreign relations), 92-6; *NGB,* VII, 141, 322.
19. For example, Earl R. Bull, *Okinawa or Ryukyu: the Floating Dragon* (Newark, Ohio, 1958), 43
20. NGB, V, 373-6.
21. NGB:TH. I, 222-3; STK. 185.
22. George H. Kerr, *Okinawa: The History of an Island People* (Rutland, 1958), 362-3.
23. RS, 9-10; NGB:TH. I, 104.
24. Narahara Kogoro shokan (Letters of Narahara Kogoro) handwritten copy, a photostatic copy now deposited *in* Higaonna Bunko, Naha, Okinawa.
25. JD, De Long to Soyeshima, October 20, 1872. Inclosure no. 1 of De Long to Fish, November 6, 1872.
26. *Ibid.,* Inclosure no. 2, Soyeshima to De Long, 5th of the 10th month of the 5th year of Meiji.
27. *Ibid.*
28. CD, W. W. Williams to Fish, May 26, 1874; the record of the conversation can also be found in NGB:TH, I, 105-200.
29. NGB, VII, 5.
30. Watanabe Ikujiro *et al.* (comp.), *Okuma Documents* (Tokyo, 1958), I, 25-6, 41.
31. Sandra Caruthers Thomson, 'Filibustering to Formosa: General Charles LeGendre and the Japanese,' *Pacific Historical Review* XL, 4 (November 1971), 449.
32. For details, see: LeGendre, *Is Aboriginal Formosa a Part of the Chinese Empire?* (Shanghai, 1874); Tei Ei-nei (Cheng Yung-ning), 'Soejima taishi teki Shin gairyaku' (Summary of Ambassador Soejima's China mission) (1873), reprinted in *Meiji bunka* zenshu (Tokyo, 1967) VI, 61-75.
33. JI, Fish to De Long, December 3o, 1872.
34. NGB, III, 178-251; TV, 159-266.
35. LeGendre to Commodore David Ammen, May to, 1873, Memo. Bk. 1, Appendix 5, *LeGendre Papers,* quoted in Thomson (see note 31), 445.
36. TCK, III, 176-7.

37. Tabohashi Kiyoshi, 'Meiji gonen no "Maria Rusu" jiken' (The *Maria Luz* incident of 1872), *Shigaku zasshi* 40.2 (February 1929), 230-46; 40.3 (March 1929), 364-75; 40.4 (April 1929), 483-508.

38. Wagner C. McWilliams, 'East meets East: the Soejima Mission to China, 1873,' *Monumenta Nipponica* XXX.3 (Autumn 1975), 267.

39. T. F. Tsiang, 'Sino-Japanese Diplomatic Relations, 1870-1894,' *The Chinese Social and Political Science Review XVII* (1933), 17, states: 'So far as I know there is only one complete version of the fateful [Yanagihara—Yamen] conversation, namely the one given by Professor Nagao Ariga' (in 'Diplomacy' in Alfred Stead (ed.), *Japan by the Japanese* (London, 1904), 101-3). Writing in 1965, Sophia Yen in her *Taiwan in China's Foreign Relations, 1836-1874,* 353, n.35, noted: 'The Chinese archives heretofore published, do not have the record [of this discussion].' The fact that the Chinese government, when disputing Soejima's claims in the following year, referred only to their recollection of the discussion but produced no written record to back their contentions suggests that the Tsungli Yamen did not in fact make any record of the interview. See Tsiang, 19 and 26-7, and *North China Herald,* August 15, 1874.

40. The official record of the discussion is found in Soejima Taneomi's 'Shi Shin nikki' (Diary of my China mission), in NGB, VI, 176-9; Tei Ei-nei (see note 32), 70-1.

41. 'Shi Shin nikki,' 178.

42. Soejima Taneomi, 'Soejima Haku keireki gudan,' (Soejima talks on his experiences), in *Toho kyokai kaiho* 44 (1898), 30; Ariga (see note 39), 163.

43. Edward E. House, *The Japanese Expedition to Formosa* (Tokyo, 1875), 12-13.

44. 'Soejima Haku keireki gudan,' 27, Soejima also noted, on page 30: 'Some people (in Japan) expressed the view that we should have secured an official note from the Chinese government stating clearly that aboriginal Formosa was beyond the limits of Chinese sovereignty, but this would have been quite difficult, and I decided that a written statement was not absolutely necessary and that a verbal statement would suffice.' See also Ariga (see note 39), 161.

45. NGB:TH, I, 105.

46. Monbusho, *History of the Empire of Japan,* compiled and translated for the Imperial Japanese Commission of the World's Columbian Exposition, Chicago, 1893 (Tokyo, 1893), 401.

47. *Okayama-ken no rekishi* (History of the Okayama Prefecture) (Okayama-shi, 1962), 768.

48. NGB:TH, I, 105; Kokuryukai (comp.), *Seinan kiden* (An account of the Satsuma Rebellion) (Tokyo, 1969), I, 1, 612-13; Tashiro Mikio, *Taiwan gunki* (A military account of the Japanese Formosan expedition) (1874), I, 6b.
49. NGB, VII, i; NGB:TH, I, 122-24; OTB, V, 343-6; *Okuma Shigenobu kankei bunsho* (The Okuma Papers) (Tokyo, 1971), II, 247-50.
50. *Sanjo Sanetomi Ko nenfu*, 27, 52a-53b.
51. *Seinan kiden*, I, 1, 612-3.
52. TCK, III, 181-2.
53. CTSM, I, 4-5.
54. *Ibid.*, 6-8.
55. LWCK, II, 91-2.
56. NGB:TH, I, 143; *Sanjo; Sanetomi Ko nenfu*, 28:1a.
57. LWCK, V, 53.
58. CTSM, II, 141.
59. Shanti S. Gandhi, 'U.S. Diplomatic Relations with China, 1869-1882' (unpublished Ph.D. dissertation, Georgetown University, 1954), 308.
60. *Ibid.*
61. NGB, VII, 316-17.
62. Chow Jen-hwa (see note 16), 174-5.
63. Now collected in CLCC, II, 277-82.
64. LWCK:PL, 19, 1b-2b.
65. OTB, VI, 237-9.
66. *Ibid., VI*, 152-61; KK, 237-41.
67. OTB, VI, 237; *Inoue Tsuyoshi den (Tokyo*, 1966-75), I, 186-8.
68. OTB, VI, 158-60.
69. KK, 243.
70. *Okubo Toshimichi nikki (Diary of Okubo), last part*, 339-42.
71. SP, 56.2, January 13, 1880, Terashima's talk with Parkes.

2

Li Hung-chang and the Liu-ch'iu (Ryukyu) Controversy, 1871-1881

Li Hung-chang's role in China's foreign affairs during the late Ch'ing period has been a subject of much study. Little is known, however, about his role in the Sino-Japanese dispute over the Liu-ch'iu (Ryukyu) Islands in the period between 1871 and 1881. What was Li's attitude toward the tributary states in general, and toward the ex-tributary state, Japan, in particular, during the period of controversy? What was Li's influence on China's foreign policy decision-making during this period? How did Li resolve (or not resolve) the seeming dilemma at a time when China was thrust into the modern nation-state system while maintaining the traditional tributary state system? Specifically, what was Li's policy toward Liu-ch'iu *vis-a-vis* Japan?

This chapter attempts to answer these questions by focusing on the Liu-ch'iu controversy. The controversy arose because of Liu-ch'iu's "dual-subordination" to both China and Japan, a status that was at best confusing in modern international law.[1] While the Liu-ch'iu king sought to preserve his kingdom in the face of Japanese annexation by turning to China for protection, the deteriorating Ch'ing monarchy obviously was incapable of sending a rescue mission to the faithful Liu-ch'iu. As this chapter will show, however, Li Hung-chang, during the period of the Liu-ch'iu controversy, contemplated the idea of forming an "alliance" between China and Japan against the encroaching Western powers. He considered this possible Sino-Japanese "alliance" as a policy priority over the "empty name" of Chinese suzerainty over the tributary state Liu-ch'iu. With pragmatism and care, he cultivated this idea with visiting Japanese leaders throughout the 1870s, only to learn, after Japan's annexation of Liu-ch'iu in 1879, that the Meiji government was actually not willing to go along. Li's miscalculation of the Japanese interest, in retrospect, weakened China's position *vis-a-vis* Japan in the protracted Liu-ch'iu dispute, even though his original design was to ally with Japan in order to strengthen China's position against the Western imperialists. As this chapter will also show, many Japanese leaders showed reciprocal interest in Li's "alliance" idea, convincing Li that he was not alone in trying to achieve this goal. Japan's forceful actions in Liu-ch'iu, therefore, shocked Li Hung-chang into the realization that a Sino-Japanese alliance was not possible. Toward the end of the Liu-ch'iu controversy, Li quickly and pragmatically shifted his pro-Japan policy to counter the rise of Japanese power in the Asian world order.

Official Sino-Japanese relations had been held in abeyance for the three hundred years preceding 1871. Japan was also a tributary state of China for a time during the Ming period. The Japanese shogun, Ashikaga Yoshimitsu, accepted the tributary status in order to enrich his coffers from trade—from 1433 to 1549 eleven tribute and trade missions sailed to China. Subsequently, however, nationalistic Japanese statesmen found such relations humiliating, and discontinued the practice after the middle of the sixteenth century, thus ending official contact with the mainland.

The year 1871 marked a new change in Sino-Japanese diplomatic relations. Soon after the newly created Japanese Foreign Ministry came into being in 1870, Yanagiwara Sakimitsu was sent by his government to Peking to seek a commercial treaty similar to China's treaties with Western nations. He was instructed, in particular, to secure the most-favored-nation clause in the treaty. Although his mission was viewed by the ultra-conservative elements in the Chinese government as opportunistic and ill-timed, it was received with warmth by the more pragmatic and progressive leaders, like Li Hung-chang, newly appointed governor-general of Chihli and superintendent of trade for the Northern Ports. Li felt that:

> Japan, which was not a dependency of China, was totally different from Korea, Liu-ch'iu, and Annam. That she had come to request trade without first seeking support from any Western power showed her independence and good will. If China refused her this time, her friendship would be lost and she might even seek Western intervention on her behalf, in which case it would be difficult for China to refuse again. An antagonized Japan could be an even greater source of trouble than the Western nations because of her geographical proximity. It was therefore in China's interest to treat Japan on a friendly and equal basis and send commissioners to Japan who could look after the Chinese there, watch the movements of the Japanese government, and cultivate harmonious relations between the two states.[2]

Li Hung-chang toyed with the idea of a possible Sino-Japanese "alliance" in the wake of Western encroachments in Asia. His suggestion to "cultivate harmonious relations" with China's ex-tributary state was not out of love for Japan but out of a cold realization of the need to strengthen China's position in order to ward off the Western threat. Li was also aware that "an antagonized Japan could be an even greater source of trouble than the Western nations because of her geographical proximity."[3]

For these reasons, the Yanagiwara mission was well received. In fact, to show Chinese good will, a Sino-Japanese treaty with eighteen articles and a trade regulation of thirty-three articles was finally signed in 1871 by Li and Yanagiwara's successor, Date Munenari. Among other provisions, the treaty allowed for the exchange of envoys and consuls and the rendering of good offices to each other should a third party intimidate or threaten either of the contracting parties. By careful negotiation, Li Hung-chang purposely excluded from the treaty the most-favored-nation clause.[4]

Article One of the Treaty was an important provision: "In all that regards the territorial possessions of either country, the two governments shall treat each other with proper courtesy, without the slightest infringement or encroachment on the other side."[5] China took for granted that the term "territorial possessions" was meant to include those tributary states around China's frontiers. But this Chinese assumption was not to be shared by the Japanese. This ambiguity was not realized until the controversies over Liu-ch'iu and Korea arose in later years.

In 1874, Japan sent an expeditionary force to Taiwan to "punish" the aborigines there who had earlier maltreated the shipwrecked Liu-ch'iuans and Japanese. One incident occurred in 1871 concerning Liu-ch'iuan citizens; the other, in 1873, involved Japanese nationals. The Japanese government, on the pretext of these two incidents, decided to take action in an attempt to resolve Liu-ch'iu's "dual-subordination" problem. By sending forces to Taiwan in the name of "protecting its nationals [meant to include the Liu-ch'iuans]," the Japanese government would first challenge the Chinese suzerainty in Liu-ch'iu and then legitimize its claim by stating that it had already exercised sovereignty over Liu-ch'iu. The detailed story of Japan's Taiwan expedition, however, is beyond the scope of this study.[6] Suffice it to say, not only did the Japanese expeditionary forces sent to Taiwan fail to accomplish the objective of "punishing" the aborigines by being "trapped" there, but the episode also touched off a crisis between China and Japan—a development that worried Li Hung-chang, as well as many Japanese leaders. What followed was the dispatch of Okubo Toshimichi to China by the Japanese government to settle the crisis.

Okubo reached Peking on August 27, and immediately entered into negotiations. An agreement between Japan and China, with reference to the island of Taiwan, was finally signed on October 31, 1874; the Liu-ch'iu Islands, however, were never mentioned in the treaty.[7] As far as the Liu-ch'iu sovereignty problem is concerned, it is debatable as to whether or not China, by signing this agreement, had "accepted ... the Japanese contention that the Lew Chews [Liu-ch'iuans] were Japanese subjects...."[8] One historian has remarked that "the phraseology of the first article clearly affirmed the Japanese right to protect 'her subjects,' which was a clear recognition that the inhabitants of Lew Chews [Liu-ch'iu] were subjects of Japan."[9] The question stands: Was the treaty really a "clear recognition" that the Liu-ch'iuans were Japanese subjects? More specifically, had Okubo and the Chinese negotiators intended to find a solution to the Liu-ch'iu problem during the course of their negotiations? It is highly unlikely that either side, at least in 1874, had intended to clarify the ambiguous political status of the Liu-ch'iu Islands at the risk of directly opposing the other.

In retrospect, the later Japanese "distortion" of the 1874 treaty arose from the ambiguities of the treaty itself. Moreover, these ambiguities were tailored by the Meiji government in Japan's favor on the advice of Gustave Boissonade—a trusted legal advisor—in March 1875).[10] In 1874, however, Okubo Toshimichi himself, while in Peking, was unaware of the possible implication that China, by recognizing the Japanese Taiwan expedition as "righteous" and by paying the consolation money to the victims, was to recognize Japan's sovereignty over Liu-ch'iu. He made a frank confession on December 15, 1874, that the treaty he had just signed with China had no legal basis for Japan's sovereign claim over Liu-ch'iu.[11]

Earlier, in a letter to his friend Kuroda Kiyotaka, written on October 30—a day before the signing of the 1874 Sino-Japanese Treaty—Okubo had suggested that a good sum of the relief money be paid to those who displayed valor in battle. The remainder of the indemnity should be returned to China to be spent in Taiwan for the administration of the area inhabited by the aborigines and for the protection of navigators against future outrages.[12] Although his proposal was not acted on, it shows that Okubo did not consider the payment of consolation money *an* indication of China's agreement to abandon her suzerainty over the Liu-ch'iu Islands. What concerned the Japanese home minister at this point was not the Liu-ch'iu problem, but a quick conclusion of the Taiwan expedition. In fact, during the course of negotiations with the Chinese officials, Okubo even deliberately avoided raising the Liu-ch'iu issue in their discussions.[13]

Okubo's outward semblance of affecting a sense of humanity by remitting the relief money was not the real reason behind his gesture; rather, it was based on political considerations. By this unprecedented move, he hoped to dispel China's suspicions toward Japan, while at the same time revealing to the world Japan's magnanimity.[14] He was anxious to reach a rapprochement with China, a country with which Japan would have to cooperate to assure Japan's future prosperity.[15] Okubo's expression of good will toward China, conveyed in the course of his November 3 talk with Li Hung-chang in Tientsin, was not a mere formality but a genuine declaration of his feelings.[16] This undoubtedly impressed upon Li Japan's desire for a closer relationship with China. Li Hung-chang was receptive, yet equally aware of the rapidly rising power of Japan and its threat to China's security. But Li feared the Western maritime powers even more; initially Li had directed his schemes for self-strengthening against the West, not Japan. It was logical for him to think of Japan *as* a possible "ally" to ward off the Western threat, as China and Japan were geographically closer and culturally similar.

Throughout most of the 1870s, Li Hung-chang was relatively tolerant of Japanese expansionism. But, by 1879, when Liu-ch'iu was annexed against China's will, Li was forced to realize that a Sino-Japanese "alliance" was impossible.

After the settlement of the Taiwan crisis in 1875, Li Hung-chang remained convinced that his "alliance" idea would find supporters in Tokyo, even though the conditions in Liu-ch'iu deteriorated progressively. In his letter to the Tsungli Yamen on September 14, 1875, Li again pointed out the difference between Japan and the Western powers in their relations to China: Japan was close to China and an immediate source of anxiety and trouble for her, whereas the West was a long distance away.[17] Although fully aware of Japan's expansionist ambitions toward Liu-ch'iu, as well as toward Korea, Li still entertained the hope of Sino-Japanese cooperation against the Western powers throughout most of the 1870s. He believed that with its continuing unrest and huge financial deficits at home, Japan was in no position to undertake a new venture abroad. He was also aware of Japan's fear of Russia. In November 1876, Li was visited by Mori Arinori and Soejima Taneomi, two Japanese diplomats. Expressing concern over Russian expansionism, the visitors told him of Japan's desire for cooperation with China and Korea in warding off the Russian threat.[18] Okubo had expressed similar ideas to Li in 1874. Although it is unlikely that Li was lulled into complacency by Japan's professed desire for cooperation, he still hoped that Japan could be placated and would remain friendly to China in the latter's disputes with the Western powers. In 1877, when the Satsuma Rebellion broke out in Japan, Li readily loaned a hundred thousand cartridges to the Japanese government.[19] He could not have foreseen that the Japanese government, after the suppression of the Satsuma Rebellion, would annex Liu-ch'iu. In retrospect, Li's policy of tolerance toward Japan weakened China's position in the Liu-ch'iu dispute.

In Liu-ch'iu, drastic changes had taken place by 1877. The Japanese had steadily extended their authority over the Islands. All their efforts had been directed toward the establishment of a legal basis for Japan's claim, including the termination of Liu-ch'iu's tributary ties with China, as well as the creation of a Japanese Home Ministry office in Okinawa.[20] The pressure from Tokyo therefore constituted an unprecedented national crisis for the Liu-ch'iuan king Sho Tai. Consequently, he secretly sent two envoys, Kochi Pechin (Hsiang Te-hung) and Lin Shih-kung, to China to seek aid.[21] They arrived in Fukien on April 12, 1877, and informed governor-general Ho Ching and governor Ting Jih-ch'ang that the tribute missions had been interrupted by the Japanese.[22] Ho and Ting, in a June 14 memorial to the throne, observed that a refusal to aid Liu-ch'iu might be construed by the Western powers as a sign that China was unable to protect her tributary states. They recommended that Ho Ju-chang, recently appointed minister to Japan, take up the matter with the Japanese.[23] This recommendation was acted on the same day that the memorial was received.[24] As will be seen later, China, in actuality, was unable to resort to military means against Japan in defending Liu-ch'iu because of naval and financial reasons.

Ho Ju-chang's mission to Tokyo to open negotiation with the Japanese government regarding Liu-ch'iu admittedly did not produce any result. The Meiji government refused to negotiate on the grounds that the Liu-ch'iu affair was an internal matter of Japan, and that Ho Ju-chang was a foreign diplomat.[25] In April 1879, Japan finally annexed Liu-ch'iu, forcing the Liu-ch'iuan king to take up residence in Tokyo. The Liu-ch'iu Kingdom ceased to exist as a nation.[26]

News of the Japanese annexation of Liu-ch'iu came as a shock to Li Hung-chang, yet he still did not totally abandon the "alliance" idea. He reasoned that he could use the good offices of former U.S. president Ulysses S. Grant, who was scheduled to visit China at that time, to mediate in China's behalf. If the mediation were successful, Li thought, the "alliance" idea could still be viable.

Li met with Grant on May 28 in Tientsin. Grant's first impression of the governor-general was a favorable one; as he recollected some years later, he ranked Li first of the four great men whom he had met in his world tour.[27] This personal factor probably influenced the American ex-president on matters relating to the Liu-ch'iu affair during his visit to China.[28] Accepting Li's request to mediate in the Liu-ch'iu dispute, Grant went on to Japan to take up the case with the Japanese leaders.

Grant's mediation, as it turned out, also did not produce any concrete result.[29] It was difficult for him, as a Westerner, to be able to comprehend fully the concepts of tributary relationships. Furthermore, after hearing the Japanese side of the story, he simply could not make a judgment on the dispute. There were rumors that Grant had made a concrete suggestion to the Chinese and Japanese leaders for the peaceful settlement of the dispute: the partition of the Liu-ch'iu Islands between China and Japan.[30] Extant records do not support this claim. Grant, however, did suggest that China and Japan each should appoint a representative to meet and work out a solution to the Liu-ch'iu problem, a suggestion that was finally accepted by the Japanese government.[31] The Ch'ing government welcomed the suggestion, for it was Japan that had repeatedly refused to discuss the matter through diplomatic channels.

In 1880, the Japanese government decided to send Shishido Tamaki to China, and this decision was considered, at least by Li Hung-chang, as a sign of Japan's willingness to negotiate directly with the Chinese government. Prince Kung, head of the Tsungli Yamen, was appointed by the Ch'ing government as its representative to negotiate with Shishido. Negotiations began on August 15 and lasted for about two months. On October 21, a draft treaty was agreed on by the two representatives.[32] It appeared that, once ratified, the agreement would finally settle the Liu-ch'iu dispute between China and Japan.

As soon as the draft treaty was sent to the Peking court for ratification, however, it created a storm within Chinese officialdom. For, according to the terms of the draft treaty, China would grant Japan trading privileges and concessions (specifically the most-favored-nation clause) in exchange for keeping two southern islands of Liu-ch'iu, while Japan would keep the rest of the seventy-three islands permanently. The Liu-ch'iu Kingdom, the center of the controversy, would not be allowed to be restored. This agreement clearly represents unnecessary concessions made by Prince Kung to his Japanese counterpart. It was also inconsistent with China's policy toward Liu-ch'iu in terms of protecting the tributary states. On the other hand, it reflects Japan's ambition and aggressiveness, as well as its insincerity in dealing with China. This draft treaty shattered whatever hope Li Hung-chang still had toward Japan; he therefore strongly opposed its ratification.[33]

The timing of Li Hung-chang's rejection of the draft treaty is significant: China, in late 1880, was on the edge of settling a dispute with Russia over Ili in the northwest frontier.[34] With the Russian threat seemingly to be removed in the immediate future, and with his disillusionment over Japan's unwillingness to cooperate, Li now advocated peace with Russia instead of with Japan. He had learned from Commodore Robert Shufeldt of the U.S. navy that a Russian fleet of two ironclads and thirteen fast ships was already in Nagasaki and had purchased $500,000 worth of fuel.[35] Li believed Japan was ready to fish in the Sino-Russian troubled waters. Consequently, on September 30, 1880, he urged the Tsungli Yamen to adopt a conciliatory policy toward Russia, and to allow Marquis Tseng Chi-tse (the Chinese representative in St. Petersburg) greater power in negotiations with the Russians, so that a peaceful settlement over Ili might be reached.[36] Li also clarified his stand on the Liu-ch'iu issue: "I think China had better not receive the southern part of Liu-ch'iu and return it to the Liu-ch'iuans themselves. It seems to me Japan will never yield."[37] On November 11, at the request of the Grand Council (November 6), Li sent a powerful memorial to the throne which stated explicitly that because the two southern islands of Liu-ch'iu, to be retained by China, were of such little value, the granting of so broad a concession as the most-favored-nation clause to Japan was unwise.[38] Li feared that once the Japanese started to make trouble, other countries might follow suit. Li impressed upon the court:

> The whole situation hinges on whether the Russian question can be settled. If it can, Japan and all other countries will be hesitant [to move]; if it cannot, they will plot [against us]. Rather than make concessions to the Japanese who cannot help us resist Russia—thereby we lose to both Japan and Russia—would it not be preferable to make some concessions to Russia and secure her help in checking Japan? The strength and weakness of Russia and Japan differ by a hundred fold. Judging by the injustice of their claims, the Japanese also insulted us far more [than the Russians].[39]

An analysis of this statement reveals a basic change in Li Hung-chang's foreign policy: peace with Russia and resistance to Japanese aggression. The question arises: Why did Li's long-time "pro-Japan" policy change overnight? The answer has to be sought in light of both strategic and institutional considerations. First, Li did not consider the Liu-ch'iu problem a serious threat to China's security. From the very beginning, he regarded Liu-ch'iu's tribute as too insignificant an issue to cause China to go to war. He clearly expressed his view in a letter to Ho Ju-chang:

> Liu-ch'iu is a small place, beyond the seas and completely cut off from all other places ... near to Japan and far away from China....

> Even if China wished to assist and rescue her neighbors, the geographical situation prevents it. China receives no great benefit from the Liu-ch'iu tribute. Moreover, if China accepted tribute from Liu-ch'iu but could not protect it, then China would be looked down on by all countries. Japan would not listen to arguments. It would not only be a waste of time but also absurd for China to use force to fight for a small tribute from a small country, and for the sake of an empty name.[40]

It is here that Li first spoke of the tributary state system as an "empty name." In his letter to Tseng Chi-tse of October 19, 1879, Li also wrote that China's naval capacity and financial conditions crippled her ability to wage war against Japan. What concerned Li even more, therefore, was China's domestic effort for self--strengthening—a theme that had consistently been shared by a number of progressive officials: "Since we [China] cannot threaten war with Japan [over Liu-ch'iu], we have to adopt a soft policy, and at the same time to try our best effort for self-strengthening in order to strive for later strength and power."[41]

Li seems to have stressed the possibility that China's protest and Japan's fear of foreign intervention would restrain Japan from taking further action in Liu-ch'iu.[42] Accordingly, he instructed Ho Ju-chang to engage in diplomatic maneuvering, despite the latter's repeated suggestion for China to take military action. Another reason why Li did not advocate a show of force, as we have discussed, was his secret desire for a Sino-Japanese "alliance" to ward off the Western threat. But the news of Japan's annexation of Liu-ch'iu took him by surprise in 1879, and he was disillusioned by Tokyo's lack of cooperation. He also realized that he had underestimated Japan's strength. Nevertheless, he misconstrued the arrival of

Shishido Tamaki at Peking as a sign of Japan's willingness to negotiate directly with the Chinese government. He therefore ordered Ho Ju-chang to remain in Tokyo and continue to seek help from the various foreign ministers in Japan.[43]

Li was totally disillusioned, however; by the 1880 draft treaty negotiated by Shishido Tamaki and Prince Kung. Why should China give Japan the pernicious most-favored-nation clause in exchange for the two small islands of Liu-ch'iu? Because Japan's annexation of the Liu-ch'iu Kingdom did not correspond to China's national interest, why should China sign the draft treaty, thus endorsing Japanese rule over the greater part of Liu-ch'iu?

For practical purposes, Li began to shift his policy, hoping that Russia could be appeased and thus support China in her disputes with foreign powers, especially with Japan. Li's concept appears similar to the traditional stratagem of "controlling barbarians with barbarians" *(i-i chih-i),* because both relied on the use of alien power to protect Chinese interest. This traditional policy was also akin to the European balance-of-power concept.

The balance of interest among several Western powers in China, as Li discovered in the summer of 1876 during his negotiations at Chefoo for the settlement of the Margary affair, might even serve to restrain the demands of so dominant a power as Britain.[44] He also knew that the combined interests of several Western powers in China helped stabilize China's position at this time. He was apparently acquainted with the European balance-of-power concept. In the summer of 1887, Ma Chien-chung, Li's protege who had gone to France the previous year to study international politics with a group of Chinese naval cadets from the Foochow Shipyard, wrote from Paris expounding the balance-of-power principle and explaining that the Western nations had historically endeavored to maintain it in the conduct of international relations.[45] Li and Ma, along with other "progressive" Chinese (such as Huang Tsun-hsien, a councilor of the Chinese embassy at Tokyo),[46] were apparently impressed by the British intervention in the Russo-Turkish War and the Berlin Congress of that summer, which saved the Ottoman Empire from complete dismemberment and destruction, and helped preserve the existing balance of power in Europe.[47]

This "modern version" of the traditional Chinese stratagem of "using barbarians to control barbarians" provided Li Hung-chang with a rational basis for his new policy of peace with Russia and resistance against Japanese aggression. He was aware of Japan's fear of Russia and believed it was strategically more important to defend Korea in order to secure China from Japanese aggression.[48] This was a new variety of *i-i chih-i,* beyond traditional usage.

Another explanation for Li Hung-chang's opposition to the 1880 draft treaty seems to have been his rivalry with the Tsungli Yamen over foreign policy formulation. The Tsungli Yamen had been established after the Treaty of Peking in 1860 specifically to deal with foreign affairs. But, since its creation in 1861, its main policy had been to try to evade questions rather than face them.[49] As a result, issues were dealt with according to expediency, rather than well-conceived plans.

In contrast, Li Hung-chang by the late 1870s had become not only the implementer of policies but also their initiator. While the Tsungli Yamen was incapable of handling foreign affairs, Li had emerged as the most influential man of his time. His position as superintendent of trade for the Northern Ports, together with his right to handle foreign affairs, made him a one-man foreign office competing with the Tsungli Yamen.[50]

Li began acting as a powerful rival to the Tsungli Yamen. The official reports of Chinese ministers abroad were often addressed to both the Yamen and Li.[51] Li could directly issue orders to ministers abroad without the Yamen being informed.[52] The operation of the "two foreign offices" was an indication of the great trust Empress Dowager Tz'u-hsi placed in Li Hung-chang, but it constituted an anomaly in the administration of China's foreign policy. In actual practice, therefore, the superintendent of trade for the Northern Ports was in charge of the Ch'ing court's diplomatic activity in Sino-Japanese relations. The Chinese envoys abroad were directly under the command of the superintendent of trade for the Northern Ports, and the court's orders prepared by the Grand Council were sent to Li Hung-chang for transmission to ministers abroad. In effect, the Tsungli Yamen was bypassed.[53]

Li believed that he understood the Sino-Japanese problem and the Liu-ch'iu issue better than the Yamen ministers. It was Li Hung-chang, not the Yamen ministers, who signed the Sino-Japanese Treaty of Friendship (1871)—a treaty without the most-favored-nation clause, which he considered to be one of his greater diplomatic achievements. It was Li who advocated the importance of coastal defense against Japan, as illustrated in the great policy debate of maritime defense versus frontier defense in 1874.[54] It was also Li who initiated the idea of requesting the former American President Ulysses S. Grant to mediate the Liu-ch'iu dispute in the interest of China. Understandably, Li felt humiliated by not being given the power as special commissioner to work out the settlement with Shishido Tamaki over Liu-ch'iu. The frustrated man might have decided to use his opposition to the 1880 draft treaty as a means to embarrass the Tsungli Yamen in their contest for power. In any event, because of strong opposition from Li, the Ch'ing court announced that it would not ratify the draft treaty.[55]

Because the Ch'ing court refused to ratify the draft treaty, Shishido Tamaki decided to leave China as a protest in early 1881.[56] The Sino-Japanese dispute over Liu-ch'iu, therefore, remained unresolved legally. Although there were some further discussions and counter proposals at Peking, Tientsin, and Tokyo, this was the end of the Liu-ch'iu controversy.[57] From 1881 on, the Okinawa Prefecture of Liu-ch'iu, created by Japan after the annexation, has technically been an integral part of the Japanese empire. From the Chinese point of view, however, the Liu ch'iu question was never settled.

The episode of the Sino-Japanese controversy over the fate of the Liu-ch'iu Kingdom significantly illustrates China's dilemma in juxtaposing the new modern nation-state with the old tributary state system. In reading the Chinese statements relating to the dispute, one cannot fail to observe the confusion in the minds of these statesmen as to the actual status of the Liu-ch'iu Islands.

These islands were sometimes considered an independent state, at other times a part of China, or even worse, a "common dependency" of both China and Japan. This confusion, to be sure, reveals not only the ambiguous political status of Liu-ch'iu, as defined by Western international law, but also the incompatibility of the tributary state system with the modern nation-state system.

That the Chinese leaders had not comprehended in the 1870s that the tributary relationship had no status in Western international law may seem incredible. As a noted historian asserted: "By 1867 the Tsungli Yamen knew ... that the tributary tie was a logical impossibility in the modern world."[58] As far as Liu-ch'iu's tributary relationship with China was concerned, Li Hung-chang believed it was not worth fighting for. As was cited above, in his letter to Ho Ju-chang in Tokyo, Li pointed out that "it would not only be a waste of time but also absurd for China to use force to fight for a small tribute from a small country ... for the sake of an empty name."[59] Indeed, Li Hung-chang began to question China's moral obligation to defend the tributary system, it appears that the ideological structure of the Chinese Confucian universal empire had begun to crumble.

Li Hung-chang believed that a war with Japan over Liu-ch'iu would be detrimental to China's national security, as well as the self-strengthening movement. As was cited above, Li remarked, "... we have to adopt a soft policy, and at the same time to try our best effort for self-strengthening in order to strive for later strength and power."[60] From the very outset, he carefully and pragmatically tried to form a Sino-Japanese "alliance" against the West, for fear that "an antagonized Japan could be an even greater source of trouble than the Western nations because of her geographical proximity" to China. He hoped that the appeasement of Japan could better serve the Chinese interest. Li's design, therefore, must be understood in light of his pragmatism and his analysis of the international situation. And when it appeared that this goal could not be reached, as evidenced by Japan's decision to annex Liu-ch'iu against China's will and the subsequent draft treaty of 1880, Li began to shift pragmatically his "pro-Japan" policy by appeasing Japan's enemy (Russia) in order to counter the rise of Japanese power in Asia. This modern version of *i-i chih-i*, as explained in terms of balance of power, provided Li with the rationale for his foreign policy change. In retrospect, however, Li's abortive attempt to appease Japan in the 1870s weakened China's position *vis-a-vis* Japan in the Liu-ch'iu dispute. In the long run, China's "loss" of Liu-ch'iu to Japan contributed to the disintegration of the tributary state system in Asia.

Abbreviations

CKCJ Ch'ing *Kuang-hsu ch'ao Chung-Jih chiao-she shih-liao (Historical* materials concerning Sino-Japanese negotiations during the Kuang-hsu period, 1875-1908) (Taipei, 1963*).*

CTSM *Tung-chih chia-hsu Jih ping chin-T'ai shih-mo (A* complete account of the Japanese Formosan Expedition of 1874) (Taipei, 1959*).*

HA *Hiratsuka Atsushi, Zoku Ito Hirobumi hiroku* (Supplement to the confidential records of Ito Hirobumi) (Tokyo, 1930*).*

IWSM *Ch'ou-pan i-wu shih-mo* (The complete account of the management of barbarian affairs) (Peking, 1930).

KK Kiyosawa Kiyoshi, *Gaiseika toshite no Okubo Toshimichi* (Okubo Toshimichi as a diplomat-politician) (Tokyo, 1942).

LWCK *Li Wen-chung kung ch'uan-chi* (Complete works of Li Hung-chang) (Shanghai, 1921).

NGB *Nihon gaiko bunsho* (including *Dai-Nihon gaiko bunsho)* (Diplomatic papers of Japan) (Tokyo, 1937-40, 1949-).

NGB:TH *Nihon gaiko bunsho: Meiji nenkan tsuiho* (Diplomatic papers of Japan: Supplement to the Meiji period) (Tokyo, 1964).

OKSG Ota Chofu, *Okinawa kensei gojunen* (Fifty years of Okinawan prefectural administration) (Tokyo, 1932).

OTB *Okubo Toshimichi bunsho* (The Okubo Toshimichi papers), 10 vols. (Tokyo, 1967-69).

RST Endo Tatsu and Goto Keishin, eds., *Ryukyu shobun teiko* (Salient points in the disposition of Ryukyu) (1879); reprinted in *Meiji bunka zenshu,* vol. 25.

THL *Ch'ing Kuang-hsu ch'ao tung-hua lu* (The Tung-hua records of the Kuang-hsu period in the Ch'ing dynasty) (Taipei, 1963).

WCSL *Ch'ing-chi wai-chiao shih-liao* (Historical materials of late Ch'ing diplomacy) (Peking, 1932-35).

Notes

1. Liu-ch'iu had not only acknowledged China's suzerainty since 1372, but, since 1609, also paid tribute to the Satsuma domain of Japan. This dual dependency on two overlords was the result of Liu-ch'iu's military and economic weaknesses. While China remained ignorant of Liu-ch'iu's

dual subordination until the Sino-Japanese dispute arose, the Satsuma domain deliberately allowed Liu-ch'iu to continue the tribute missions to China so that it could reap the profits from Liu-ch'iu's trade with China.

2. *IWSM,* T'ung-chih, 77:35.

3. *Ibid.*

4. For details, see Wang Hsi, *Li Hung-chang yu Chung-Jih ting-yo* (Li Hung-chang and the Sino-Japanese Treaty of 1871) (Taipei, 1981).

5. *NGB:TH,* I:142; *IWSM,* T'ung-chih, 96:27-32.

6. For details, see Edwin Pak-wah Leung, "The Quasi-war in East Asia: Japan's Expedition to Taiwan and the Ryukyu Controversy," *Modern Asian Studies* 17.2 (April 1983), 257-81.

7. *CTSM,* II, 141.

8. Shanti S. Gandhi, U.S. Diplomatic Relations with China, 1869-1882 (unpublished Ph.D. dissertation, Georgetown University, 1954), 308.

9. *Ibid.*

10. For Boissonade's advice to the Japanese government, see *HA,* 32-36.

11. *OTB,* VI, 237-39.

12. *Ibid.*, VI, 152-61; *KK,* 237-41.

13. *OTB,* VI, 237.

14. *Ibid.*, VI, 158-60.

15. *KK,* 243.

16. *Okubo Toshimichi nikki* (Diary of Okubo), last *part,* 339-42.

17. *LWCK Tsungli Yamen Letters,* 4:24-25.

18. *Ibid.*, 6:31-32.

19. *Ibid.*, 7:3-4.

20. For aspects of the "Disposition of Ryukyu," see Endo Tatsu and Goto Keishin, eds., *Ryukyu shobun teiko* (Salient points in the disposition of Ryukyu) (1879); reprinted *in Meiji bunka zenshu,* vol. 25.

21. Lin Shih-kung (Rin Seiko, 1841-80), *Pei-shang tsa-chi* (Miscellany of my northward trip) (1884).

22. *CKCJ,* I:21-22.

23. *Ibid.*

24. *Ibid.*, I:22.

25. On October 7, 1878, the frustrated Ho Ju-chang sent the Japanese Foreign Ministry *a* note of strong protest. Although Ho's note was men-

tioned *in WCSL* 15:12, the full text of the note is nonexistent in Chinese documents. It can be found, however, *in Japanese* documents: *NGB*, XI, 271-72; Tada Komon, ed., *Iwakura Ko jikka* (A factual account of Iwakura Tomomi) (Tokyo, 1968), III, 578-79.

26. *RST*, 132-33; *OKSG*, 43-44.

27. Grant recalled, "I have met on this journey four great men, Bismarck, Beaconsfield, Gambetta, and Li Hung-chang. I am not sure, all things considered, but Li is the greatest of the four." In John Russell Young, *Men and Memories: Personal Reminiscences* (New York, 1901), II, 303.

28. According to Young, the relations between Grant and Li had almost the element of romance, *Ibid.*, 319; Liang Chung-ying, *Li Hung-chang tui Jih wai-chiao chueh-ts'e chih yen-chiu* (Studies on Li Hung-chang's foreign policy toward Japan) (Taipei, 1974), 79.

29. Edwin Pak-wah Leung, "General Ulysses S. *Grant* and the Sino-Japanese Dispute over the Ryukyu (Liu-ch'iu) Islands," *Proceedings of the First International Symposium on Asian Studies* (Hong Kong, 1979), II, 421-49.

30. Richard T. Chang, "General Grant's 1879 Visit to *Japan,*" *Monumenta Nipponica* XXIV.4 (Winter 1969), 381.

31. See Grant's identical letters of August 13, 1879, to Li Hung-chang and Iwakura Tomomi, *in Grant Papers* (in microfilm, Library of Congress), Reel 2, S.IB, 6312-15.

32. *CKCJ*, II, 8a-10b.

33. *Ibid.*, 14b-17; *LWCK Memorials.*, 39:1-15.

34. For details, see Immanuel C. Y. Hsu, *The Ili Crisis: A Study of Sino-Russian Diplomacy, 1871-1881* (Oxford, 1965).

35. *LWCK Tsungli Yamen Letters*, 11:26-28b.

36. September 30, 1880, *Ibid.*, 11:36b.

37. *Ibid.*, 10:26a-27a.

38. *CKCJ*, II, 14.

39. *Ibid.*, II, 14b-17; *LWCK Memorials*, 39:1-15.

40. *LWCK Tsungli Yamen Letters*, 8:5.

41. *LWCK Letters, 9:1b-2b.*

42. *LWCK Tsungli Yamen Letters*, 8:1-2.

43. *CKCJ*, no. 32.

44. See S. T. Wang, *The Margery Affair and the Chefoo Convention* (London, 1940).

45. Ch'en San-ching, "Lueh-lun Ma Chien-chung ti wai-chiao ssu-hsiang," (A brief discussion on the diplomatic thought of Ma Chien-chung), *Chung-yang yen-chiu-yuan chin-tai-shih yen-chiu-suo chi-k'an* III.2 (1972), 548.

46. Mai Chung-hua, comp., *Huang Ch'ao eking-shill wen hsin-pien* (A new compilation of writings of our imperial dynasty) (Taipei, 1972), 72:9a-13a.

47. Ch'en San-ching, "Lueh-lun Ma Chien-chung," III.2, 548.

48. *LWCK Tsungli Yamen Letters,* 8:1a, 4b-6a.

49. Ssu-ming Meng, *The Tsungli Yemen: Its Organization and Functions* (Cambridge, Mass., 1962), 3-4.

50. Liu Hsin-hsien, "Chung-kuo wai-chiao chih-tu ti yen-ke," (The evolution of Chinese diplomatic institutions), *in Chung-kuo chin-tai shih luntsung,* II.5, 23-28.

51. Tabohashi Kiyoshi, *Kindai Nissen kankei no Kenkyu* (A study of Japanese-Korean relations *in* modern times) (Keijo, 1940), 13, 565.

52. *LWCK Memorials,* 1:23, 2:10, 6:26, 15:26.

53. *THL,* I.295 (November 1876) 45; I.319 (November 1876) 135; I.1037 (February 1881), 7.

54. See Immanuel C. Y. Hsu, "The Great Policy Debate in China, 1874: Maritime Defense vs. Frontier Defense," *Harvard Journal of Asiatic Studies* 25 (1964-65), 212-28.

55. *LWCK Memorials,* 39:1-5; *NGB,* XIII, 379-80.

56. Shishido Tamaki's communications with the Chinese government are now collected *in* the *Shishido Tamaki kankei bunsho in* the National Diet Library at Tokyo.

57. Liang Chia-pin, "Liu-ch'iu wang-kuo Chung-Jih cheng-ch'in kao-shih," (An investigation of the Sino-Japanese dispute over Liu-ch'iu and the fall of the Liu-ch'iu Kingdom), *Ta-lu tsa-chih* 48.5 (May 15, 1974), 193-218; 48.6 (June 15, 1974), 263-90.

58. Mary C. Wright, "The Adaptability of Ch'ing Diplomacy: The Case of Korea," *Journal of Asian Studies* 17.3 (May 1958), 381.

59. *LWCK Tsungli Yemen Letters* 8:5.

60. *LWCK Letters*, 9:1b-2b.

3

General Ulysses S. Grant and the Sino-Japanese Dispute over the Liu-ch'iu (Ryukyu) Islands

The present paper is the first comprehensive study on American ex-President Ulysses S. Grant's mediation of the Sino-Japanese dispute over the Ryukyu (Liu-ch'iu) Islands in 1879.[1] An attempt has been made in this study to exhaust Chinese, Japanese, Ryukyuan and American sources in order to provide a balanced and judicious account. By focusing on the role played by General Grant, this paper attempts to shed light not only on the Ryukyu crisis but also on the initial diplomatic intercourse between China and Japan. For the sake of better understanding Grant's position at the time of his mediation in 1879, it is all necessary to trace the background of the dispute.

I

For more than two and a half centuries before the Meiji Restoration in 1868 Ryukyu had not only been a fief of the Japanese Satsuma-han but also a faithful member of China's tributary state system.[2] It had paid tribute to China since 1372 and had been a protectorate of Japan since 1609.[3] Ryukyu's status of dual-subordination to two overlords continued to exist insofar as the

East Asian world was isolated and Japan remained in seclusion. By the late nineteenth century, these conditions no longer existed![4]

Caught between two powerful neighbors, the Chuzan Kingdom of Ryukyu was well schooled in diplomatic evasion, which helped to keep its political status in confusion. When the question of sovereignty over the little kingdom created a crisis between China and Japan in the 1870's, the *Sanshikan* (the three senior officials in Ryukyu) wrote the Japanese Ministry of Foreign Affairs that the Ryukyuans regarded China as a "father" and Japan as a "mother."[5]

Westerners in Asia were confused and uncertain as to the precise relationships between the Ryukyu Kingdom and the courts of China and Japan. Commodore Matthew C. Perry, for example, after some confusion, resorted to treat the king of Ryukyu as an independent sovereign after his arrival on the island country. As he wrote on July 18, 1854, "Lewchew (Ryukyu), it appears, is in a measure an independent sovereignty, holding slight allegiance either to Japan or China, but preferring rather its relations to the latter Empire."[6] Representing the American government, he signed a treaty with Ryukyu the same year.

Another American diplomat shared a similar feeing with the commodore. S. Wells William, while serving as a *Charge d'Affaires* for the American legation in Peking, observed in 1866 that: "The long continued existence of Lewchew (Ryukyu), with a population of less than two hundred thousand inhabitants, as an entirely independent government lying between two such powerful nations as Japan and China might perhaps be impossible."[7] Nevertheless, he believed that the Ryukyuan "attainments in self-government and civilization during six or seven centuries past, have doubtlessly been owing to their relations with China."[8] As confusing and uncertain as these observations about the political status of Ryukyu may first appear, they represented a prevailing opinion among the international communities, which in turn shaped General Ulysses S. Grant's judgment of the issue at the time of his arrival in China and Japan.

II

Grant left the White House in March 1877 after some sixteen years of continuous public service, first as a soldier and then as a two-term president.[9] In May 1877, he and Mrs. Grant, accompanied by John Russell Young (who from 1882 to 1885 served as the minister to China)[10] and others, began a round-the-world tour, something Grant had dreamt of during his years as president.[11] Having set out with no definite itinerary in mind, the general and his party continued the tour for two and a half years. On April 4, 1879, Grant wrote the following from Singapore to Elihu B. Washburne, his former secretary of state: "I shall then visit Chinese ports as far north as Shanghai, and possibly go to Pekin [Peking] before visiting Japan."[12] At this point, he became involved in the Asian dispute, for on the same day Japan finally annexed the Ryukyu Islands against Chinese will.[13]

Thus, when the distinguished general arrived in China with Robert Hart, the Inspector General of the Chinese Customs,[14] he found that he had been cast as the judge in the dispute between the two Asian countries. Although a private citizen, Grant was intrigued by the dispute and decided to accept China's request as a mediator.

It is evident that before General Grant visited China and Japan, Tokyo had no intention of settling its differences with Peking by means of negotiations. As mentioned earlier, Japan abolished the Ryukyu-han and created the Okinawa Prefecture on April 4, 1879. Sometime earlier, on October 7, 1878, Ho Ju-chang, the Chinese Minister in Tokyo, had demanded, in a strongly worded note, that Tokyo refrain from establishing a prefecture over the islands; Tokyo had rejected the demand. When Shishido Tamaki, the newly appointed Japanese Minister to China, went to Peking in April 1879, Foreign Minister Terashima Munenori instructed Shishido to avoid negotiating with the Tsungli Yamen on the Ryukyu question, and told him to seek instructions from Tokyo before answering inquiries from the Yamen about that question.[15] As can be imagined, these steps were conceived by Chinese leaders as indications of Japanese insincerity in settling the matter through peaceful means. As a result, the Chinese looked forward to Grant's visit as an appropriate opportunity for mediation and aid.

Earlier, Peking had attempted to have the British Minister in Japan mediate the dispute, but to no avail. While hoping for the Western powers' mediation, Peking was fearful of a demand for concessions that such mediation often entailed. Li Hung-chang[16] reasoned that the American ex-president's mediation would be more effective than that of foreign envoys; moreover, since he was now a private citizen, a demand for concessions would not accompany his mediation.[17] His letter to the ministers of the Tsungli Yemen reflects this Chinese intention: "I hope I can persuade

General Grant to visit Peking, so that you will get acquainted with him and establish relations of cordiality. His good offices may be useful in the Ryukyu question. The Japanese are very friendly with the Americans and Grant is the foremost of them."[18]

Upon his arrival in China in May, General Grant and his party were warmly greeted by the Chinese officials. On May 23 and June 12, he was met by Li in Tientsin. Grant's first impression of the governor-general was a favorable one, as he recollected some years later he ranked Li first of the four great men whom he had met in his world tour.[19] This personal factor probably influenced the ex-president on matters relating to the Ryukyu affair during his visit to China.[20]

It was on these occasions that Li communicated Grant the Chinese government's desire for Grant to act as arbitrator in the Ryukyu question. Knowing that the general would later meet with the Japanese emperor and talk with the principal ministers of state in Tokyo, the governor-general hoped to invoke General Grant's interest and sympathetic support. He planned to associate Grant and the United States with the Chinese claims by inference if not by facts.[21] Li appears to have misunderstood, in some degree, the position of a former president and to have attributed to him a greater influence in political matters than he actually enjoyed.

Li noted that the Ryukyu Islands were semi-independent and that China had never exercised sovereignty, although she accepted tribute payments. He observed that the king and people of Ryukyu were not Chinese, although a few people of Chinese descent played an important role in government and education there.

China had no officials stationed in the islands, levied no taxes, and in the event of war neither received or extended aid. Ryukyu had always benefitted through the special trading facilities on the China coast, and the leading men of the kingdom sent their sons to Peking to study. Li assured General Grant that the Ryukyuan people preferred to be associated with China. From this, Li turned to a discussion of the strategic importance of the islands, noting that they were a screen for the China coast and straddled the international shipping lanes. He predicted that if Japan were allowed to remain in the Ryukyu Islands, Taiwan would some day be taken as wel1.[22]

In addition, the Chinese "prime minister" shrewdly made the point that American trade would suffer in the event of war between China and Japan. He knew very well that China was in no position, judging from her military and naval strength, to become involved in a war with Japan unless it were certain that the Western powers would aid China.[23] According to Li, General Grant agreed to mediate in the Ryukyu dispute if China would alter its laws governing Chinese migration to California.[24]

In answer to a query by Grant whether the sending of tribute by Ryukyu was considered by China as grounds for war, Li replied: "The sending of tribute is no problem, but since the king of Ryukyu has hitherto received investiture from the Chinese court, the abolition of this practice arbitrarily by Japan at this time is a violation of public law."[25] Li cleverly realized that Westerners who were familiar with enthronement and inauguration ceremonies and symbols could better understand the implications of investiture than they could the significance of tribute missions. Thus, he minimized what was considered so vital by the Chinese government.

In early June, Grant met and talked with Prince Kung in Peking. Advised by Li, the prince pleaded with Grant to exercise his good offices in the interest of peace in the Ryukyu controversy. He explained that the policy of his government was peace, but not peace at any price. He noted that though China claimed suzerain rights in Ryukyu, Japan had pursued an arbitrary policy there without any reference to the Middle Kingdom. The efforts of the Chinese government to arrive at a satisfactory understanding had hitherto proved unsuccessful, he said, and warned that unless Japan withdrew from the position she had assumed, China must declare war. His government was nevertheless willing to be guided by General Grant's decision in order to resolve the dilemma.[26]

In response, General Grant promised that when he arrived in Japan, he would study the Japanese side of the case and do whatever he could for the peaceful solution of the dispute. He expressed hope that the two Asian countries would reach a peaceful settlement instead of a military confrontation. War between China and Japan, Grant added, could only benefit third parties. Indeed, there were many who would welcome the war.[27]

The general then referred to an outstanding achievement of his administration—the arbitration between Great Britain and America on the *Alabama* Claims dispute—as an example for China and Japan.[28] "That arbitration," he stated, "may not satisfy either party at the time, but it satisfies the conscience of the world, and must command itself, as we grow in civilization, more and more, as the means of adjusting international disputes.[29]

Soon after this meeting, O.N. Denny, the American consul at Tientsin, accompanied Grant to Japan to act as liaison. Li Hung-chang requested that Denny take to Ho Ju-chang a record of his and Prince Kung's conversations with Grant as well as a letter from Li, which contained some interesting comments about the general: "Grant and I have become great friends... He was President and controlled American policy for eight years. When he returns home his countrymen will undoubtedly re-elect him. If he should voice his impartial judgment about this question (of Ryukyu), it may be *unnecessary* for him to refer back to the American Congress."[30] Li was mistaken. Technically, from an American point of view, Grant's involvement in the Ryukyu dispute was a violation of the Logan Act. Li overrated the power which ex-president Grant actually enjoyed; and he hoped that the general's prestige would outweigh technicalities.

The Logan Act, passed by Congress in 1799, prohibits American citizens from trying "to influence the measures or conduct of any foreign government or any officer or agent thereof" without the authority of the United States government.[31] The law, which carries a maximum penalty of a $5,000 fine and three years in prison, also bars a citizen from defeating "the measures of the United States" in any correspondence or talks with a foreign government or its agents. It prohibits any American, except the President and the Secretary of State, to discuss matters relating to foreign relations. Legally, Grant made a mistake in acting as he did at that time.

III

Judging by his tone toward both the Chinese and Japanese leaders during his visit in the Orient, General Grant was aware of his possible violation of the Logan Act. In fact, he expressed this fear to Li on June 12, when he talked to him the second time in Tientsin before sailing to Japan. He said that the Chinese may have overrated his power, but not his wish to preserve peace, and especially to prevent such a deplorable thing as a war between China and Japan.[32] He explained that he was a private citizen, with no authority to enter into negotiation or to speak for the government.[33]

In Japan, General Grant had an audience with Emperor Meiji on August 10. The general repeated to the emperor that he had been requested by the Chinese leaders to use his good offices with the Japanese government on the question of Ryukyu. He said he would rather not trouble himself about the matter, as it belonged to diplomacy and governments. At the same time, however, he could not ignore a request made in the interest of peace.[34] "The importance of peace between China and Japan is so great," the general said, "that each country should make concessions to the other."[35]

Since Grant's dialogue with Emperor Meiji is of considerable importance in terms of his mediation of the Ryukyu dispute, it is recorded here.[36]

General Grant:	It may not be improper in this connection to say that, while I was in China I had several interviews with Li Hungchang and Prince Kung. They spoke to me at length regarding the Loo Chu [Ryukyu] question; and requested me to speak to the members of the Japanese

Government in favor of its proper and moderate settlement. I promised them I would do my best, though I declined to act as their agent in the matter. I then told them I would first speak to the U. S. Minister Mr. Bingham which I did, and many times too. I also had a talk on the subject with Mr. Ito and General Saigo while at Nikko. And I have of late informed myself more fully on the subject then before. As is the case in all controversies—there are two sides—and what I have learned in Japan is fardifferent from what I was told in China. I am not, of course, in a position to know definitely the merits of the case. On that I would not feel myself justified in expressing an opinion. I can see how impossible it is for Japan to recede from her position. I can see how her case has features that cannot be answered.—A nation having gone as far as Japan, and having acted as she believed in her unquestioned sovereignty, must consider what is due to her people. But while all that should be recognized and conceded, there is an aspect to the Loo Chu [Ryukyu] affair, which seen from the Chinese point of view is worthy of attention. That is the only point that I would care to mention. China feels that she has not received from Japan the consideration due to her as a sovereign power—as a friendly nation—and as a nation which had for a long time enjoyed a certain relation to Loo Chu [Ryukyu]. She feels this more keenly now, because she feels that the case of Formosa was a humiliation. Suffering from that remembrance, she looks upon Japan's action as wanting in respect and friendship, and as indicating a disposition upon the part of Japan to again occupy Formosa and in doing so bar the channel between China and the Pacific Ocean. The result of this is that the Chinese statesmen feel a sense of wrong and irritation towards Japan. Now without, as I was saying, entering into the discussion, nor denying to Japan every right claimed by the government, it seems to me that this feeling in the minds of Chinese statesmen should be well-considered by Japan, and that Japan in a spirit of magnanimity and justice should make concessions to China. The importance of peace between China and Japan is so great that each country should make concessions to the other. I have heard it suggested, but I have no authority to speak on the subject, that a boundary line running between the islands so as to give China a wide channel to the Pacific would be accepted. I have no idea how true it is. I mention it to show that while in the minds of Chinese statesmen there is a feeling of anger, they are open to accommodation.

Emperor Meiji: As regarding Loo Chu [Ryukyu], Ito etc. are authorized to talk with you and will do so shortly.

General Grant: I would say one word more on this question. In your discussions with China on Loo Chu [Ryukyu), and on matters at issue, do not invite or permit so far as you can avoid it, the intervention of a foreign power. European powers have no interests in Asia, so far as I can judge from their diplomacy, that do not involve the humiliation and subjugation of the Asiatic people. Their diplomacy is always selfish, and a quarrel between China and Japan would be regarded by them as a quarrel that might ensue to their own advantage. China and Japan—approaching this question in a spirit of friendship and concession, as ancient allies and of the same race, can adjust it in a manner honorable to both, and lay the foundations of a lasting peace. I may add that nothing would give me more pleasure than to be able to carry back to my own country to which I am about to sail, the knowledge that peace between China and Japan had been assured.

Emperor Meiji: (Expressed his hope for the most peaceful and harmonious relations with China)....

This record reveals that General Grant's motivation to accept China's request for mediation arose from his kind feelings towards both China and Japan.[37] For he reasoned that a war between these two Asian nations would bring in foreign nations, who would end it to suit themselves. The history of European diplomacy in Asia, according to Grant,[38] was unmistakable on that point: "European powers have no interests in Asia, so far I can judge from their diplomacy, that do not involve the humiliation and subjugation of the Asiatic people. Their diplomacy is always selfish, and a quarrel between China and Japan would be regarded by them as a quarrel that might ensue to their own advantage."[39] Such an idea could not have failed to leave an impression on the Japanese leaders, as evidenced in Ito's letter to Shishido Tamaki, dated August 12, 1879—two days after the Meiji-Grant conversation.[40]

Earlier, on July 22, Grant had met in his inn in Nikko with the Japanese special envoys: Ito Hirobumi, then home minister, who was accompanied by War Minister Saigo Tsugumichi (who had led the 1874 Formosan expedition), and Yoshida Kiyonari, Japan's minister to the United States. In this Nikko Conference, Grant made two points.[41] First, he advised Japan to settle the Ryukyu question amicably with China without introducing a third party into the controversy. The only parties who might benefit from a Sino-Japanese war, argued Grant, would be those European powers whose policy aimed at reducing Japan and China to the status of dependency. Secondly, he pointed out that in the eyes of Peking, Tokyo's disposition of the Ryukyu Islands had violated the provision of the Sino-Japanese friendship treaty (1871) which bound each party to respect the territorial integrity of the other.[42] Grant judged that the two governments should discuss the issues and come to an understanding without foreign intervention. "Your weakness and your quarrels are their opportunity," concluded the general, "such a question as Loochoo [Ryukyu] offers a tempting opportunity for the interference of unfriendly diplomacy."[43]

Ito, after thanking General Grant for his counsel, presented Japan's side of the case.[44] He and other Japanese officials in this Nikko Conference responded to three major issues raised by the Chinese. They challenged the Chinese assertion that Japan's treatment of Ryukyu constituted a breach of the 1871 treaty between China and Japan, which provided that each nation should respect the territory of the other. This charge, the Japanese assured General Grant, could be refuted simply. They said that the Japanese rulers had for centuries protected and governed their people, had legislated for them and had received taxes from them. Therefore, China had no reason to claim Ryukyu as Chinese territory. Such a claim, they contended, needed no argumentative refutation. It was sufficiently met by a bare statement of facts. It emphatically told General Grant that there was no wish more dear to Japan than peace and good will with China. If any question of Chinese territory had been concerned, he said, the government of Japan would have acted with a proper regard for the rights of the Chinese empire and for the 1871 treaty of friendship.

Another issue discussed with Grant involved China's desire to maintain Ryukyu as a dual dependency of the two empires subject to the jurisdiction of the separate governments. To this the Japanese replied that such a situation would be a political anomaly quite unique. Different empires could assert rival claims to sovereignty over the same territory. In such a case one of the two claimants must have been deceived. In this instance, it was clear which of the two had been deceived. The Chinese government had accepted the mere statement of the Ryukyu king that he was independent of any other nation, and, under this belief, China maintained a purely nominal protectorate over the islands. Japan, on the other hand, having from time immemorial exercised a certain kind of sovereignty over the islands, eventually asserted her authority by force of arms, reduced the country to a proper obedience, gave it laws and a "constitution" and bound its rulers to a perpetual allegiance which had never been questioned, but had always been openly adhered to by Ryukyu and insisted upon by Japan.

Finally, the Japanese challenged the Chinese assumptions that Ryukyu was a nation and that no other power had any right to interfere with her independence. China admitted that she had long been aware that Ryukyu had paid tribute to Japan. Although it was regarded as inconsistent with the relations between her own sovereign and the people of these islands, especially since Ryukyu kings habitually received investiture from the emperors of China, yet out of respect for the autonomy of Ryukyu, China had refrained from calling her to account for this dereliction of duty. But the Chinese inferred that Japan also should take the same view, and that the Japanese government had no right to interfere with the freedom of the islands. Japan responded that she recognized no such independence in Ryukyu and could not do so without ignoring her own ancient and ancestral rights. It was nothing new for the emperor of China to assume a shadowy right of nominal suzerainty over small territories in the neighborhood of their empire by merely investing the local chiefs with the ceremonial insignia of kingship. History afforded other examples of this custom. The relations of Japan with Ryukyu had been of a very different character. It was impossible to reconcile China's nominal relations with Ryukyu and the claim of actual historical ownership. On this point, according to Ito, it was appropriate to recall that Japan had, even in recent times, dealt with the people of Ryukyu as with their own subjects. When famine visited the islands, Japan sent grain and money to support the people. A few years ago, when some of the Ryukyuan people were massacred by savages on the island of Formosa, the Japanese government fitted out an expedition to punish the authors of this outrage. China did not dispute the right of the Japanese government to send out this expedition. On the contrary, she even went so far as to pay, on behalf of the Formosans, an indemnity to Japan for outrages committed upon the Ryukyuan islanders.

Skillfully applying international law to challenge the Chinese walls of the tributary system, Ito Hirobumi and his colleagues, by frequently omitting or distorting some of the historical facts, succeeded in persuading General Grant of Japan's side of the Ryukyu story. It assured Grant that Tokyo would give most careful consideration to his counsel.[45] Grant, in turn, promised to advise Peking if necessary. On August 1 he wrote from Tokyo to Li Hung-chang about the Nikko, conversations and urged China and Japan to settle the matter by direct negotiations without the mediation of a third party.[46]

IV

In retrospect, General Grant's involvement in the Ryukyu dispute was not only a violation of the Logan Act, but was also at odds with American foreign-policy goals in East Asia. The main concern of the American State Department was maintaining the "co-operative policy" and treaty rights in the Orient.[47] Although some Americans encouraged the expansionist impulses of Japan, the State Department showed little interest. Washington directed Bingham to make no formal representation to the Japanese government, but to hold himself ready to assist in smoothing over the problem of Ryukyu if he were asked to use his good offices. Bingham believed the Japanese to be in the wrong, but the State Department maintained that as long as the 1854 *compact* provisions were observed, the United States could not interfere. But the dispute continued, and at the time of Grant's involvement, the American government directed its minister in Tokyo to again review and report on it.[48]

Meanwhile, in a letter of July 8, Ho Ju-chang formally sought the good offices of the United State to bring about an amicable arrangement of the matter with Japan. But the Chinese high officials had previously asked General Grant to present their case to the Japanese authorities, and he had done so. Bingham now asked for instructions as to whether or not he should use his good offices officially.[49]

The reply of Secretary of State William M. Evarts expounded the principles involved in this request of the good offices of the United States.[50] Evarts believed that: "The present dispute (over Ryukyu) grows out of that fruitful cause of international dissensions, the right of possession or jurisdiction over territory to which both lay traditional claim." He made it clear that: "To assume that such divided claim works injustice to one party or the other, and to officiously tender the good offices of this government in virtue of such assumption, would be practically to take sides in the question, which in view of its nature, is a course neither called for by the treaty,[51] nor admissible under the uniform policy of this government with regard to disputes between foreign nations."

According to the secretary of state, the attitude of the American government toward the Ryukyu question was clear; it was a policy of non-involvement. "It would, therefore," concluded Evarts, "be impossible for this government to tender its good offices at the instance of only one of the parties to the question, or to impose its influence for the settlement of a dispute of this character, without, in effect, disparaging the independent sovereign rights of the other. Such a course, whether limited to a tender of good offices, or extending to mediation or arbitration, could only be adopted on the certain assurance that it would be agreeable to both parties." This analysis indicates that Grant's involvement in the Ryukyu dispute was not in line with American policy. But the American representatives in Tokyo took no action against Grant's arbitration, probably because of the general's position as ex-president.[52]

V

General Grant continued his mediation activities during his stay in Japan. He wrote Li Hung-chang several times, reporting his progress with the Japanese officials concerning the Ryukyu question.[53] There were rumors that Grant had made a concrete suggestion to the Japanese and Chinese leaders for the peaceful settlement of the dispute: the partition of the Ryukyu Islands between China and Japan.[54] Extant records do not support this claim.

Evidence contrary to the rumor is contained in Grant's identical letters of August 13, 1879, to Iwakura Tomomi, the Japanese prime minister, and to Li Hung-chang and Prince Kung. He suggested in these letters that China withdraw certain offensive correspondence which had been addressed officially to the Japanese government on October 7, 1878. Believing that arbitration would resolve the issue, he hoped that China and Japan would each appoint commissioners to appraise the problem and arrange for impartial arbitration. Finally, Grant desired that no foreign countries or foreigners be allowed to become parties to the dispute itself, or to be employed in any way in connection with the affair, except, perhaps, as interpreters.[55] This important letter reads in full as follows:

"Since my arrival in Japan I have been favored with several interviews with the Cabinet of His Majesty The Emperor, on the subject which His Highness Prince Kung, and His Excellency the Viceroy Li Hung Chang have so much at heart, to wit, an honorable and satisfactory settlement of the Loo Choo [Ryukyu] question; a settlement which will be alike honorable to both nations. While the statement of facts relating to this question, as stated by the Japanese side differ, in many material points from the statements made to me, both in Peking and Tientsin yet I feel that what I have heard here will justify me in saying that the Japanese are most anxious to preserve the most amicable relations with China, and to this end would magnanimously make sacrifices of what she believes to be her just rights if China would meet her in the same spirit. But in the heated controversy which has already taken place between the two governments, on the Loo Choo [Ryukyu] question there has been one or more communications on the part of China, so threatening in tone, or if not threatening so offensive, that I do not believe that the Japanese would consent to treat with any commission from the other side, until China consented to withdraw such despatch or despatches. This being done I believe Japan would gladly appoint a commissioner, or commissioners from among her able citizens, to meet a like commissioner or commissioners, appointed in like manner by China from among her own representative citizens.

They would not only meet to confer, but would meet determined to bring about permanent good feeling among the two peoples—if China would meet them half-way in concessions."

"No foreign power should be brought into such a convention, nor should any foreigner, except it might be as an interpreter; and with the consent of both parties. It might be that such a convention would fail to agree entirely, or fail upon some minor points, in which contingency the two nations might agree upon an arbitrator whose decision on the disputed points, after hearing both sides, should be binding. In such case, while it is entirely the business of the two nations, I would earnestly suggest that no representative of a foreign government abroad should be selected."

"In the vast East, embracing more than two-thirds of the human population of the world—there are but two nations even partially free from the domination and dictation of some one or other of the European powers, with intelligence and strength enough to maintain their independence—Japan and China are the two nations. The people of both are brave, intelligent, frugal and industrious. With a little more advancement in modern civilization, mechanics, engineering, etc. they could throw off the offensive treaties which now cripple and humiliate them, and could enter into competition for the world's commerce. Much more employment for the people would result from the change and vastly more effective it would be. They would become much larger consumers as well as producers, and then the civilized world would be vastly benefited by the change; but none so much as China and Japan."

"Japan is rapidly reaching a condition of independence and if it had now to be done over such treaties as exist could not be forced upon her. What Japan has done, and is now doing, China has the power—and I trust the inclination—to do. I can readily conceive that there are many foreigners, particularly those interested in trade, who do not look beyond the present and who would like to have the present condition remain, only grasping more from the East, and leaving the natives of the soil merely 'hewers of wood and drawers of water' for their benefit. I have so much sympathy for the good of their children if not for them, that I hope the two countries will not disappoint them."

"I leave Japan in two weeks from now, for my American home. If I could hear there that amicable and most friendly relations had been established between China and Japan I should feel delighted. If anything I may have said or done should have any effect in producing so desirable a result I shall feel that my visit has not been in vain, though made without any thought of taking any part in the affairs of the two countries."

> "With many thanks for the great courtesy shown me by all Chinese officials during my visit to the country, and with the assurances of my highest consideration,
>
> I am very truly and respectfully,
Your obedient servant,
[Signed] U.S. Grant"

This formal communication clearly shows that the ex-president, as mediator, did not make a concrete proposition for the partition of the Ryukyu Islands between China and Japan as a solution to the dispute.

Other evidence contrary to the rumor can be seen in Inoue Kaoru's letter to Bingham, dated April 19, 1880.[56] In this letter the new Japanese foreign minister sought to confirm Ho Ju-chang's statement that Bingham, after full consultation with General Grant, had suggested the partition of Ryukyu: "Riu-Kiu [Ryukyu] is naturally divided into three parts: The Middle part would be returned to the King of Riu-Kiu [Ryukyu) to restore the Kingdom and its sovereignty; China and Japan may appoint their respective consuls to protect her in common; the Southern part is situated near to Formosa and very important to China; it will therefore be subjected to China; the Northern part is situated near to Satsuma and very important to Japan; it will therefore be subjected to Japan."[57] This letter of inquiry, which brought Bingham's letter of denial,[58] indicates Japan's ignorance of such a proposition. Had General Grant suggested partition, the Japanese foreign minister would not have had to ask Bingham for confirmation of the news.

VI

From the above description of General Grant's mediation of the Ryukyu dispute, we see that all the ex-president did was to try his best to avoid any chance of a Sino-Japanese war, with relatively little regard to the political status of the Ryukyu Kingdom. The basic problems of Japan's frontier security and territorial expansion, as well as China's effort to defend the Sino-centric tributary state system, were beyond Grant's comprehension.

General Grant's mission was doomed to fail: he could not please both the Chinese and Japanese. Clearly, he was in a dilemma. He was in an even more difficult position than he realized. For the Chinese leaders were trying to use him, if possible, to embarrass Japan and to estrange Washington and Tokyo. No sooner had this distinguished guest arrived in China than Li Hung-chang made a determined effort to reopen the Ryukyu sovereignty question, ostensibly on behalf of Sho Tai—the last emperor of the island kingdom.[59]

Li believed that poverty-stricken Ryukyu was not worth a war.[60] Yet he perceived that the Western powers were closely following the course of the dispute and could be counted on to draw some pregnant conclusions from the outcome.[61] Furthermore, to declare war with a rising Japan was risky since the international environment of the late 1870's was unfavorable to China due to the crisis with Russia over Ili.[62] It should be recalled that Russia had posed a major threat to China's security from 1878 on, so much so that war clouds hung low over both Peking and Moscow. Under such circumstances, Japan posed an additional problem for Peking: the Chinese feared possible collusion between Japan and Russia. Li Hung-chang was apprehensive that China might face Russia and Japan simultaneously, and the Western powers might fish into the troubled water and make further demands.[63] The use of the former American president's good offices was, therefore, perceived by Li as an effort to elevate the question to a level of international discussion in order to block the Japanese design on the Ryukyu Islands.

Some evidence of European interest in the controversy was shown by newspaper reports which Bingham transmitted to the State Department. One advocated an alliance between Germany and China (from the German *Army Gazette*), another alleged that Russia and Japan had formed an alliance (from the *Pall Mall Gazette*), and a third, based on a telegram from London, asserted that the United States had offered to mediate (from the *Japan Daily Herald*), which Bingham regarded as a piece of British meddling.[64] The latter brought an instruction for Bingham to deny the statement.[65]

A letter from Max von Brandt (formerly at Tokyo but then German minister to Peking) to Sir Harry Parkes,[66] dated July 3, 1879, gives the typical European opinion of the situation at that time: "A little war between China and any foreign Powers would do it an immense amount of good and would make it progress more in six months' time than it would do otherwise in twenty years."[67]

It is doubtful that a war between China and Japan could have enabled the Chinese to modernize. General Grant was in particular apprehensive that if war should ensue between China and Japan, European powers would end it in their own way and to their own advantage, and not to the advantage of the two Asian nations. He said to Emperor Meiji on August 10, shortly before he headed for America, "I may add that nothing would give me more pleasure than to be able to carry back to my own country, to which I am about to sail, the knowledge that peace between China and Japan had been assured."[68]

There was to be no such assurance when he sailed homeward. But credit for easing the 1879-80 Sino-Japanese tension over the Ryukyu Islands goes to General Grant. Although he did not make any concrete proposition for settlement, his mediation helped the Japanese and Chinese commissioners to meet and make mutual concessions; and this in turn eliminated the risk of Sino-Japanese conflict. By prevailing upon Tokyo to negotiate with Peking, Grant furthered the cause of peace in East Asia. It is difficult to refute Grant's view that such a conflict would have ended to the advantage of European powers and to the detriment of China and Japan. By and large, the aftermath of the Sino-Japanese war of 1894-95 proved him a prophet.[69]

Notes

1. For an earlier study, see: Mikuniya Hiroshi, "Ryukyu kizoku ni kansuru Guranto no chotei" (General Grant's mediation of the Ryukyu issue), *Toho gakuho* (Kyoto) 10.pt.3 (Oct. 1939), 29-64. This article however uses no American source and little Chinese and Ryukyuan source.
2. For Sino-Ryukyuan relations, see: Ta-tuan Ch'en, "Sino-Liu-ch'iuan Relations in the nineteenth century," (unpublished Ph.D. dissertation. Indiana University, 1963) (in microfilm).
3. Cf. Ta-tuan Ch'en, "Investiture of Liu-ch'iu Kings in the Ch'ing Period," in John K. Fairbank (ed.) *The Chinese World Order: Traditional China's Foreign Relations* (Cambridge, Mass.: 1968), 135-164: Robert K. Sakai. "The Ryukyu (Liu-ch'iu) Islands as a Fief of Satsuma," in *Ibid.*, 112-134.
4. For a Ryukyuan point of view, see: Kishaba Choken. *Ryukyu kenbun-roku* (or *Haihan jiken*) (An eye-witness account of the disposition of Ryukyu, 1872-1879). Tokyo: reprinted, 1952.
5. Shidehara Hiroshi, "Ryukyu no Shina ni tsuzeshi tancho," (The beginning of Ryukyu's relations with China) *Shigaku zasshi* 6.9 (Sept. 1895). 680.
6. Quoted from George Kerr, "Sovereignty of the Liu-chiu Islands," *Far Eastern Survey* 14.8 (April 1945). 97.
7. S. Wells Williams, "Political Intercourse between China and Lewchew," *Journal of the North China Branch. Royal Asiatic Society (Shanghai)* III (New Series) (Dec., 1866), 81-93.
8. *Ibid.*
9. Charles Tansill, *United States and Santo Domingo* (Baltimore: 1938), 340: see also Allan Nevins, *Hamilton Fish: the Inner History of the Grant Administration.* (N.Y.: 1936).
10. Jack L. Hammersmith, "American Attempts to prevent a War over 'Vietnam': the Experience of John Russell Young, 1882-85," *The Historian* 38.2 (Feb., 1976), 253-67.
11. Nevins, op. cit., 893: "The ex-President as Secretary of State Hamilton Fish records in his papers, had made $25,000 from a fortunate mining investment, and resolved to exhaust it in travel."
12. *General Grant's Letters to a Friend, 1861-1880* (N.Y.: 1897). 89-91.

13. Hyman Kublin, "The Attitude of China during the Liuchiu Controversy, 1871-1881," *Pacific Historical Review* XVIII.2 (1949), 213-31.

14. Robert Hart's letter to his London agent and confidant, James Duncan Campbell, from Shanghai, dated May 6, 1879, *The I.G. in Peking: Letters of Robert Hart, Chinese Maritime Customs. 1866-1907*, edited by J.K. Fairbank, K.F. Bruner and E.M. Matheson (Cambridge, Mass.: 1975). 1, 294.

15. *Segai Inoue Ko den* (Biography of Marquis Inoue Kaoru) (Tokyo: 1933-34), III, 404.

16. Then governor-general of Chihli and superintendent of trade of Northern Ports.

17. Mikuniya Hiroshi. op. cit, 34.

18. *Li-wen-chung-kung ch'uan-chi* (Complete works of Li Hung-chang), *I-shu han-kao* (Shanghai: 1921), 8:36, 40.

19. Grant recalled that: "I have met on this journey four great men, Bismarck, Beaconsfield, Gambetta, and Li Hung Chang. I am not sure, all things considered, but Li is the greatest of the four," in John Russell Young, *Men and Memories: Personal Reminiscences* (N.Y.: 1901), II, 303.

20. According to Young, the relations between Grant and Li had almost the element of romance. *Ibid.*, 319: Liang Chung-ying, *Li Hung-chang tui-Jih wai-chiao chueh-t'se chih yen-chiu* (Studies on Li Hung-chang's foreign policy toward Japan) (Taipei: 1974), 79.

21. *Li-wen-chung-kung ch'uan-chi, I-shu han-kao*, 8:36a-b.

22. *Ibid.*

23. Record of Li's talk with Grant, *Ibid.*, 8:41a-44a.

24. *Ibid.*, 8:4313.

25. *Ibid.*, 8:42a.

26. Frank Brinkley. "The Story of the Riukiu (Loochoo) Complication," *Chrysanthemum* III. 3, March 1883), 142; New York *Herald*, Aug. 15, 1879.

27. Brinkley, op. cit., 142.

28. In the Treaty of Washington (1871) settlement of various dispute between the U.S. and Britain was agreed upon, including arbitration of the *Alabama* Claims in Geneva. And the following year, an international tribunal awarded the U.S. $15,000,000 as result of this arbitration. For details, see: Goldwin A. Smith, *The Treaty of Washington, 1871: a study in important history* (Ithaca, 1941), 91-113.

29. John Russell Young, *Around the World with General Grant* (N.Y., 1879), II, 412. Strangely, General Grant recalled this matter in late April. 1879, shortly before he arrived in China, as follows: "...The *Alabama* arbitration was an illustration of what those in authority are compelled sometimes to do as a matter of expedience." (*Ibid.*, 279-81) This view is contradictory to what Grant later expressed to Prince Kung.

30. *I-shu han-kao*, 8:48-49.

31. *The Public Statutes at Large of the U.S.A.* (Boston, 1854). I, 613; see also *United States Code* (Washington, D.C., 1971), IV, 4271.

32. *Around the World*, II, 416.

33. Joel T. Headley, *Life and Travel of General Grant* (Philadelphia, 1879), 145.

34. For a complete record of this conversation, see: Gaimusho, *Nihon gaiko nenpyo narabini shuyo bunsho* (Chronology and major documents of diplomatic affairs in Japan) (Tokyo, 1955), I, 74-8; *Around the World*, 545.

35. "Memorandum of the Conversation between His Majesty and General Grant, August 19th 1879 at Hama Rikiu," English-language transcript in Kokumain Seishin Bunka Kenkyu-jo, *Guranto Shogun to no gotaiwa hikki* (The Meiji Emperor's discourse with General Ulysses S. Grant, hereafter cited as *Hikki*) (Tokyo: 1937), 22.

36. *Hikki*, 20-23.

37. *Around the World*, II, 559.

38. *Ibid.*, 546.

39. *Hikki*, 22; Ito's letter to Shishido Tamaki, dated August 12, 1879, shows that Ito was impressed by Grant's idea. Hiratsuka Atsushi, *Zoku Ito Hirobumi hiroku* (Supplement to the confidential records of Ito Hirobumi, hereafter cited as *ZIHH*) (Tokyo: 1930), 23-24.

40. *ZIHH*, 23-24.

41. See John Russell Young's report on the Nikko Conference, from Nikko on July 23, 1879, the New York *Herald*, Sept. 1, 1879.

42. Around the World, II, 558-62.

43. Recorded in Matsui Junji, *Ryukyu jiken* (The Ryukyu Affair) (Tokyo: 1880), 77; *Around the World*, II, 560.

44. The New York *Herald*, Sept. 1, 1879.

45. *Ito Hirobumi den* (Biography of Ito Hirobumi), II, 132.

46. T.F. Tsiang, "Sino-Japanese Diplomatic Relations, 1870-1894," *The Chinese Social and Political Science Review* XVII (1933), 43.

47. For an interesting discussion of the "cooperative policy" see: Mary C. Wright, *The Last Stand of Chinese Conservatism: the Tung-chih Restoration, 1862-1874* (N.Y.: 1967), 21-42. The policy expounded (1) cooperation among Western powers; (2) cooperation with Chinese officials; (3) recognition of Chinese legitimate interests; and (4) enforcement of the treaty rights.

48. George Kerr. *Okinawa: the History of an Island People* (Rutland, Vermont: 1959), 385-6.

49. *Despatches from U.S. Ministers to Japan, 1855-1906.* (Department of State, National Archives, M13, in microfilm), no. 970, Sept. 18.

50. Evarts' reply to Bingham, Oct. 25, 1879, *Diplomatic Instructions of the Department of State, 1801-1906, Japan.* (Department of State. National Archives, M77, in microfilm), no. 465.

51. Evarts: "It is observed that the Chinese Government bases its appeal on the text of the first article of the treaty of June 18, 1858 between the U.S. and China, wherein it is provided that if any other nation shall act unjustly or oppressively, the United States will exert their good offices, on being informed of the case, to bring about an amicable arrangement of the question." *Ibid.*

52. Especially Grant's first two weeks in Japan, and to a lesser degree throughout his stay, his schedule was filled with formal entertainment, ceremony, and visits from American and Japanese officials.

53. Grant's two letters to Li can be found in *I-shu han-kao* 9:32b-33; 9:40b-41b, which are translated into Chinese. The original copies of the letters are not in the *Grant Papers.*

54. Richard T. Chang, "General Grant's 1879 Visit to Japan," *Monuments Nipponica* XXIV.4 (Winter 1969), 381.

55. This letter can be found in the *Grant Papers* (in microfilm, Library of Congress), Reel 2, S.IB, 6312-15. See also *Okinawa-ken shi* (History of the Okinawa Prefecture) XV, 149-151.

56. Inoue to Bingham, April 19, 1880, Tokyo, *Archives in the Japanese Ministry of Foreign Affairs, years 1839-1945.* Microfilmed by the Library of Congress. PVM 10: "The Problem of the Reversion of the Ryukyu Islands, Jan. 1854-Sept, 1887," 604. Sometime earlier, on June 28, 1880, Inoue had also talked to Ho Ju-chang, the Chinese minister, on the same question, see Document 56.21, handwritten original copy in *Shishido Tamaki kankei bunsho* (The Shishido Tamaki Papers, unpub-

lished materials on and related to the Ryukyu dispute), located in the Kensei Shiryo Shitsu, National Diet Library, Tokyo.

57. Ho to Li, Enclosure of Inoue to Bingham, *Archives in the Japanese Ministry of Foreign Affairs*, PVM 10:604. See also Documents 70, 72, 75, 76, 77, 80, 83, in *Okinawa-ken shi* XV.

58. Bingham to Inoue, U.S. Legation, Tokyo, April 20, 1880, *Archives in the Japanese Ministry of Foreign Affairs*, PVM 10:606-3; *Okinawa-ken shi*, XV, 183-185.

59. Kerr, op. cit., 385.

60. Tsiang, op. cit., 37-8.

61. Kublin, "Chinese Attitude...," 224-226.

62. Immanuel C.Y. Hsu, *The Ili Crisis: A Study of Sino-Russian Diplomacy, 1871-1881*, Oxford at the Claredon Press, 1965.

63. *Ibid.*, 102-3, 116-7.

64. *Despatches from U.S. Ministers to Japan*, No. 1013, Nov. 12; No. 1016, Nov. 18; No. 1027, Dec. 8, 1879.

65. *Diplomatic Instructions of the Department of State, 1801-1906, Japan*, No. 478, Jan. 1880.

66. Then British minister in Tokyo.

67. F.V. Dickens and S. Lane-Poole, *The Life of Sir Harry Parkes* (London: 1903), II, 283-285.

68. *Hikki*, 22; *Nihon gaiko bunsho* (Diplomatic Papers of Japan), XII, 152.

69. For instance, the Sino-Japanese war of 1894-95 brought on the Triple Intervention of Russia, France, and Germany, to force Japan to give up the Liaotung Peninsula.

4

From Prohibition to Protection: Ch'ing Government's Changing Policy Toward Chinese Emigration

I. Introduction

The influx of Chinese laborers into Southeast Asia and America is an important phenomenon in modern world history. Millions of Chinese in the 19th century left their homes for the Gold Mountain (America) and the South Ocean (Nanyang) looking for better opportunities abroad, or for the sake of sheer survival. However, most of them experienced exploitation and discrimination in the new lands, as some of them were treated virtually as slaves, while others worked as coolies or contract laborers.[1] Their lives were full of indescribable hardships and sufferings, since their rights and safety were not protected by the foreign governments, nor their home government.[2]

The following table indicates the number of Chinese contract laborers emigrating abroad between the years 1800 and 1925, and the major areas of distribution:

Table 1

Chinese Contract Laborers Abroad, 1800-1925

Area	*Number of Chinese Laborers*	*Remarks*
1. 1801-1850 (320,000 total)		
a) Southeast Asia (including British Penang, Singapore, Malaya, Siam the Philippines, Java)	200,000	most laborers on board Chinese ships, some took British ships to Singapore mostly leaving from Hong Kong
b) U.S.A.	18,000	
c) Peru	10,000	
d) West Indies	15,000	
2. 1851-1875 (1,280, 000 total)		
a) Malaya Penn. (including Singapore)	350,000	
b) The Philippines	45,000	including those later transferred to Cuba
c) U.S.A.	160,000	
d) Hawaiian Islands	25,000	
e) Canada	30,000	
f) East Indies	250,000	
3. 1876-1900 (750,000 total)		
a) U.S.A.	12,000	
b) Hawaiian Islands (1876-1898)	5,000	
c) Malaya Penn.	360,000	
d) The Philippines	20,000	
e) Canada	4,000	including those to U.S.A. via Canada
f) East Indies	320,000	
4. 1901-1925 (650,000 total)		
a) Malaya Penn.	125,000	
b) East Indies	300,000	

Source: Ch'en Tse-hsien, "Shih-chiu shih-chi sheng-hsin ti ch'i-yo hua-kung chih" (The popular contract Chinese laborer system in the 19th century), *Li-shih yen-chiu* 1 (1963), pp. 176-178.

The above table reflects at best only a conservative estimate, since many Chinese were kidnapped illegally by the foreign agents in China, while hundreds and thousands died in the high sea due to inhuman treatment by crew members. Professor Chen Tse-hsien gives a figure of 3 million Chinese emigrants in the period of 1800-1925.[3] But Professor Mary Somers Heidhues believes that just between the years 1876 and 1901, already 4.8 million Chinese had left China.[4] While the actual number can never be known because of the lack of reliable and comprehensive statistics, it is obvious that the magnitude of 19th century Chinese emigration was significantly large indeed.

One basic question naturally arises: why did so many Chinese leave their homes for foreign lands? That is, under what circumstances did they emigrate, risking their government's prohibitory emigration laws (such laws were still in the Ch'ing statute book until 1893)? And, how did the Chinese government respond to such illegal and massive Chinese emigration?

This paper will explore the changing policy of the Chinese government towards emigration: from that of the initial prohibition, to that of the later protection of Chinese abroad. In analyzing such a shift in government policy, the socio-economic and other relevant factors will also be examined in order to understand why the Chinese emigrated and how they presented a problematic reality to both the central and local governments.

II. The Ch'ing Government's Prohibitory Emigration Policy

When the alien Manchus overpowered Mainland China and founded the Ch'ing Dynasty in 1644, the prohibitory emigration policy was used initially as a political measure to ban Chinese from going overseas to join opponents of the Ch'ing court, particularly Cheng Ch'eng-kung's resistance movement in Taiwan. Understandably, the punishment for those who emigrated was severe. According to the Ch'ing statutes: "Those who find excuses to sojourn abroad and then clandestinely return home, if captured, shall be *executed* immediately".[5]

A frequently quoted edict of Emperor K'ang-hsi, promulgated in 1672, shows the harshness of the Ch'ing policy towards emigration:[6]

> All officers of government, soldiers, and private subjects, who clandestinely proceed to sea to trade, or remove to foreign islands for the purpose of inhabiting and cultivating the same, shall be punished according to the law against communicating with rebels and enemies, and consequently suffer death by being beheaded. The governors of cities of the second and third orders shall likewise be beheaded, when found guilty of combining with or artfully conniving at the conduct of such persons. When only a neglect of their duty, in not taking measures to prevent the same is the offense imputable to them, they shall not suffer death, but be degraded and dismissed forever from the public service. Governors of cities of the first order, and other officers having the same rank, when guilty of a similar neglect, shall be degraded three degrees and removed from their stations. Governor-generals and other great magistrates of provinces shall, in similar cases of imputed neglect, be degraded two degrees, but retain

> their offices. Nevertheless, the neglect of all such officers shall be pardoned, if afterwards succeed in securing the offenders, and in bringing them to condign punishment.

Although Cheng's resistance movement failed in 1683, the prohibitory emigration policy continued to be in force. However, since the policy had now lost its original meaning, its enforcement was not as strict as before. At one point, the Ch'ing government even relaxed the prohibitory emigration law, as evidenced in Emperor Yung-cheng's 1727 decree.[7] At other points, emigration was tolerated if applications were made for a permit to travel abroad.[8]

But the relaxation of the prohibitory emigration policy was largely due to the local governments' handling of the emigration problem in their respective regions, particularly along the coastal areas. Because most of the Chinese who went abroad were from South China (especially Kwangtung and Fukien provinces), and because the central government in Peking was unable to enforce the prohibitory emigration laws by itself, the local officials in the south therefore had a relatively free hand in handling the emigration problem at their discretion.[9]

Before the 19th century, the problem of Chinese emigration was not serious, since there was no great demand for Chinese labor in Southeast Asia and America.[10] Nor were there any compelling forces motivating large numbers of Chinese to seek a better life abroad. Many local officials, in dealing with the problem of Chinese emigration, either kept an eye closed or accepted bribes in exchange for their silence.[11] It was not until the 19th century, with the increasing number of Chinese leaving the country, and the problems caused by the coolie trade and the maltreatment of the

Chinese laborers abroad, that the central government finally became alarmed by the exodus of its people. This was particularly true after the news of the California Gold Rush had reached China by the late 1840's,[12] and when the Chinese economy was upset by the invasion of Western imperialism and by domestic upheavals.

III. The Pre-conditions and Causes of Chinese Emigration

The pre-conditions of the massive Chinese emigration must be examined in order to understand the causes and motivations of such a significant outward movement of population in 19th century China.

Professor Ho Ping-ti points to the pressure of the ever-increasing population in China, which rose from 275 million in 1779 to 430 million in 1850.[13] Together with a shortage of arable land, this increase led to a rice shortage throughout the country. In Kwangtung Province alone, population came close to doubling between 1786 and 1882.[14] According to Professor Chen Ta, "the pressure of population weighs heavily on the side of emigration."[15]

Many social and economic historians seem to have neglected the impact of opium-smoking on Chinese emigration. Opium-smoking was a widespread problem in South China as a result of heavy importation of the lucrative drug by British and other Western merchants. On the eve of the Sino-British Opium War (1839-

42), it is said that nine out of ten people in Kwangtung and Fukien provinces had become addicts of opium![16]

The economic repercussions of opium-smoking were most serious. Spending on opium caused a stagnation in the demand for other commodities, with a consequent general sluggishness in the market. Moreover, the constant in-flow of opium caused a continuous out-flow of silver. For example, between 1831 and 1833 nearly 10 million taels of silver flowed out of China.[17] The silver depletion upset the domestic economy, and rocked the exchange rate between silver and copper in the market.

The phrase *"yin-kuei ch'ien-chien"*, expressing the rising cost of silver and falling value of copper cash, abounds in the Chinese officials' memorials to the Emperor.[18] The strains that it put on the Chinese economy bore most heavily on the peasantry. For while taxes and rents were calculated by a silver standard, produce brought in increasingly worthless copper. By the late 1840's the cost of silver had risen to three times its official value.[19] Furthermore, the Opium War added the burden of tax surcharges, increases that are chronicled in the *hsien* gazetteers?[20]

The social effects of the Opium War were equally devastating, as they provoked a wave of disorder in South China. Professor C. K. Yang has done a quantitative analysis of mass actions (i.e. social protests or disturbances threatening public order) reported in the *Ta-Ch'ing li-chao Shih-lu* (Veritable records of the Ch'ing Emperors), which indicates the following frequencies:[21]

Years	1836-1845	1846-1855	1856-1865	1866-1875	1876-1885	1886-1895	1896-1911
Incidents	246	933	2332	909	385	314	653

The disturbances created disorder in the countryside and contributed to the further deterioration of the Chinese economy. There were also serious natural calamities reported in 1849, 1876, and 1878.[22] All these developments turned many peasants into bandits, while many others chose to emigrate instead and work abroad for sheer survival or better opportunities.

IV. The Coolie Trade and the Change of Chinese Emigration Policy

As early as 1827, there were reports indicating Chinese coolies were being deceived and sold overseas.[23] By the mid-19th century, the kidnapping of Chinese for exportation as laborers had become so lucrative that many Western transportation companies decided to organize their fleets, for the shipping of Chinese coolies.[24] This also included the transportation of those Chinese laborers who decided to emigrate at their own free will and paid the voyage tickets in advance or through the credit-ticket system.[25]

However, the voyage to the new land was usually a horrifying experience to the Chinese, as many of them described their carrying ships as the "floating hells": overcrowding, starvation, and inhuman treatment of the coolies by crew members were rampant.[26]

Naturally, the Kwangtung authorities were the first to learn about the illegal kidnapping and the maltreatment of the Chinese. As such, they were more active than the central government in coping with the coolie problem. Out of experience, they were also more sensitive than the Peking court in recognizing the need for a change in the emigration policy.[27]

Extant Chinese records show that it was Kwangtung Governor Lao Ch'ung-kuang who first "legalized" Chinese emigration. On October 28, 1859, Lao issued a proclamation in which he claimed that voluntary emigration was *legal* if the emigrants "proceeded themselves to the emigration houses and there made a clear report" examined by the Chinese officers.[28] Lao's proclamation constituted the first official recognition of the right of the Chinese legally to leave their homeland and settle abroad. Governor Lao at the meantime also came up with twelve regulations governing Chinese emigration, which became the blueprint of the regulations drawn up by the central government in 1866.[29]

The Chinese central government in 1860 also approved voluntary Chinese emigration, as evidenced in Article 5 of the Convention of Peking signed with Great Britain.[30] A similar agreement was included in the treaty between China and France signed also in 1860. The Spanish secured similar rights in a treaty signed in 1864, while the Sino-American Treaty of 1868 even permitted free immigration between the Chinese and the Americans.[31]

Although these treaties legally ended China's prohibitory emigration policy, they were not effective in controlling the emigration. Illegal kidnapping in Kwangtung still persisted, so the Governor-general of Liang-Kuang, Mao Hung-pin, proposed to Peking in October 1864 to impose a heavy punishment upon all native kidnappers apprehended in the act of carrying off Chinese for sale for foreign countries.[32] The proposal was accepted, and the Tsungli Yamen subsequently drew up a set of regulations for management of the coolie trade in any port of China. These regulations, twenty-two in number, were codified in the "Convention to Regulate the Engagement of Chinese Emigrants by British and French Subjects" signed on March 5, 1866.[33]

Essentially, the 1866 Convention was based on Governor Lao's proclamation and regulations of 1859. If strictly enforced and observed, the Convention could have established a sound emigration system, for the regulations insisted that only voluntary emigrants could go abroad and only if they were engaged by authorized foreign emigration agents under the joint supervision of the foreign consuls and the Chinese authorities.[34]

The Convention was approved by Russia, America and Prussia, though they were not parties to it. However, both the British and French governments refused to ratify the Convention on grounds of some unacceptable provisions.[35] Nevertheless, the regulations of the Convention formed the basic new policy of the Chinese government toward Chinese emigration. The Convention of 1866 not only opened the way for Chinese emigrating abroad, but also led to a change in the attitude of the Chinese government towards Chinese abroad: while earlier the government had disregarded them, it now showed a desire to protect them. This can be seen by certain provisions of the treaties later signed with Peru (1874), Spain (1877), and the United States (1880 and 1894).[36]

V. Conclusion: the Protection of Chinese Abroad

The desire of the Chinese government to protect its nationals abroad corresponds to the maltreatment of the Chinese outside China and to the sending of Chinese diplomatic representatives abroad. The Ch'ing government was particularly concerned with the anti-Chinese movement in America, which culminated in the passage of the Chinese Exclusion Act in 1882 by the U.S. Congress.[37] The Chinese Associate Minister in Washington, Yung Wing, registered a strong protest to the U. S. government in 1880 about the conditions of the Chinese in America: ". . . at the present time, the [Sino-American] Treaty of 1868 is practically a dead letter in one of the states of the Union where tens of thousands of my countrymen are by law deprived of shelter and prohibited from earning a livelihood and are in hourly expectation of being driven from their homes to starve in the streets . . . ."[38] It was under these unfortunate circumstances that the Chinese government finally learned of its responsibility in taking a more active role in protecting its nationals overseas. By the 1880's, therefore, China had sent its diplomatic representatives to major countries: United States, Spain, Peru, England, Germany, France, Italy, Japan.[39] As far as the protection of the Chinese in Southeast Asia is concerned, a Chinese consulate office was opened in Singapore in 1877, with

Hu Hsuan-tse[40] as the head officer. All these indicate the Ch'ing government's attempt to better protect its nationals abroad.

Ironically, the Ch'ing statute book still contained the item of prohibitory emigration. The first Chinese statesman suggesting the abolition of this law, in a memorial from London on June 29, 1893, was the Chinese Minister to England, Hsueh Fu-ch'eng. "The old prohibitory law has not been repealed," Hsueh remarked, "but it has repealed itself".[41] His suggestion was sent to the Tsungli Yamen for consideration by Emperor Kuang-hsu on August 21, 1893. At the same time, the diplomatic representatives of Great Britain, France, Italy and Belgium in Peking jointly petitioned the Chinese Emperor to abrogate this law.[42] The Chinese government by this time had realized that Chinese emigration had not only eased the problem of unemployment inside China, but also benefited China by millions of ounces of gold a year sent in by the overseas Chinese. As a result, the outdated prohibitive emigration law was finally annulled on September 13, 1893.[43]

Notes

1. Cf. Shih-shan Henry Tsai, *China and the Overseas Chinese* in *the United States, 1868-1911* (Fayetteville, 1983); Stuart C. Miller, *The Unwelcome Immigrant: the American Image of the Chinese, 1785-1882* (Berkeley, 1969); Victor Purcell, *The Chinese* in *Southeast Asia,* 2nd edition (London, 1965); Song Ong Siang, *One Hundred Years' History of the Chinese* in *Singapore* (London, 1923); and Persia C. Campbell, *Chinese Coolie Emigration to Countries within the British Empire* (London, 1923).
2. For documentation, see: Chu Shih-chia, *Mei-kuo p'o-hai hua-kung shih-liao* (Historical materials concerning America's Persecution of Chinese laborers) (Shanghai, 1958); and Chen Han-sheng, et. al. (eds.) *Hua-kung*

chu-kuo shih-liao (Historical materials concerning Chinese laborers abroad) (Peking, 1981).

3. Ch'en Tse-hsien, "Shih-chiu shih-chi sheng-hsin ti ch'i-yo hua-kung chih" (The popular contract Chinese laborer system in the 19th century) *Li-shih yen-chiu* (Historical Studies) 1 (1963), p. 178.
4. Mary F. Somers Heidhues, *Southeast Asia's Chinese Minorities* (New York, 1975), p. 16.
5. Tsai, *op. cit.*, p. 8.
6. The Ch'ing code has been translated into English by Sir G. T. Staunton, *Ta Tsing Leu Lee* (London, 1810), pp. 643-644.
7. Tsai, *op. cit.*, p. 10.
8. *Ibid.*
9. Purcell, *op. cit.*, pp. 26-27.
10. *Ibid.*, pp. 25-26.
11. Robert L. Irick, *Ch'ing policy toward the Coolie Trade, 1847-1878* (San Francisco, 1982), pp. 11-14.
12. Michael Hunt, *The Making of a Special Relationship: the United States and China to 1914* (New York, 1983), p. 64.
13. Ping-ti Ho, *Studies on the Population of China, 1368-1963* (Cambridge, MA, 1959), Appendix 1.
14. Yearly figures by province for 1786 to 1898 are given in Yen Ching-p'ing, et. al., *Chung-kuo chin-tai ching-chi shih t'ung-chi tzu-liao hsuan-chi* (A selection of statistical materials on modern Chinese economic history) (Shanghai, 1955).
15. Ta Chen, *Chinese Migrations, with Special Reference to Labor Conditions* (Washington D.C., 1923), p. 5.
16. Immanuel C. Y. Hsu, *The Rise of Modern China* 2nd edition (New York, 1975), pp. 223.
17. Hsin-pao Chang, *Commissioner Lin and the Opium War* (Cambridge, MA, 1964), p. 41.
18. See for example the memorial of the Liang-Kuang governor-general contained in *Ch'ing shih-lu chingchi tzu-liao chi-yao* (Economic materials from the Veritable Records of the Ch'ing) (Peking, 1959), p. 478.
19. Chang, *op. cit.*, pp. 39-40.
20. See Wang Yu-ch'uan, "The Rise of Land Tax and the Fall of Dynasties," in *Pacific Affairs 9* (1959-60), for a concise summary of this phenomena.

21. C. K. Yang, "Some Preliminary Patterns of Mass Action in 19th-century China," in Frederick Wakeman, Jr., and Carolyn Grant (eds.) *Conflict and Control in Late Imperial China* (Berkeley, 1975), p. 190.
22. Sing-wu Wang, "The Attitude of the Ch'ing Court toward Chinese Emigration," *Chinese Culture* IX. 4 (December 1986), p. 64.
23. Chang Hsin-tai, *Yueh-yu hsiao-chih* (Journal of my travel to Kwangtung) (1827), chapter 8, as quoted in Ch'en Tse-hsien, *op. cit.*, p. 163 note 5.
24. Hunt, *op. cit.*, p. 65.
25. Campbell, *op. cit.*, xvii: "Under the credit-ticket system Chinese brokers, paid the expenses of the coolie emigration. Until the debt so incurred by the coolie was paid off the broker had a lien on his services -- a lien that might or might not be sold to a bona fide employer of labor."
26. H. B. Morse, *The International Relations of the Chinese Empire Vol.* 2 (London, 1918), p. 170.
27. For more details, see Irick, *op. cit.*, pp. 81-150.
28. *Ibid.*, pp. 99-101.
29. The 12 Regulations can be found in *Chung-Mei kuan-hsi shih* (History of Sino-American relations, periods of Chia-ch'ing, Tao-Kuang, and Hsien-feng) (Nanchiang, Taipei, 1968), pp. 351-353.
30. Wang, *op. cit.*, p. 67.
31. Details of the 1868 Treaty in Frederick Wells Williams, *Anson Burlingame and the First Chinese Mission to Foreign Powers* (New York, 1921), Appendix I.
32. Wang, *op. cit.*, p. 67.
33. The 22 Regulations can be found in *Ch'ou-pan l-wu shih-mo* (The complete account of the Management of barbarian affairs), T'ung-chih period (Peking, 1930), 39: pp. 13-20.
34. See details of the 22 Regulations.
35. Wang, *op. cit.* p. 70.
36. *Ibid.*, p. 72.
37. For more details, see Hunt, *op. cit.*, pp. 227-257.
38. Yung Wing to U. S. Secretary of State William M. Evarts, March 9, 1980, Notes from the Chinese Legation to the Department of States, *National Archives* 98, Roll 1.
39. Immanuel C. Y. Hsu, *China's Entrance into the Family of Nations: the Diplomatic Phase, 1858-80* (Cambridge, MA, 1960), Appendix B.

40. Hu Hsuan-tse, also known as Hoo Ah Kay, was a Singapore merchant, see: Michael R. Godley, "The Late Ch'ing Courtship of the Chinese in Southeast Asia," *Journal of Asian Studies* 34.2 (February, 1975), pp. 363-364.

41. Hsueh Fu-ch'eng, *Yung-an ch'uan-chi* (Collected works of Hsueh Fu-ch'eng) 1:319-20, *as* translated in Tsai, *op. cit.,* pp. 10-11.

42. Ta Chen, *op. cit,* p. 18.

43. Wang, *op. cit.*, p. 75.

PART II

POLITICS AND LEADERSHIP

5

The Characteristics of Political Leaders in Modern China

Confucius has said: "the rule of virtue can be compared to the Polc Star which commands the homage of the multitude of stars without leaving its place" (*Analects* 12.1). This saying is significant insofar as it refers to one aspect of Chinese political leaders (both ancient and contemporary), namely, the desire for order through the authority of one key figure: the ruler. This introduction discusses the characteristics of the political leaders of the late imperial period, the Republican period, and the Communist period. Though each period is marked by different specific ideological elements, all three periods reveal their common heritage in a tradition that favors a strong central government. While this belief is not necessarily unique to the Chinese per se, its expression, through a deep historical understanding of what it means to be "Chinese," is. And this reverence for Chinese culture reveals how even the most radical elements of contemporary politics did not shake off the residue of some traditional Chinese values and ideas.

Common Characteristics

One common characteristic of these leaders that should not be too surprising to anyone familiar with the political history of any culture is the desire for power. None of the major political figures in each of these three periods, no matter how virtuous or ruthless, was free from the overwhelming desire to control China's fate. Of course, not everyone who aspired for power succeeded in attaining it. Hong Xiuquan, the leader of the Taiping Uprising of the 1850s and 1860s, led a religious/social rebellion against what he saw as an unworthy, corrupt government. Though his motives may have been mostly or partly religious, there is no denying his desire to control China. He may have wanted to bring China salvation, but his self-proclamation as the "Heavenly King" of a new dynasty demonstrated an ulterior motive of power.

Another example of power lust is the similarly brief and failed attempt by Yuan Shikai to start a new dynasty in the early Republican period. Yuan saw the opportunity to take advantage of the budding republic for his own personal gain. Unlike most of China's modern leaders, Yuan did not seem to be driven by any sense of nationalism toward China, but only by his own desire for power. He defied constitutional procedures and dissolved parliament in an attempt to consolidate his power. It was indeed a tragedy in China's early Republican history.

By far, the most famous battle for power in recent decades was between Jiang Jieshi (Chiang Kai-shek) and Mao Zedong in the civil war of the 1930s and 1940s. Both sides painted noble pictures of their struggles for the people of China. But behind the scenes lay a fight for control not only between the parties, but also within the parties themselves. After the Communist takeover and subsequent exile of the Nationalists to Taiwan, Jiang ruled the island with an iron fist. It was not until his son, Jiang Jingguo, came to power that Taiwan began to move toward democracy. Likewise, on the mainland, Mao struggled to consolidate his power, becoming "deified" in the eyes of the people. As some in the party and in the general public became disillusioned with Mao's failed "Great Leap Forward," he sought to regain authority by sowing the seeds of the Cultural Revolution of the 1960s and 1970s, which attempted to reenergize support for Mao. During this time, Mao, who had been brought up with Confucian values, ostracized all of those with traditional Confucian ideals. As Mao grew older his main focus seemed to stray from doing what was best for China and turned toward maintaining his own power.

Most recently, in 1989, the struggle for power in China was plastered on television screens around the world during the student demonstrations at Tiananmen Square. But the Tiananmen Square demonstration also points to another more fundamental characteristic of Chinese politics from the late imperial period to the present: a desire for reform. In fact, "reform" embodies the tone and nature of not only the political climate of these periods, but also the social and intellectual climates as well. It is widely accepted that China is now in a period of rapid change and development, which has been sparked by recent desires for improved social and political conditions.

Even in the mid-nineteenth century, the theme of reform was evident. Lin Zexu, for example, pushed for reform by trying to rid China of foreign influence, especially in the opium trade. Lin was given orders to rid China of the addicting substance in whatever way possible. Unfortunately, he was eventually made the scapegoat of the Chinese government when Great Britain retaliated against his heroic efforts to destroy the opium coming into China. However, subsequent generations hailed him as a hero of social reform.

Reform can also be seen as a driving force for the other political leaders. Hong Xiuquan, through the Taiping Uprising had a mission to change China, and also rid the country of corruption and foreign influence. The fall of the Qing Dynasty in 1912 and the rise of Republican China came out of the spirit of reform. Sun Yat-sen and Jiang Jieshi after him envisioned a new republic rather than a new dynastic system. But with reform inevitably came disagreement as to what kind of reforms should be implemented. Again, the dispute between the Nationalists and the Communists was ideological insofar as both sides envisioned different remedies for China's ills. And even when the Communists prevailed in 1949, Mao still faced internal opposition to his own ideas of reform, since many of them had failed.

After Mao's death in 1976 and until 1989, Deng Xiaoping was hailed by many as a great reformer. Deng's pragmatism led to the opening of China to modernization, despite his aversion to democratization. His main concern was economic reform, which led him to coin the phrase "socialism with Chinese characteristics," an idea that is still promoted by Chinese political leaders today.

The Uniqueness of the Chinese Political Leaders

The special emphasis on "Chinese characteristics" was a common trait among the late modern and contemporary political leaders in China, which made them unique in world politics. It stemmed from a deep sense of cultural heritage and history. These leaders recognized and took pride in China's long and rich political and cultural legacy, and made it a staple of their reform efforts. No matter how China needed to change, China always needed to remain "Chinese."

The "Chineseness" of the reformers came in two broad categories: conservative and liberal. In the conservative category were reformers who wanted to take China back to a "golden age" of moral integrity. Many leaders during the Qing saw a corruption in the original moral order of society caused by some (usually foreign) element that needed to be exterminated. For Lin Zexu and others, it was opium, which profited foreign traders while it plagued the Chinese people. Opium enslaved the common people into addiction and corrupted government officials, who squandered the people's money in search of a constant drug-induced "fix." The key for Lin was to rid China of this social ill, and thereby return to a more idealized, a more "purified," social condition— one that was free from foreign influences.

In the liberal category were leaders like Mao and Deng, who both tried to reform China not by rejecting foreign influences, but rather by embracing them—but with a catch. The Chinese Communists could not pride themselves in rejuvenating an "old world" China. Socialism was a new idea, a foreign idea, an idea that appeared to reject everything the Chinese had tried before. But in order to make it palatable to the common people, the Communists had to show that it could be adapted to the Chinese context. Hence "Marxism" became "Maoism," which led to Deng's "Socialism with Chinese characteristics." Both Mao Zedong thought and Deng Xiaoping thought were far from classical Marxism, according to which China was far from ready for a Socialist revolution. But Mao's faith in the power of the Chinese peasant class and Deng's pragmatic concerns for China's specific economic problems provided grounds for enough adaptation of classical Marxist theory to make it work.

The Impact of Tradition

But what exactly does it mean to be "Chinese"? A truly satisfactory answer is too complex for this chapter, but suffice it to say that there is an element of indigenous tradition, especially Confucian tradition, in what brings out the "Chineseness" of the culture. Of course, the Confucian tradition is a long and complex one involving political, moral, and even religious elements, so to say that China has remained somewhat "Confucian" throughout the ages is vague. It is best to specifically point out the "family resemblances" of diverse individuals which make up a composite "Confucian" tradition.

The most obvious examples came out of the Qing with individuals who explicitly styled themselves Confucian. Lin Zexu's moral crusade against opium was a distinctly Confucian crusade. Lin and others such as Zeng Guofan and Li Hongzhang were schooled in the Confucian classics and were trained to view the world through the lens of Confucian moral and political discourse.

This discourse, since its beginnings in the Warring States period (468-221 B.C.), viewed proper government as a moral government, a government structured with ritual codes of conduct. And the government itself was supposed to be a monarchy that operated within the "dynastic system."

Even in Qing rebellions, such as that of Hong Xiuquan and the Taipings, the residue of Confucianism remained. Though Hong considered himself Christian and even destroyed Confucian temples, his creative "misunderstanding" of Christianity revealed his Confucian upbringing. Hong's view of the Trinity, for example, interpreted the three persons of God not as one substance, but as a "holy family," much like what was prevalent in traditional Chinese ancestor worship.

But what of the periods after the Qing? Did they not abandon Confucianism for more progressive worldviews? They did if Confucianism were strictly defined as an inherently hierarchical system of government that entailed monarchy. But first of all, traditions like Confucianism, which have evolved over millennia, tend to be flexible. Second of all, it is almost impossible to abandon any cultural tradition completely.

One Confucian cultural element that was never abandoned completely in both the Republican and Communist periods was the notion that social stability presupposed homogeneous thought patterns throughout society. In other words, "pluralism" was not acceptable. The notion of "choice" was never dominant in Confucian thought, so the idea that one had some fundamental "freedom" of thought or "right" to think never arose. Basically then, since the institutionalization of Confucianism, there were two ways of thinking: the right way and the wrong way, and there was only *one* right way.

This idea did not die with the end of the dynastic system. It remained popular to both the Nationalists and the Communists. As mentioned above, both Jiang Jieshi and Mao Zedong strove to consolidate their own power within their respective parties. But they and their parties also strove to maintain control over the people. Jiang kept Taiwan under martial law and firmly resisted local desires for democracy, which carried with it the danger of potentially numerous dissenting voices within society.

The Communists were just as controlling on the mainland. Dissension from the party line was not tolerated, especially within the general public. Mao did appear to support free expression with his "let a hundred flowers bloom, let a hundred schools contend" policy, but neither he nor the party tolerated any harsh criticism. Many critics were persecuted. Similar persecution occurred under Deng Xiaoping's reform movement, which involved allowing the people to speak out about reform. But as the "Democracy Wall" became more critical than Deng could tolerate, it was quickly shut down.

Even though the Nationalists and especially the Communists rejected Confucianism as an explicit solution to China's problems, both reverted back to strong government-controlled systems. Social harmony meant getting the people to think in the "right" way, and any deviation from this rigid standard was seen as a threat to social order. Though Confucius was absent in name, his spirit lingered on in different forms.

Conclusion

Chinese political leaders from the late imperial period to the Communist period were, on the whole, complex personalities who strove for their own personal gain while also fighting for China itself and trying to work within China's own particular social and intellectual circumstances. Although many Chinese leaders did not consider themselves nationalistic, their main interest seemed to lie in doing what was best for China. This nationalistic sentiment seemed to be a common bond among most of China's leaders, past and present. The tradition of Confucianism also carried through the generations of leadership. While none truly attained the "Pole Star" status that Confucius idealized for the rulers, many of them made remarkable attempts to steer China into its present status as a world power. And as China continues to develop politically and economically, it is clear that present-day and future Chinese political leaders will not only shape Chinese history, but also world history.

6

Chiang Kai-shek, 1887-1975

On April 5, 1975, Chiang Kai-shek, who was president of the Republic of China for almost half a century, died in Taipei, Taiwan.

Born into a merchant family in Fenghua, Chekiang Province, Chiang Kai-shek received training at the National Military academy in Paoting before leaving for Japan in 1907 to attend the Military Staff College in Tokyo. There he met Dr. Sun Yat-sen, a republican leader opposing the reigning Manchu dynasty. Chiang joined Sun's United Revolutionary League *(T'ung-meng hui)*, a secret organization and the forerunner of the Kuomintang (Nationalist Party, or KMT). When the Wuchang Uprising broke out in 1911, Chiang returned to China to take part in the overthrow of the imperial Ch'ing government and the establishment of the Republic of China. He also participated in the subsequent Second Revolution, and the campaign against the dictator President Yuan Shih-k'ai, in 1915 and 1916. In 1923, while seeking assistance from the Soviet government, Sun sent Chiang to the USSR to study the Soviet military and social systems, and also appointed him superintendent of the newly founded Whampoa Military Academy, the training center for the KMT army.

After Sun's death in 1925, Chiang emerged as the most powerful leader of the party as he became commander-in-chief of the National Revolutionary Army. In 1926, he embarked on the Northern Expedition to crush the warlords in the north and to unify the country. While the campaign was still underway in 1927, Chiang ended the KMT's alliance with the Communists by ordering their liquidation.

After he had temporarily unified China under his own presidency, Chiang launched a new series of campaigns against the Communists, while offering only token resistance to the Japanese, who had invaded Manchuria in 1931. This policy forced the Communists on their Long March in October 1934. It also induced the Manchurian general Chang Hsueh-liang to kidnap Chiang—the so-called Sian Incident—in December 1936. He was released only when he reportedly promised to form a united front with the Communists against Japan.

Chiang emerged from a national to a world leader when the China War escalated into World War II in 1941. In 1942, he was appointed supreme commander of the Allied forces in the China theater and represented China at the Cairo Conference. While mobilizing China's national resources in an effort to resist the Japanese invasion, Chiang continued trying to contain the Communists.

When the Japanese were finally expelled in 1945, Chiang was immediately confronted with the Communist challenge for supremacy, and the civil war erupted again. US attempts to mediate between the two sides failed, and in 1947, the Communist army conducted a general offensive, scoring victories in Honan and northern Hupeh. The Battle of Huaihai was another disaster for Chiang, and when General Fu Tso-yi, commander of the Peking-Tientsin region, surrendered to the Communists in early 1949, the Nationalist forces collapsed. The Communists rapidly won control of the entire country, and Chiang was forced to seek refuge on the island of Taiwan.

On Taiwan, still claiming to be the rightful president of China, Chiang was protected against Communist invasion by the US Seventh Fleet. He was thus able to stabilize the situation on the island and carry out an ambitious economic development program. Under his leadership, and with US aid, Taiwan began to modernize its agriculture and industry and became highly competitive in foreign trade.

In the late 1960s, Chiang began to groom his elder son, Chiang Ching-kuo, to be his successor. Even though he never abandoned his dream of an eventual return to the mainland, he made no serious effort to achieve that objective. But his dream was totally shattered in 1972, when the US president, Richard Nixon, began to improve relations with the Chinese Communist government. Chiang died embittered after a prolonged illness in 1975.

Reference Sources

- "Chiang Kai-shek," by Edwin Pak-wah Leung and Winston L. Y. Yang. In vol. 6 of *Funk & Wagnalls New Encyclopedia*. New York: 1983.

- "Chiang Kai-shek." In vol. 1 of *Biographical Dictionary of Republican China,* edited by Howard L. Boorman and Richard C. Howard. New York: Columbia University Press, 1967.
- "Chiang Kai-shek," by Ssu-yu Teng. In vol. 4 of *Encyclopedia International.* New York: Lexicon Publications, 1979.
- "Chiang Kai-shek," by Parks M. Coble, Jr. In vol. 1 of *Encyclopedia of Asian History,* edited by Ainslie T. Embree. New York: Charles Scribner's Sons, and London: Collier Macmillan Publishers, 1988. ISBN: 0-684-18898-8.

Works by Chiang

- *Resistance and Reconstruction: Messages During China's Six Years of War, 1937-1943,* by Chiang Kai-shek. Translated by Albert French Lutley, Frank Wilson Price and Ma Pin-ho. Freeport, NY: Books for Libraries Press, 1970 (©1943).
- *Soviet Russia in China: A Summing Up at Seventy,* rev. ed., by Chiang Kai-shek. Translated under the direction of Madame Chiang Kai-shek. New York: Farrar, Straus, & Giroux, 1965.
- *China's Destiny,* by Chiang Kai-shek. Translated by Wang Chung-hui. New York: DaCapo Press, 1976 (©1947).

Adult Works about the Subject

- *Chiang Kai-shek: His Life and Times,* by Keiji Furuya. Translated by Chun-ming Chang. New York: St. John's University, 1981. The most detailed study of Chiang Kai-shek.

- *The Man Who Lost China: The First Full Biography of Chiang Kai-shek,* by Brian Crozier, with Eric Chou. New York: Scribner's, 1976. A comprehensive study, but with a lot of errors.
- *Chiang Kai-shek: Asia's Man of Destiny* by Hsin-hai Chang. Garden City, NY: Doubleday, Doran, & Company, 1944. Focuses on Chiang's accomplishments.
- *Chiang Kai-shek: Marshal of China,* by Sven Hedin. Translated by Bemard Norbelie. China in the 20th Century Series. New York: The John Day Company, 1940. Reprint. New York: DaCapo Press, 1975.
- *The Early Chiang Kai-shek: A Study of His Personality and Politics, 1887-1924,* by Pichon Pei Yung Loh. New York: Columbia University Press, 1971. An interesting study of Chiang's early life. First published in the occasional papers of the East Asian Institute at Columbia University.
- *Chiang Kai-shek,* by Hollington K. Tong. Taipei, Taiwan: China Publishing Company, 1953. The "official" biography of Chiang in Taiwan.
- *Government and Politics in Kuomintang China, 1927-1937,* by Tien Hung-mao. Stanford, CA: Stanford University Press, 1972. ISBN: 0-8047-0812-6.
- *The Sian Incident: A Pivotal Point in Modern Chinese History,* by Wu Tien-wei. Michigan Papers in Chinese Studies, no. 26. Ann Arbor: University of Michigan, 1976. ISBN: 0-89264-026-X.

Children's Works about the Subject

- *Jiang Jie-shi (Chiang Kai-shek): 1887-1975* by J. S. Gregory. Leaders of Asia Series. St. Lucia, Australia: University of Queensland Press, 1982. Includes bibliographical references.
- *Chiang Kai-shek*, by Richard Curtis. New York: Hawthom Books, 1969. Illustrated with selected photographs.
- *President Chiang Kai-shek: His Life Story in Pictures.* Taipei, Taiwan: Government Information Office, 1972. A pictorial history of Chiang.

Audio-Visual Resources

- *President Chiang Kai-shek.* (*Government* of Taiwan). Available from the Chinese Cultural Center Library. 25 min. Sources of Further Information: Chinese Cultural Center Library 159 Lexington Avenue New York, NY 10016 (212)725-4950 Houses a rich collection of books on or related to Chiang Kai-shek.

Key Datcs

- 31 October 1887: Chiang Kai-shek was born. (Some sources cite 1886 as the year of Chiang's birth.)
- 15 August 1900: The Imperial court of Empress Dowager Tzu Hsi left Peking. (For more information on this topic, see "Chinese Imperial Court Leaves Peking" in this volume.)
- 12 February 1912: Sun Yat-sen promised to step down from his position as the first president of the Republic of China.

(For more information on this topic, see "Sun Yat-sen and the Chinese Nationalist Communist Reign in Mainland China" in *Book of Days, 1987.)*

- 21 March 1927: Shanghai taken by the Nationalist Chinese forces of Chiang.
- 15 April 1927: Chiang, and conservative members of the KMT, split with the Communists at Hankow, China.
- 18 April 1927: Chiang inaugurated the moderate Nationalist government of China at Nanking.
- 20 September 1927: Chiang formed the right-wing National Revolutionary Government, which signaled the end of the "warlord" era in China.
- 10 October 1928: Chiang was inaugurated president of China in Nanking.
- 12 December 1936: Chiang declared war on Japan.
- 1 March 1950: Chiang resumed the presidency of Chinese National Government.
- 5 April 1975: Chiang Kai-shek died in Taipei, Taiwan.

7

The Politics of Chinese Communism during the Kiangsi Period, 1931-1934

The Politics of Chinese Communism: Kiangsi under the Soviets. By Ilpyong J. Kim. Berkeley and Los Angeles: University of California Press, 1973. 232 pages, Introduction, Glossary, Bibliography, Index. $12.50.

Despite the efforts of a growing corps of specialists on China, large areas of the early history of Chinese communism have unfortunately still remained obscure to the reading public. The most obvious example of this obscurity may perhaps be the story of the Kiangsi Soviet Republic (1931-1934). For even the revealing work of James R. Townsend's *The Political Participation in Communist China* (1967) pays little attention to the Kiangsi period. The standard work of *A Documentary History of Chinese Communism,* edited by Conrad Brandt, Benjamin Schwartz and John K. Fairbank, also provides little information on the subject.

But in the course of the Chinese Communist movement, the Kiangsi period is of particular importance: it was then that the Chinese Communist leaders, for the first time in their struggle for power, acquired control over a definite geographic area comprising approximately 150 *hsien* and a population of twelve to fifteen million people. Moreover, the Central Soviet government in Juichin experimented with various economic and social problems, and the institutional theories and administrative practices that have since developed in China are deeply rooted in the programs evolved in the Kiangsi period, including Mao Tse-tung's concept of mass mobilization.

With the recent release of the Ch'en Ch'eng archival materials on microfilm by the Hoover Institution, a burgeoning interest on the Kiangsi Soviet Republic has emerged within the academic circle. This collection of documents contains Communist sources from the CCP and the Chinese soviet government that were collected on the spot by KMT troops under the command of General Ch'en Ch'eng in the early 1930's. The microfilm also contains *A Collection of Red Bandit Reactionary Documents,* compiled by the KMT for private circulation in 1935.[1] The Ch'en Ch'eng Collection has so far provided bases for at least three important and fascinating monographs: one by Derek J. Waller, *The Kiangsi Soviet Republic: Mao and the National Congresses of 1931 and 1934* (1972), one by Trygve Lotveit, *Chinese Communism, 1931-1934: Experience in Civil Government* (1973), and the third one by Ilpyong J. Kim, *The Politics of Chinese Communism: Kiangsi under the Soviets* (1973) which is under review.

A Korean-born professor of the Political Science Department at the University of Connecticut, Dr. Kim has published articles like: "Mass Mobilization Policies and Techniques developed in the period of the Chinese Soviet Republic."[2] He also did research work in Hong Kong and Taiwan in 1964-65, parts of it being an interview with the former CCP leader Chang Kuo-tao, and a review of documents from the Collection of the Bureau of Investigation, Ministry of Justice in Ch'ing-tan, Taiwan.

If the social revolution in contemporary China's rural area consisted of three stages: land reform, cooperation (for collectivization) and communization,[3] then the Kiangsi Soviet Republic witnessed the initial experiment of the first two movements. Professor Kim explores the evolution of the Kiangsi soviet, especially its organizational concepts and development of "mass-line" politics. He seeks answers to the questions such as: what notions of organization shaped the Kiangsi political system? Who formulated the policies? How were they implemented at the "rice-roots" level of government? The result is an extensively documented and carefully written monograph.

Treating the Kiangsi soviet system as a "formal organization" (P.21), the author skillfully applies Max Weber's organizational theory throughout the course of analysis. The primary concern, as Kim indicates, is to identify comparable characteristics of organizations and ascertain whether the Western theory of organization has any relevance to the analysis of Chinese administrative behaviour (P.20). He comes up with a negative conclusion.

In what way, then, is the Kiangsi soviet system different from its Western counterparts? To seek answers to this question, one has to examine whether Mao's activities and organization theories in the Kiangsi period were but a response to Comintern instructions. From Kim's viewpoint, Mao never believed that the CCP leadership (such as Li Li-san, Wang Ming and other Russian-returned students) or the Comintern authority could correctly understand and analyze the deep-seated peasant problems of China better than he did himself (P.110). As a result, his "mass-line" approach developed during his revolutionary experiences in rural China from 1925-1930 (during and after the CCP-KMT collaboration) has formalized, by himself, as the principles and procedures of operating the soviet system of government in the Kiangsi base.

What emerges from Mao's extensive writings and reports for the period between 1927-34 is that his theory of organization minimized elaborate, specialized bureaucratic structures, and was thus contrary to the Western notion of structural differentiation and functional specificity in modern organization.[4] It also combined the functions of government and mass organization into one "mass line" style of work, as a solution to administrative problems, and it mobilized the masses to participate in the policy-formulation process at the basic level of government. According to both Kim and James P. Harrison, Mao's creation of the "mass line" politics, together with the "revolutionary nationalism," remain today as the "twin pillars of Chinese Communism."[5]

One particularly fascinating theme illuminates the book's main concern—that of the "collective leadership" theory. Challenging the commonly held view that Mao's power was eclipsed by the Returned-student clique, the study (especially Chapters 3 and 4) persuasively argues that a complex relationship of conflict and cooperation existed between the two groups based on mutually reinforcing functions and differential experience. In Kim's classification, there were three major elements of power within the Kiangsi soviet leadership: the first one was the Russian-returned-student group headed by Ch'en Shao-yu (Wang Ming), Ch'in Pang-hsien (Po Ku), and Chang Wen-t'ien (Lo Fu); the second group consisted of the leaders and organizers of the soviets and the Red Army units headed by Mao and Chu; the third group was the veteran leaders of the CCP such as Hsiang Ying and Ch'en Yun. Nevertheless, neither an individual leader nor a single group wielded absolute power or dictated the political processes during the Kiangsi period, so that a situation existed in which the concept of collective leadership was fully worked out and the balance of power between the contending groups was carefully maintained (P.56). As a result of this collaboration, the Chinese Communist leaders as a whole were able to develop highly sophisticated administrative techniques in the process of operating the complex organizations of the many soviet governments that were widely scattered throughout the soviet area (P.178).

There were, as presumed, ideological conflicts within this collective leadership, on the one hand, Mao was inclined to take the "mass line" approach because of his practical experience in organizing the peasant masses, whereas on the other hand some of the returned-student leaders such as Ch'in Pang-hsien took the "class line" approach because of their theoretical education and ideological training in orthodox Marxism in the Soviet Union. The solution to bridge their differences was the politics of compromise. They reached an agreement that the poor-peasant corps on the "rice-roots" level should be fully developed to function as the vanguard of the poor peasant masses, to establish a powerful alliance between the poor and the middle peasants, and to carry out the broadest possible mass mobilization, based on Mao's concept of "mass line"; however, the class struggle based on the concept of "class line" was not ignored or abandoned, for the cadres at all levels of the soviet government were also directed "to take seriously the anti-rich-peasant policy as the form of class struggle and as the means to generate the latent power of peasant masses in the struggle to carry out the Chinese revolution." (P.139)

One basic question arises: how did the central leaders mobilize the peasant masses from the passive to the active? During the Kiangsi period, the peasants were actively involved in the processes of mass-participation (such as land confiscation and distribution) largely through two auxiliary organizations under the *hsiang* soviet government's jurisdiction: the poor-peasant corps and the farm labor-union. Kim finds that these two organizations had considerable success in arousing class consciousness and a sense of participation on the part of the masses of ordinary peasants. He agrees with Harold Isaacs[6] that this was the first time in Chinese history that any serious attempt had been made to involve the ignorant mass of ordinary mass in meaningful activities aimed at social change and modernization.

Based primarily on the information obtained from an interview with Chang Kuo-tao,[7] the author (particularly in Chapter 6) tries to draw an administrative picture of the Kiangsi system on each level of interaction, especially the three case studies of the provincial soviet government of the O-yu-wan, the Hsingkuo *hsien* soviet government, and the Changkang *hsiang* soviet government. In reading this chapter, one gets the impression that "the electoral process ... and elections obviously reflected effort on the part of the soviet organizers to create a sense of mass participation among the entire population." (P.176) The whole idea seems to be consistent with the main thesis of the "mass line" politics, even though Kim does not say whether this is the factor, for instance, why some of the rich peasants sought refuge in the soviet border areas after escaping from the white (non-communist) areas (P.122).

In line with the Weberian organizational concept, one of the most important tasks of the Kiangsi soviet system was to maintain its long-term existence first by institutionalizing its new concepts of leadership and then by training its new cadres according to these new concepts. Since the central concepts of the Kiangsi political system were the mobilization of the entire population to preserve the revolutionary base and the development of organizational techniques that would release the latent power of the masses for the revolutionary cause, the organizational achievements of mass organization therefore depended largely on local organizations and their cadres, who were trained and charged with the responsibility of maintaining close relationship with the peasant masses. They not only appealed to the peasants psychologically but also created an organizational outlet to channel their energies into revolutionary change. It is interesting to note that the Inspection Committee in dual ways played a special role: it provided the opportunity for the Party committees, at the provincial and district levels, to ascertain whether each committee practised collective decision, and it gave "intellectual" cadres practical experience. All of which, in Kim's viewpoint, were in close accord with Mao's organizational concept of "mass line" (P.181). It is to the author's belief that Mao's mass-line style of work in Yenan was derived from his policies developed in the Kiangsi base, for there are strikingly similar concepts of leadership and organization strategy during these two distinct periods in the history of the Chinese Communist movement. For example, the reform movement of 1931-33 in the Kiangsi soviet was so like the Cheng-feng rectification campaign of 1942-44,[8] in both goals and methods, that one is led to speculate on whether Mao Tse-tung himself contributed the basic ideas for both.

Like many leaders in contemporary developing countries, Chinese communist leaders were preoccupied, during the Kiangsi soviet period, with the problems of institution-building: the creating of a new political party, the organizing of it, the establishing of governmental agencies, and the structuring of mass organizations. Professor Kim's book fully demonstrates the dynamics of organizational power in modern China. His distinctive contribution lies in his concern with the issue of how the Chinese Communist leaders maintained a balance of power among the party, the government, and the Red Army while administering an expanding territorial base and managing complex organizations. In another area, he skillfully analyzes the development of policies, political institutions, empirical organization theory, and cadre recruitment methods which contributed greatly to the Communists' acquisition of a mass base of support during the Kiangsi period.

This book together with Mark Selden's *The Yenan Way in Revolutionary China* (1971) and James P. Harrison's *The Long March to Power* (1972) further substantiates the thesis of the political maturity of the Chinese Communist movement at the time of its coming to power in 1949.

The volume is not without flaws, however. First, although Kim admits that: "the evacuation of the soviet base in the fall of 1934 was more a result of relentless Nationalist military pressure than of the inability of the Communist leaders to mobilize the masses" (P.200), he does not seem to be paying adequate attention to the five KMT encirclement campaigns which should be considered as the external challenges threatening the very existence of the Kiangsi soviet system. One is inclined to think that, as Jerome Ch'en has suggested,[9] this might be an important factor contributing to the collaboration of the heterogeneous elements of leadership.

Secondly, after the passing away of Ch'en Shao-yu (Wang Ming), the most controversial head of the Russian-returned-student clique, at the old age of seventy in Moscow on March 27, 1974, there seems to have occurred a debate between China and the Soviet Union concerning Ch'en's past activities. According to the Moscow authority, Ch'en went to the Oriental University when he was sent to Moscow between 1927-29.[10] But this certainly is a mistake. Both the Hong Kong and Taiwan sources indicate that Ch'en went to the Sun Yat-sen University, where he had an opportunity to become acquainted with Pavel Mif, the President of the University and an active Stalinist.[11] It was thereafter that, as Kim also confirms, there developed a Mif-Wang (Ch'en) alliance (P.56). But Kim's very thesis of "collective leadership", convincing as it may be for the Kiangsi period, does not provide any further explanation for the later struggle between Mao and Ch'en, say, from the Yenan period to as late as the early 1970's.[12]

Thirdly, Kim makes very little effort to explore Mao's understanding of Marxism, partly because he focuses too much on Mao's indigenous aspect of philosophical and developmental thought. He points out the CCP has always been a non-proletarian party. How, then, can Mao call his revolution "communist" or "Marxist"? The *Communist Manifesto* speaks of "the idiocy of rural life" and points to the proletariat as the revolutionary class. But Mao and some of his comrades were intellectuals who relied on the peasantry and guerrilla warfare to gain power. What has all this to do with Marx or Marxism? And what does it say about Mao's conception of the role of ideology? Kim leaves these questions almost unexplored.

Finally, Kim's generalization of the Kiangsi soviet governmental structure, based primarily on the case studies of the "model governments" of the Hsingkuo *hsien* and the Changkang *hsiang,* certainly sheds light to our understanding of the Kiangsi soviet administrative procedures. But it would be misleading for the reader of Professor Kim's book to take an ideal or "model" description of one or two parts of early Communist China's development as the whole system. For example, can one say that the Tachai Commune is a typical example of contemporary China's agricultural development?

Notes

1. For detailed holdings, see: Tien-wei Tu, "The Kiangsi Soviet Period: a Bibliographical review of the Ch'en Ch'eng Collection," Journal *of Asian Studies* XXIX.2 (Feb., 1970), 395-412.
2. In A. Doak Barnett (ed.) *Chinese Communist Politics in Action* (N.Y.: 1969), 78-98.
3. Franz Schurmann, *Ideology and Organization in Communist China* (Berkeley and Los Angeles: 1966), 493.
4. For the characteristics of modern organizations, see: Philip Selznick, *Leadership in Administration: a Sociological Interpretation* (N.Y.: 1957); Amitai Etzioni, *Modern Organizations* (Englewood Cliffs, N.J.: 1965); James D. Thompson, *Organization in Action: Social Science Bases of Administrative Theory* (N.Y.: 1967); Peter M. Blau and W. Richard Scott, *Formal Organization: a Comparative Appraoch* (London: 1969).
5. James P. Harrison, *The Long March to Power* (N.Y.: 1972), 514.
6. Harold Isaacs, *The Tragedy of the Chinese Revolution* (Stanford: 1961), 20.
7. For Chang Kuo-tao's own interpretation, see his *The Rise of the Chinese Communist Party: the Autobiography of Chang Kuo-tao.* 2 vols. (Lawance, Kansas: 1971-72).
8. See, for example, Mark Selden, *The Yenan Way in Revolutionary China* (Cambridge, Mass.: 1971), 188-276.
9. Jerome Ch'en, Mao *and the Chinese Revolution* (London: 1967), 160-184.
10. For the Chinese translation of the Moscow broadcasting, see: Huai Yuan, "Wang Ming, Mao Tse-tung yu So-Lien," *Fei-ch'ing yueh-pao* 17.3 (Taipei, May 1974), 7-10.
11. See: *Ming Pao* (Hong Kong), March 29, 1974; and *Chung-Kung jen-ming lu* (Taipei: 1967), 407-8.
12. For a brief description by the Peking authority, see: Yun Nan, "Yao tsung ssu-hsiang shang lung-ch'ing-ch'u lu-hsien shih-fei," *Hung-ch'i* (Peking, Nov. 1972), 13-16.

8

The Chinese Civil War: Microscopic and Macroscopic Perspectives

The Chinese Civil War is a topic of fundamental importance to the study of modern Chinese history. This protracted struggle between the Chinese Communist Party (CCP) and the Chinese Nationalist Party (better known as Kuomintang, or KMT) ultimately led to the Communist victory on the Mainland and the Nationalist retreat to the island of Taiwan in 1949. In retrospect, the Chinese Civil War served as both the demarcation line and the catalyst for the revolutionary changes of the 20th century within China.

1. The Chinese Civil War—the Microscopic Perspective

Many existing studies on the Chinese Civil War have focused on the four-year period between 1945 and 1949, from the Japanese surrender in the Sino-Japanese War to the Communist victory on the Mainland. This approach constitutes the microscopic perspective on the Chinese Civil War. The following is a historical summary of the major developments during those years.

The Sino-Japanese War (1937-1945) seriously affected the political fortunes of the two main contenders for power in China.

The Japanese attack evoked a nationalistic response which brought the KMT and CCP temporarily together in a unified anti-Japanese resistance movement. The Communists, however, emerged from World War II the most dynamic political force in China, developing guerrilla warfare and peasant revolution. As a result, the years 1945-1949 marked the culmination of Mao Tse-tung's new democratic revolution, which was complicated by both American involvement and Soviet intervention in China during that time.

The Chinese Civil War began immediately after the ending of World War II. As the Communists and Nationalists competed to receive the Japanese surrender, the tensions between the opposing factions became more apparent. The Communists were in a better position to do this because they had set up operations behind the Japanese lines during the prolonged war. This geographical advantage infuriated Chiang Kai-shek because his rivals were gaining in strength. Chiang attempted to equalize the situation by asking the United States to airlift his troops to sites where they could accept the Japanese surrender. President Harry S. Truman responded by sending a special envoy to China.

General George C. Marshall arrived in China in December 1945 to mediate a truce between the warring Chinese factions. His mission was to encourage the Chinese to discover means for promoting peace; to assist in reestablishing the authority of the Nationalist government; and to inform the Chinese that American aid was contingent upon a peaceful resolution of the internal problems.

The first meetings between Chiang, Mao, and Marshall seemed an enormous success. Marshall's proposals to restore the peace included the following: to secure a cease-fire; to initiate a forum to investigate a viable coalition government; and to integrate the KMT and CCP forces into a single national army. But the Communists would not surrender the territory they had recovered from the Japanese. Nor would the CCP agree to integrate its army with that of the Nationalists until it was assured of some political power in a coalition government. Chiang, on his part, refused to consider a coalition until the Communists had given up the land and their army. Neither side was willing to move from its basic position and risk a greater degree of vulnerability. In addition, each had a different vision of the form that the coalition government should take.

Despite the fundamental differences the negotiations continued. The cease-fire was arranged and a Political Consultative Conference (PCC) was convened to consider the problems of a coalition government. The PCC lasted from January 10 through January 31, 1946, while 38 members of different parties deliberated. The PCC came to an agreement about the form of government which would be universally acceptable. This government would be of the cabinet type with a legislative and an executive yuan. They also discussed the future constitution, which would stipulate a balance of power between the central and local governments.

Marshall was also able to get the CCP and the KMT to come to an agreement about the relative strengths of their armies. It was resolved that within a year the KMT forces were to be reduced to

90 divisions and the CCP forces to 18, followed in the next six months by a further reduction of forces to 50 and 10 divisions, respectively. These troops would be stationed in certain strengths throughout China and Manchuria.

While Marshall returned to the United States to arrange a loan to China, the CCP and KMT opted to reinitiate hostilities. Both sides were attempting to improve their military position in order to better their bargaining position. Although the negotiations lasted until early 1947, they were ultimately unsuccessful. Marshall was recalled in January 1947.

The Nationalists anticipated a quick and resounding victory over their adversaries due to their superior weapons and numbers. While they prepared for a short war, the Communists anticipated and prepared for a longer confrontation. In the beginning the conditions favored the KMT, who even captured the Communist capital of Yenan. Encouraged by his military victories, Chiang set about consolidating his political power by convening a National Assembly in November 1946. The assembly drafted and adopted a constitution but the Communists boycotted the meeting. Ignoring the Communist protests, Chiang went ahead with the plan to have himself elected president. His presidency began on April 19, 1948. However, despite the new governmental structure, the country was still in disarray and the KMT's forces were no longer assured of victory.

For two years the Communist forces increased. They were supplied by the Soviets from the war booty the Soviet Union had obtained from the Japanese. The Nationalist forces, on the other hand, began to dwindle as the civil war dragged on. In addition to smaller numbers, the Nationalists committed many of their men to guarding lands they had re-conquered. This further weakened the forces which were able to fight. With this numeric advantage the Communists began to engage in large-scale battles against the KMT rather than guerrilla warfare that was previously a large part of their strategy.

The KMT attempted to overpower the Communists in the area of Manchuria before north China was secured. The fighting in Manchuria was particularly bitter and the KMT began losing the war. Chiang Kai-shek refused to pull out of Manchuria even when his position was impossible to maintain. The Manchurian campaign cost him 470,000 of his best troops and dealt a mortal blow to the morale of the entire government army. Thus, this was a most decisive defeat for the KMT in late 1948.

The Communist forces moved into other areas as well. They captured the Shantung Peninsula in September 1948 and then moved on to fight the Battle of Huai-Hai. The location of the battle was between the Lunghai Railway in the north and the Huai River in the south, centering around the city of Hsuchow. In Hsuchow, the heavy weapons and machinery of the KMT forces were useless due to the poor weather conditions. The demoralized and immobilized Nationalist troops were handily defeated, and Hsuchow fell to the Communists in December 1948. The Campaign and Battle of Huai-Hai turned out to be one of the most historic battles of the entire Chinese Civil War.

Riding on the tide of victory, the Communists moved on toward Nanking, the capital of Chiang's government. The Nationalists continued to lose more battles and large numbers of men. They retreated to south China in an attempt to hold the southern regions but that also failed. Chiang resigned as president in favor of Vice President Li Tsung-jen in the hope that there could be some negotiations about saving the southern part of the country for the Nationalists.

The Communists were not interested in the negotiations, however, and continued to force their way south. Mao's army—led by Liu Po-ch'eng and Ch'en Yi—easily crossed the Yangtze River in April and took Nanking on April 23, 1949. The Nationalists fled from Nanking to Canton and then to Chungking to avoid the Communist forces. Chiang, his forces, and some of the Chinese citizens loyal to the Nationalist cause were forced off the Mainland to the island of Taiwan on December 9.

Mao's clear and pragmatic long-range strategy in conjunction with the Communists' organizational abilities, the disastrous effect of inflation on the KMT, and the assistance rendered by the Soviet Union in aiding and arming the Chinese Communists were all factors of the Communist success. With these successes, Mao Tse-tung formally proclaimed the victory of the Communists by establishing the People's Republic of China (PRC) on the Mainland on October 1, 1949. However, Taiwan remained in the control of the Chinese Nationalists.

2. The Chinese Civil War—the Macroscopic Perspective

Some historians differ from the adherents of the microscopic perspective and they contend that the Chinese Civil War actually began in 1921 with the founding of the CCP and lasted until 1949 with the Communist victory on the Mainland. This broader macroscopic perspective can lend a more complete understanding of the burgeoning conflict between these two political entities. When viewed in this way it becomes clear that there was a long period where both the Communists and the Nationalists were vying for power as each attempted to impose their will on the people of China.

The developments during those 28 years of bitter struggle between the CCP and KMT—from the May Fourth Movement to the First United Front, and from the Sian Incident to the Second United Front—clearly reveal the unbridgeable and irreconcilable differences between the two feuding parties. The continuous competition and recurrent confrontation between the parties must be seen, in retrospect, from the perspective of a greater, or macro, civil war—in the making.

A macroview of the Chinese Civil War can be divided into the following three periods.

A. First Period (1921-1927)

The Bolshevik Revolution in Russia not only influenced the establishment of the Chinese Communist Party but also the reorganization of Dr. Sun Yat-sen's Chinese Nationalist Party. Throughout the early Republican period, Dr. Sun was troubled by the three-part problem of foreign imperialism, party disunity, and civil strife. In search of a solution he found the success of the Soviet Revolution inspiring, and the Soviet offer of friendship and abolition of the unequal treaties attractive. He attributed Soviet success to good party organization and strict discipline. He blamed his failure on the lack of these two qualities, and was anxious to reorganize his party based upon the Soviet model. This led to the dramatic alliance between the KMT and CCP in 1923—the First United Front, which was made possible by the Communist International (Comintern) and Soviet leader Joseph Stalin.

But the KMT-CCP collaboration was only a marriage of convenience, each needing the other. The KMT desired Soviet aid in revitalizing the party, in developing a party army, and in carrying out the National Revolution that Dr. Sun wanted so much. It also aspired to the utilization of Communist ties with workers, the peasants, and the masses. The CCP, smaller in size, wanted to use the KMT base to expand the CCP's influence and eventually subvert the KMT from within. In the tenuous relationship, cooperation lasted as long as it was in the interest of both; each hoped to emerge the victor when the other had outlived its usefulness. Dr. Sun's stature and prestige were decisive factors in holding together the various elements. But once he passed away, divisive forces emerged. Dr. Sun reorganized his party and was eager to resume the much delayed Northern Expedition to rid China of competing warlords vying for power, and to frustrate the warlords' imperialist supporters. However, his untimely death on March 12, 1925, halted this move.

Dr. Sun's political successors were Wang Ching-wei and Hu Han-min, who were the left- and right-wing leaders of the KMT, respectively. The military power rested with Chiang Kai-shek, the superintendent of the Whampoa Military Academy, who was in charge of developing an officer corps to staff the new party army. His cadets were given political indoctrination as well as military training so that they could correctly instruct the soldiers in the political mission of the revolution. The deputy head of the Political Education Department was Chou En-lai. The cadets were rapidly becoming a powerful military factor. In 1926, Chiang Kai-shek was commissioned by the Nationalist government to lead the Northern Expedition against the warlords in order to reunify the country. His army was called the National Revolutionary Army.

The Northern Expedition was strengthened by Soviet supplies and by CCP advance agents who mobilized peasant and worker organizations. They organized strikes and sabotaged the cities, making the Northern Expedition a success from Canton to central China. They took Wuhan in October 1926, and Shanghai and Nanking in March 1927. The nine-month campaign was a huge success, and the southern half of China was under the Nationalist control.

On January 1, 1927, the Nationalist government moved from Canton to Wuhan. But the Wuhan government was dominated by the Soviet adviser Michael Borodin and the KMT left wing, and the important ministries of workers and farmers were put under the charge of the Communists. They carried out Stalin's new order of March 3, 1927, calling for intensified mass movements, arming the workers and peasants, and mobilizing the masses to embarrass and attack the KMT rightists.

At the same time, Chiang Kai-shek, conducting a successful military campaign, was rapidly building a power base in eastern and southeastern China. He had deliberately disregarded Borodin's advice to skip Shanghai in favor of the north. Instead Chiang went straight through to Shanghai—the financial center of China. The Chinese Communists in Shanghai, who had dominated the General Labor Union, did not know whether they should cooperate with Chiang, so they awaited Moscow's orders. Hoping to avoid a split between the CCP and KMT, Moscow advised the Shanghai workers to avoid any clashes. Chiang entered the city unopposed on March 22, 1927. His forces went on to conquer Nanking and formed a new KMT power base there.

It was apparent that Wuhan and Nanking now formed two power centers within the KMT hierarchy and that a split was imminent. On April 10, 1927, with the support of the financial sector in both Shanghai and Nanking, Chiang organized a "Purification" campaign and orders were given to liquidate all the Chinese Communists. This purge was, doubtlessly, a tremendous blow to the Chinese Communist movement.

The Wuhan government, pushed by the Communist protest, dismissed Chiang as commander-in-chief of the National Revolutionary Army. Chiang, with the help of Hu Han-min, organized his own Nationalist government in Nanking. The split between the two power centers had widened into an unbridgeable gap. It was not until M. N. Roy, an agent from the Comintern, mistakenly showed to Wang Ching-wei a telegram from Stalin which instructed the Chinese Communists to seize control of power in the Wuhan government that Wang realized the true Communist intention of the KMT-CCP alliance. Wang subsequently ordered the liquidation of all Chinese Communists. Thus, the Wuhan government was dissolved in February 1928, to be merged with the Nanking government.

B. Second Period (1927-1937)

From its beginning in 1928 to the outbreak of the Sino-Japanese War in 1937, the Nationalist government in Nanking had domestic problems to contend with as well as foreign aggression. No sooner had it been established as the legal government of China than it found itself challenged by dissident politicians from within the KMT and by rebellious "new warlords." Compounding this disorder were the two larger threats of rising Communist opposition in the southeast and the Japanese aggression in Manchuria. This decade was a decade of "internal troubles and external invasion." The Nationalists under Chiang Kai-shek had failed to carry out the much needed social and economic reforms that would have alleviated the plight of the peasants. This negligence was to have far-reaching consequences a decade later.

The unification achieved by the Northern Expedition under Chiang Kai-shek was more apparent than real, for although many of the northern warlords had been wiped out, a number of others maintained themselves by nominally supporting the Expedition. In his eagerness to achieve national unification, Chiang negotiated with them for a mutual accommodation, granting them appointments which confirmed their semi-independent regional status while receiving in return their recognition of Nanking as the central government of China.

Some of these new warlords were in fact quite "progressive" in outlook, promoting modernization in their own areas of jurisdiction. But they lacked the sense of national commitment that would make them surrender their semi-independence. Cooperation with Nanking was possible as long as their interests did not collide. Each of the "new warlords" maintained a large army for territorial aggrandizement as well as for self-protection; collectively, they drained a good portion of the country's meager resources desperately needed for national reconstruction.

Apart from the problem of the new warlords, the KMT was also plagued with factional strife. The right wing, led by party elder Hu Han-min and the Western Hills faction, was in constant conflict with the left wing, headed by Wang Ching-wei. Chiang Kai-shek, the new strongman holding the military power, presented a third force. Chiang charted his course alternately favoring each with his support according to the dictates of political necessity and expediency.

Meanwhile, the Chinese Communists continued to present a serious challenge to the KMT. The Central Committee of the CCP in underground Shanghai urged the Communist members to instigate strikes and military attacks in the cities, whereas Mao Tse-tung and Chu Teh recruited new members in the countryside, particularly in the Chingkangshan and Kiangsi areas. But they joined hands in 1931 in Kiangsi to establish the Kiangsi Soviet Republic—the first Chinese soviet government ever established. It presented a real political challenge to the Nationalist government in Nanking.

In 1931, Chiang Kai-shek launched the First Encirclement and Suppression Campaign against the Communists in Kiangsi, to be followed by four more such campaigns. The Kiangsi Soviet Republic was dominated by the Twenty-eight Chinese Bolsheviks—the Russian-returned students now turned Communist leaders. Mao was still not yet the paramount leader of the Chinese Communist movement.

While the Chinese Communists were able to expand and even carried out land reform and soviet policies in the Kiangsi Soviet Republic, they continued to be encircled and attacked by Chiang's forces. In October 1934, the Communists were unable to protect themselves from the KMT's strong military challenge and began to escape by embarking on the journey known as the Long March into the interior part of China. This was the CCP's 6,000-mile retreat from Kiangsi to northern Shensi. In January 1935, at the Tsunyi Conference, Mao and Chu were able to gain their leadership in the CCP by ousting the Twenty-eight Bolsheviks from power. The Long March group finally arrived in Yenan in 1936, but its size had shrunk from 100,000 to only 8,000. The future of the Chinese Communist movement looked dim.

The Japanese invasion of China unintentionally saved and even helped the development of the Chinese Communist movement during this time. The attack on Mukden by the Japanese Kwantung Army in September 1931 and the subsequent occupation of Manchuria by Japan forced Chiang to cut short some of his campaigns against the Chinese Communists. The kidnapping of Chiang by the Manchurian general Chang Hsueh-liang in the Sian Incident of December 1936 eventually led to Chiang's reluctant decision to temporarily call off his campaigns against the Chinese Communists. The Japanese full-scale attack of China in July 1937 made it necessary for the KMT to once again work with the CCP against a national enemy of Japan. The Second KMT-CCP United Front was formed in 1937, thus giving the Chinese Communists a golden opportunity to survive and even expand during the war years.

C. Third Period (1937-1949)

The Sino-Japanese War began on July 7, 1937, when the Japanese army attacked the Chinese garrison at the Marco Polo Bridge outside Peking. On July 15, the CCP issued a "Together We Confront the National Crisis *(kung fu kuo-nan)*" manifesto and pleaded for cooperation with the KMT. On August 13, the Japanese army invaded Shanghai and opened the second battle front. Because of the United Front, the Communist Red Army was reorganized into the Eighth Route Army, led by Chu Teh and P'eng Te-huai. The Red Army south of the Yangtze River was reorganized into the New Fourth Army, and was led by Yeh T'ing and Hsiang Ying. In

December, Nanking was taken by the Japanese army. The Rape of Nanking took place when the Japanese soldiers massacred more than 200,000 Chinese civilians. The Nationalist government retreated from Nanking to Chungking.

In 1940 and 1941, the breakdown of the short-lived cooperation between the Communists and the Nationalists began, and friction between the CCP and KMT forces in Japanese-occupied areas reached a climax. Chiang disbanded and attacked the New Fourth Army, and this ended the Second United Front between the two parties, even though it still existed in name.

The war years witnessed the rapid increase of Chinese Communist members, as the CCP engaged in vigorous recruitment activities. From the stronghold of the Yenan base in Shensi they gradually infiltrated much of north China, occupying most of Shansi, Hopei, and Shantung behind the Japanese lines. In January 1938, they were among the founders of a local anti-Japanese government, the so-called Border Region Government, that coordinated the activities of the first guerrilla base area. When Japan surrendered in 1945, there were 19 Communist base areas, most of them in north China. The Red Army had grown to 900,000 men by 1945, plus a militia force of 2.2 million men. Also by 1945, the Communists had controlled over 90 million peasants, with a CCP membership of 1.2 million, and therefore were a serious contender for power. So great was the CCP's growth during the war years that by 1945 some informed observers were asking themselves if the Communists had not already won the impending civil war.

The "macro" civil war climaxes here with the "micro" civil war of the 1945-1949 period, as described in the first part of this introduction. In retrospect, Mao Tse-tung must be given credit for his contribution to the ultimate victory of the Chinese Communist revolutionary movement. He prepared for a protracted war which allowed him to establish goals, goals which he achieved in a shorter time than he had envisioned. Mao's sweeping victory came from his recognition that, more important than the tanks, guns, and infantrymen on the battlefield, was winning over the hearts and minds of the Chinese people. Mao accomplished this through goodwill and appeasement, as he preached "unity, democracy, and peace." At the conclusion of the war, the Nationalist forces collapsed because of low morale, poor leadership, and most important, the strength of the Communist forces. Mao's long struggle found him able to impose his Communist ideology and his will upon China.

Viewing the Chinese Civil War macroscopically can also complete the picture with the global perspective of events. The episode is of great international significance because of the foreign powers' involvement in China during the period under study. Japan, the United States, and the Soviet Union were all heavily involved in World War II and the Cold War in China. Japan's invasion of China, the United States' relations with Chiang Kai-shek and the Chinese Nationalist government, and the Soviet Union's connections with the Chinese Communists are but some of the aspects of the Chinese Civil War within the global context.

As far as this dictionary is concerned, the entries and chronology are limited to the period between 1921 and 1949. However, since China is presently still a divided country, one may argue that, when viewing the current situation with the macrostudies model, a quasi-civil war in China still continues today. The Chinese Communist government's refusal to rule out the possibility of using military means to re-incorporate Taiwan is indicative of this. Thus, this book's effort to take a closer look into the long years of the Chinese Civil War will, hopefully, serve to clarify not only this period's impact on contemporary China but also the prospects for its future development.

PART III

EDUCATION AND MODERNIZATION

9

China's Decision to Send Students to the West: The Making of a 'Revolutionary' Policy

I

Before the arrival of Western imperialism in the nineteenth century, China stood unchallenged in Asia. Known as the Middle Kingdom, it had proved to be strong and powerful over the centuries.[1] The Chinese believed that their superiority over other peoples stemmed from the cultural advancement of China since Confucius. It was Confucianism alone that distinguished the "civilized" Chinese from the "barbarians" who were ignorant of Confucian values, norms, and vituals.[2] However, "barbarians" could become "civilized" through the process of sino-cization or sinification. Therefore, it was the "barbarians" who learned from the Chinese, and not *vice versa.* This Sino-centric mentality kept China from learning from the outside and, consequently, the Confucian mandarins, in the nineteenth century found themselves totally unprepared to meet the new challenges presented to them by the industrialized Western "barbarians."

To be sure, few Chinese officials actually understood the nature of Western encroachment. When China was first defeated in 1842 by the mighty British in the Opium War, the still egoistic

Chinese generally felt that it was only an "accident."[3] The Peking court did not take any significant steps afterwards in coping with the rising Western influence in China until further defeats were painfully experienced in the 1850's and 60's.[4]

Alarmed by Western superiority in weaponry, as forcefully demonstrated during the fighting, some more progressive mandarins began to try to grasp the nature of imperialism and Western superiority in order to find ways to cope with the Western threat.[5] It was under these unpleasant circumstances that the Chinese government, for the first time and albeit unwillingly, began to realize the necessity to learn from the West.

However, there was still a considerable number of die-hard conservative elements within the Chinese officialdom who opposed any programs for Westernization. They insisted that, in the words of Grand Secretary Wo-jen, "... the way to establish a nation is to lay emphasis on propriety and righteousness, not on power and plotting. The fundamental effort lies in the minds of the people, not in techniques ... why is it necessary to learn from the barbarians?"[6] Wo-jen even expressed his shame at the idea of regarding the Western "barbarians" as teachers. He also feared that to learn from "barbarians" would eventually result in the "barbarization" of China![7]

It should be noted that those Confucian mandarins who advocated for limited Westernization did not actually dispute this view. For they considered modern projects and programs only as temporary "innovations" to strengthen China to the point that the Western "barbarians" could be driven ashore. The goal of limited

Westernization was, therefore, to make China strong enough to rebuild a valid Confucian system which had been shattered by foreign invasions and Western-inspired domestic uprisings. To be sure, even the most progressive Chinese mandarins at that time still believed in the validity of Confucianism. The limited Westernization programs for self-strengthening *(tzu-ch'iang)* were not planned to destroy Confucianism, but rather to preserve it. As far as the Self-strengthening leaders were concerned, they were engaged in the *restoration* of the Confucian system through limited Westernization, as required by the changing times.[8] The dictum of "Chinese learning for the foundation, Western learning for practical use" *(Chung-t'i Hsi-yung)* came into play.[9] With this understanding, and when the *tzu-ch'iang* leaders took power in the early 1860's, the Self-strengthening Movement aiming at limited Westernization was launched.

II

The Self-strengthening Movement was indeed China's conservative compromise with the changing times.[10] As the movement began to unfold, arsenals, modern government schools, and the T'ung-wen kuan (College of Foreign Languages) were established to enable the Chinese to acquire new knowledge from the West then mostly unavailable in China.[11]

In the process of Western learning one basic question arose: should the Chinese acquire Western knowledge inside China through the employment of foreign experts? Or should the government send students to the Western countries to learn directly from the "barbarians"? Obviously, during the 1860's, there was still strong opposition from the conservative quarters against the idea of sending Chinese students abroad. They feared not only that the Chinese students might be "barbarized" once outside the "civilized" land, but also the likelihood of China losing "face" to the Western "barbarians" once directly learning from them.

Even the *tzu-ch'iang* leaders in the 1860's were reluctant to send students abroad to acquire Western knowledge since they had high hopes from their newly-established modern programs and projects. As one historian has observed: "During the [T'ung-chih] Restoration the effort was made [by Chinese leaders] to develop new knowledge in China without sending Chinese abroad to acquire it."[12]

The major source of Western knowledge in China during this period came from the foreign experts, notably W.A.P. Martin and Prosper Giquel. Martin, a missionary from the United States, joined the T'ung-wen kuan in 1864 as an English instructor and was promoted to president in 1869. He was instrumental in spreading Western knowledge in China and the T'ung-wen kuan marked the beginning of Western education in China.[13]

The Frenchman Giquel, on the other hand, served on different capacities as adviser and particularly as chief engineer in the Foochow Dockyard which built steamships and manufactured guns.[14] With the assistance from the foreign experts, the Chinese government believed that China could be strengthened and be able to ward off the Western threat within a short period of time.

The high expectation from the Self-strengthening Movement on the part of the Chinese government, however, began to turn into frustration by the turn of the decade when it was evident that the movement fell short in accomplishing its avowed goal of strengthening the country: steamships produced could not sail fast; the modern projects depended much on foreigners for operation and maintenance; and the modern schools failed to attract qualified students since the civil service examination was still the only channel to officialdom.[15]

Obviously, at this critical juncture, the idea of sending Chinese students abroad to more effectively master Western science and technology began to loom large in the eyes of the *tzu-ch'iang* leaders. Actually, as will be seen in the following pages, the issue of sending students abroad had been extensively discussed by key officials throughout the 1860's. In the meantime, the Yale-educated Yung Wing was also busy trying unsuccessfully to present to the Chinese government his educational proposal of selecting students to be sent abroad for education.[16] But it was not until November 10, 1870, that Tseng Kuo-fan and Li Hung-chang—chief architects of the Self-strengthening Movement, having finally found Yung's proposal meaningful and acceptable, decided to memorialize the Throne suggesting that a number of intelligent youths be selected and sent to the West to be trained in the technical arts.[17]

The Imperial Court subsequently approved the proposal and in 1872 a group of thirty young Chinese students was despatched to America for education,[18] and that was indeed the first time China ever sent her students to the West.

III

Existing literature in the field gives full credit to Yung Wing for effecting such a "revolutionary" change in Chinese educational policy.[19] In reading the Chinese historical records, however, one gets a very different picture. In point of fact, Yung Wing was not the first person who put forth the "revolutionary" idea of sending Chinese students abroad to the imperial court. Throughout the 1860's, a number of Chinese officials had been engaged in extensive discussions which ultimately led to the formation of a new educational policy.

In 1863, Prince Kung of the Tsungli Yamen attached in his memorial to the Throne a proposal made by a local magistrate in Kwangtung, Kuei Wen-ts'an (1823-1884) who had had involvements with some modernization projects such as the compilation of the *Kwantung t'u-shuo* (Topographical work on Kwangtung).[20] Impressed by Japan's efforts in acquiring Western knowledge by sending students abroad, Kuei proposed that China should follow Japan's footsteps. However, Prince Kung commented that although Kuei's idea was far-sighted, the time was not yet ripe for China to undertake such an action. He explained that since preparations were under way for establishing the T'ung-wen kuan, it would be more appropriate to select students to study in the modern schools as a means to acquire new knowledge than sending students abroad.[21] Obviously, Prince Kung had high hopes and expectations from the modern schools in China in accomplishing the objective of Western learning and to meet the needs of the time.

In the spring of 1864, in his letter to the Tsungli Yamen, Li Hung-chang however renewed the discussion of sending students abroad. Like Kuei, Li began the letter by praising Japan for sending youths to Western countries to acquire new knowledge: "… the Japanese government selected the most talented young men from the royal household and high-ranking ministerial families and sent them to study technology in Western countries. Meanwhile it purchased machinery from these Western countries so that other Japanese could study it at home. Today, the Japanese not only operate steamships but also manufacture their own weaponry"[22] After making this observation, Li quickly and pointedly suggested: "If a small island kingdom like Japan can make *timely* changes and know what it should or should not adopt, it is even more necessary for a country like China to do likewise, once we come to the conclusion that only through changes can we find alternatives to meet our need, at a time when the old ways are no longer adequate."[23] Li was bold in promoting once again the idea of sending students abroad, he was however very careful with the details in implementing it, as can be seen in the following case.

On March 14, 1865, the Tsungli Yamen consulted Li about the possibility of sending officers and young men of the Banner forces abroad to learn arsenal techniques.[24] Replying on May 2, Li wrote that he had long considered sending students to Western countries "to inquire into the sources of their technology and manufacturing."[25] However, Li at the same time was worried that since few Chinese or Manchus had had the necessary preparation in mathematics and such sciences as mechanics, it would therefore not be beneficial for China to send them to the West for training at this time. Li felt compelled to advise the Yamen to have men trained first in a Chinese arsenal, where they could be introduced to these subjects. Obviously, Li meant that once the students had received the necessary and basic training inside China, they could then be sent abroad to more effectively acquire Western knowledge directly there. Li also pointed out that since sending students abroad was "unprecedented in Chinese history," therefore "extreme caution had to be exercised in order to make sure that the best plan [of sending students abroad] could be deliberated."[26]

Before any action was taken, the Tsungli Yamen had a chance to send students of the T'ung-wen kuan abroad for visits and observation. In early 1866 when Robert Hart, the inspector-general of the Maritime Customs, applied for a leave of absence to return to his home in Ireland to be married, he also suggested that two or three of the more proficient Chinese students accompanying him to observe conditions in Europe. The Tsungli Yamen quickly agreed to his suggestion. Prince Kung on February 20 memorialized that such an experience "could widen the scope of [the students'] knowledge and intellectual horizon" and therefore "beneficial to their schooling."[27] Consequently, Feng-i and Te-ming (later known as Chang Te-i), both students in the English department, and Yen Hui, a student of the French department, were appointed to go. Accompanied by three employees of the Maritime Customs—Pin-ch'un (an elderly Manchu official), E.C. Bowra (an Englishman), and E. de Champs (a Frenchman)—who served as advisers, the students left Shanghai with Hart on March 23. They spent three and a half months in England, France and other northwest European countries, visiting factories, museums, and similar points of interest and being entertained by royalty and high officials. The Chinese students returned to Peking on October 26.[28] And this was the first time China sent her students to the West. However, this time the three students' stay in Europe was short, and they did not stay there for any formal education or training. It was not until 1872 that China finally sent a group of students to the West to receive schooling.

IV

From the above description, it is plain that from 1863 to 1866, the Chinese high officials were not only just toying with the idea but in fact were giving serious consideration to the possibility of sending students abroad to acquire new knowledge. It was against this background that Yung Wing's educational proposal came into the picture. In 1867, the American-educated Yung submitted to Ting Jih-Ch'ang, governor of Kiangsu, four proposals of reform, hoping that Ting would transmit them to Wen-hsiang of the Tsungli Yamen for possible adoption. The second proposal of the four reads as follows: "The Government should send picked Chinese youths abroad to be thoroughly educated for the public service."[29] According to Yung's autobiography, the reason why the educational proposal was put in the second instead of the first place was that: "Of the four proposals, the first, third and fourth were put in to chaperone the second, in which my whole heart was enlisted, and which above all others was the one I wanted to be taken; but not to give it too prominent place, at the suggestion of my Chinese teacher, it was assigned a second place in the order of the arrangement."[30] Unfortunately, Wen-hsiang was then mourning his mother's death, and the matter was put aside temporarily.

Meanwhile, a major development affecting Chinese educational change was taking place. In late 1867 when Anson Burlingame was leaving his office as U.S. minister to China, he was asked by the Chinese government to represent China to visit major Western countries.[31] The subject of Burlingame's mission to the West is beyond the scope of the present study; suffice to say is that on July 28, 1868, Burlingame, on behalf of China, signed a treaty with the U.S. Secretary of State William Seward in Washington. Article VII of this Seward-Burlingame Treaty has an interesting provision regarding student exchange:

> Citizens of the United States shall enjoy all the privileges of the public educational institutions under the control of the Government of China; and, reciprocally, Chinese subjects shall enjoy all the privileges of the public educational institutions under the control of the Government of the United States, which are enjoyed in the respective countries by the citizens or subjects of the most favorable nations.[32]

In point of fact, this provision of the Treaty later gave legal rationale as to why the Chinese leaders selected America instead of Europe as the first home where they would send students in 1872.

According to the *North China Herald,* Governor Ting Jih-ch'ang had in 1869 attempted to submit Yung Wing's educational proposal to the central government for consideration. However, no official document could support this report.[33] It appears that

Yung's proposal did not actually reach the high officials until 1870, the year of the Tientsin Massacre which was caused by the anti-Christian movements.[34] Some of the highest officials, including Tseng, Li, and Ting, convened in Tientsin to settle this matter. Appointed interpreter because of his proficiency in English, Yung Wing worked with Ting to investigate the case. It was at this point that Yung's educational scheme finally reached the influential quarter of the Chinese officialdom as Li Hung-chang and Tseng Kuo-fan, upon learning of Yung's plan, were reportedly impressed by his effort.[35] In retrospect, however, it is perhaps more accurate to say that Yung's proposal merely added impetus to the aspirations of the more progressive leaders regarding sending students abroad. Subsequently, Tseng sent in a memorial dated November 10, 1870, in which he suggested that a number of intelligent youths be selected and sent to the various nations of the West to be trained in the technical arts.[36]

In this memorial Tseng deplored China's lack of technical knowledge and pointed out the need to acquire such knowledge from the West as a primary prerequisite to upgrading the quality of the army and the establishment of the navy. He cited the example of Russia under Peter the Great, which, when confronted with a similar lack of technical knowledge, learned from England and Holland the arts of shipbuilding. The training which Tseng seemed to have had in mind for the youths who were to be sent abroad was to be strictly utilitarian, and his intention seemed to be to make of them master workmen in the various technical arts essential to the development of an army and navy along Western lines.[37] Two days after its receipt (November 12), Tseng's memorial received imperial sanction. In the next few months the details of the project were elaborated.[38]

V

On June 26, 1871, Tseng and Li in a long letter to the Tsungli Yamen presented a draft plan for discussion and further deliberation.[39] In this proposed plan Li and Tseng explained that: "If we Chinese wish to adopt their [Western] superior techniques and suddenly try to buy all their machines, not only is our power insufficient to do this, but also there is no way for us to master either the fundamental principles or the details of the profound ideas contained in these superior techniques, unless we have actually seen them and practised with them for a long time."[40] As to how long should the students stay in the West to study, "it is roughly estimated that after more than ten years their training will have been completed, and they will return to China so that the Chinese can learn thoroughly the new techniques in which the Westerners are particularly strong, and then we can gradually plan for self-strengthening."[41]

It was also specifically suggested by Tseng and Li that the students be sent to the United States. The reason for the choice of the United States rather than one of the European countries seems to have been brought about because of the intimate knowledge Yung Wing possessed of American life and educational institutions, and also because of the reciprocal nature of the recently-concluded Seward-Burlingame Treaty between the two countries specifically providing for mutual rights of residence and attendance at the public schools in the two countries. Furthermore, Tseng and Li recommended two persons as co-commissioners to supervise the proposed educational mission to the United States: "Ch'en Lan-pin, who is an assistant secretary of the Board of Punishments, fourth rank, and Yung Wing, who is a sub-prefect of Kiangsu, are both competent for the job."[42] However, Tseng and Li anticipated two major difficulties: "One is the selection of human talents [to be sent abroad], and the other is the raising of funds."[43] As to the first, Tseng and Li advised that extreme care had to be exercised in the selection of students and that an office be created in Shanghai specifically responsible for recruiting and preparing the candidates to be sent abroad. As to the second difficulty, it was proposed that funds be appropriated from the foreign customs duties at Shanghai on a yearly basis.[44] In regards to the size of students to be sent, Tseng and Li also proposed that: "The number for each year will be thirty persons, and for four years, there will be a total of one hundred and twenty."[45]

The Tsungli Yamen's reaction to the draft plan must have been favorable, for on September 3, 1871, Tseng and Li jointly memorialized the throne. Attached to this memorial was the draft plan, together with 12 regulations for governing the students abroad.[46]

According to these twelve proposed regulations, the age of the students was limited to between 12 and 19 years. After being recruited, they were to undergo preliminary training in Shanghai, which was to last for six months. Their study in the United States was to last about fifteen years, and during that time quarterly and annual examinations were to be conducted by the commissioners. After their arrival in the United States, the students were expected to continue their study of the Chinese classics under special tutors attached to the mission; and at a specific intervals the commissioners were to summon the students together to read the "Sacred Books of Imperial Edicts." In the eighth month of each year, Chinese calendar books containing information on rituals were to be issued and sent to the students through the customs service. The customary rituals were to be performed by both the commissioners and the students in order to preserve and develop their sense of propriety and reverence. After the completion of their studies, the students would be allowed two years for travel before returning and reporting to the Tsungli Yamen. Awards of official rank and appointments to government service would then be made on the basis of evaluation reports submitted by the commissioners. As dependents of government, the students were not permitted to withdraw before completing their studies, to seek naturalization abroad, or to secure their own employment after completing the program. Generally speaking, these regulations reveal the great importance attached by the government to the continuation of Chinese studies while the students were abroad.[47]

VI

Upon receipt of the memorial and the proposed plan and regulations, the Throne exercised caution by transmitting them back to the Tsungli Yamen for further comments. On September 15, 1871, the Yamen responded by sending in their approval to the proposed plan and the regulations.[48] However, the Yamen added that in recruiting the youths, no distinction should be made between Manchus and Han Chinese and that the best qualified be selected.[49]

On February 27 (March 1?), 1872, Tseng and Li sent in another joint memorial attaching a revised set of six condensed regulations governing the proposed educational project. The Tsungli Yamen's September 15, 1871 comments were incorporated in the first revised regulations. However, except the re-wording and in a more condensed form, the rest of the regulations were somewhat similar to that of the original twelve regulations of 1871.[50]

The Tsungli Yamen once again responded on May 17, approving the condensed regulations except making one significant change. According to the Yamen, candidate selection should be limited to the ages between 11 and 15, instead of the originally proposed age limit of 12-19.[51] The Throne found no objection to the Yamen's proposed revision, and the education abroad project as well as the regulations were subsequently approved by the Imperial Court.[52]

Li Hung-chang also thought it necessary to approach Frederick F. Low, United States minister to China, to tell him of the education project and to ask him that a suitable reception be given to the young students. When Low inquired of Li why China had chosen America as the place to train these students, Li replied that from all the information obtained, he was "satisfied that [the American] schools possessed a superiority over those of Europe in imparting practical knowledge."[53]

To be sure, the proposed Chinese educational mission to America aroused much interest in the foreign community in China. A *North China Herald* editorial published in Shanghai on February 22, 1872, was typical of the general view: "The whole affair [of sending students to America] presents itself to our mind, as something being vague and misty ... ;" nevertheless, "this undertaking ... will doubtless assist materially ... in opening the whole of China to the advantages of free foreign intercourse."[54] Another editorial on August 31 added that the students would become "the means of introducing a more varied range of information into China when they return."[55]

Before leaving China for America, the first group of the students went to visit the American legation in Peking. Frederick F. Low greeted the boys warmly and asserted that the American government would try everything possible to facilitate their studies in the United States.[56] Seven days later, on August 12, the pioneer students of the Chinese Educational Mission were sent.[57]

VII

From 1863, when the idea of sending students to the West was first proposed to the Ch'ing government by Kuei Wen-ts'an, to 1872, when the first students of the Chinese Educational Mission were actually sent, it took the Chinese leaders ten years of deliberation before they put the idea into practice. Consider the "revolutionary" nature of the decision to send students abroad, such a long deliberation on the part of the Confucian officials was understandable. As has been pointed out in the beginning of this paper,

China in the 1860's and 1870's still firmly believed in the validity of Confucianism. Modern projects and programs were considered by the *tzu-ch'iang* leaders only as temporary "innovations" to strengthen China to the point that the imperialistic Western "barbarians" could be driven ashore. The purpose of "Western learning" was only for "practical use" and certainly not for replacing "Chinese learning." Indeed, the decision to send students abroad came only as the last resort, when early efforts of acquiring Western knowledge inside China turned out to be unsatisfactory,

As far as Tseng Kuo-fan and Li Hung-chang were concerned, their sponsorship of the Chinese Educational Mission had nothing to do with Westernizing China. As they understood it, they were engaged in the task of restoring the Confucian order which had been seriously shattered by the challenges from the West. In their reasoning, the restoration of Confucian China could not possibly be achieved without "learning the barbarians' superior techniques to control the barbarians." The sending of students abroad was therefore regarded as the quickest and most effective way to master the "barbarians'" superior techniques.

According to Tseng and Li's original design, as can be seen in the content of the proposed regulations governing the Chinese students abroad, in order to safeguard the students from being "enclosed by foreign learning" and to keep their Chinese learning, a staff of Chinese teachers was to accompany the Chinese Educational Mission to America and to instruct the students in the Chinese language and Confucian classics.[58] A recent discovery of the Mission students' Chinese school work confirms that these teenagers had to receive intensive and strict Chinese classical education while in America.[59]

In retrospect, the Ch'ing government's "revolutionary" decision to send students to the West was in reality conservative in nature. Despite how careful their plan was in governing the Chinese students abroad, the Confucian mandarins could not possibly have been able to anticipate the full-scale impact of the Western-educated Chinese students upon their return to China. By sending students to the West, the *tzu-ch'iang* leaders had unintentionally pushed Confucian China one step forward toward modernization, for, as remarked by one noted Sinologist: "The traumatic transformation of traditional China would not have been born without the modernization of her intellectuals led by the movement of Chinese studying abroad."[60]

Notes

1. Cf. John K. Fairbank (ed.) *The Chinese World Order: Traditional China's Foreign Relations.* (Cambridge, Mass.: Harvard University Press, 1968).
2. Jerome Chen, *China and the West: Society and Culture, 1815-1937.* (Bloomington: Indiana University Press, 1979), pp. 26-27.
3. Immanuel C.Y. Hsu, *The Rise of Modern China.* 2nd ed. (New York: Oxford University Press, 1975), p. 247.
4. For more details, see: E.R. Hughes, *The Invasion of China by the Western World.* (London: Adam and Charles Black, 1968); Immanuel C.Y. Hsu, "Late Ch'ing Foreign Relations," in *The Cambridge History of China. Vol. 11,* Part 2 (Cambridge: Cambridge University Press, 1980), pp. 70-141.
5. See my Chinese article: "Yang-wu yung-tung shih-ch'i Man-ch'ing wai-chiao cheng-ts'e chuan-pien ti shen-chueh" (A Critical study of Foreign

policy Change in Ch'ing China during the Self-strengthening Movement Period) *Shih-ch ao* (Hong Kong) 7 (October 1971), pp. 7-24.

6. *C'h'ou-pan I-wu shih-mo* (The Complete Account of the Management of Barbarian Affairs, hereafter cited as *IWSM)* (Peking: 1930), T'ung-chih Period. 47:24b-25b.
7. *Ibid.*
8. Cf. Mary C. Wright, *The Last Stand of Chinese Conservatism: the T'ung-chih Restoration, 1862-1874.* (Stanford: Stanford University Press, 1957); Jonathan Porter, *Tseng Kuo-fan's Private Bureaucracy.* (Berkeley: Center for Chinese Studies, University of California, 1972).
9. This dictum was first used by a Confucian scholar Wei Yuan in the early 1840's.
10. John K. Fairbank, *et. al., East Asia: the Modern Transformation.* (Boston: Houghton Mifflin Company, 1969), p. 404.
11. Cf. Knight Biggerstaff, *The Earliest Modern Government Schools in China.* (Ithaca: Cornell University Press, 1961); Thomas Kennedy, *The Arms in Kiangnan: Modernization in the Chinese Ordnance Industry, 1860-1895.* (Boulder: Westview Press, 1978).
12. Wright, *op. cit.*, p. 242.
13. For a study of the T'ung-wen kuan, see : Biggerstaff, *op. cit.*, pp. 94-153.
14. Steve A. Leibo, *Transferring Technology to China: Prosper Giquel and the Self-Strengthening Movement* (Berkeley: 1985).
15. The civil service examination was not abolished until 1905.
16. Yung Wing, *My Life in China and America (N.Y.:* 1909), pp. 170-180.
17. *Tseng Wen-cheng Kung ch'uan-chi* (Complete Works of Tseng Kuo-fan) (1888). *Tsou-kao.* Chuan 30, pp. 3a-4a.
18. Edwin Pak-wah Leung, "China's Quest from the West: the Chinese Educational Mission to the United States, 1872-1881," *Asian Profile* 11.6 (December 1983), pp. 527-534; Edwin Pak-wah Leung, "Education of the Early Chinese Students in America," in Jenny Lim (ed.) *The Chinese American Experience* (San Francisco: 1984), pp. 203-210.
19. See, for example, Y.C. Wang, *Chinese Intellectuals and the West, 1872-1949,* (Chapel Hill: 1966), p. 42; Jerome Ch'en, *op. cit.*, p. 151; Li Chih-kang, *Jung Hung yu Chin-tai Chung-kuo* (Yung Wing and Modern China) (Taipei: 1981), pp. 83-90; Li Shou-k'ung, Li *Hung-chang chuan* (Biography of Li Hung-chang) (Taipei: 1985), p. 151.
20. Arthur Hummel (ed.) *Eminent Chinese of the Ch'ing Period (1644 1912)* (Washington, D.C.: 1943-44), Vol. 1, p. 91.

21. *IWSM:TC,* chuan 15, pp. 31b-34b.
22. *IWSM:TC,* chuan 25, pp. 9-10.
23. *Ibid.*
24. Chung-yang yen-chiu-yuan chin-tai-shih yen-chiu-so (comp.) *Hai fang tang* (Archives on Coastal defense) (Taipei: 1957), *Chi-ch'i chu* I, pp. 13-21.
25. *Ibid.*
26. *Ibid.*
27. *IWSM:TC,* chuan 32, pp. 1-3.
28. Knight Biggerstaff, "The First Chinese Mission of Investigation sent to Europe," *Pacific Historical Review 6* (Dec. 1937), p. 307.
29. Yung, *op. cit.*, pp. 171-175.
30. *Ibid.*, p. 175.
31. Knight Biggerstaff, "The official Chinese Attitude toward the Burlingame Mission," *American Historical Review* 41.4 (1936), 682-702.
32. See Article VII of the 1868 Treaty, in Frederick Wells Williams, *Anson Burlingame and the First Chinese Mission to Foreign Powers (N.Y.:* 1912), Appendix I.
33. Lu Shih-ch'iang, *Ting Jih-ch'ang yu Yang-wu yun-tung* (Ting Jih-ch'ang and the Self-Strengthening Movement) (Taipei: 1972), p. 212.
34. For details, see: John K. Fairbank, "Patterns behind the Tientsin Massacre," *Harvard Journal of Asiatic Studies* 20 (1957), pp. 480-511.
35. Yung, *op. cit.*, p. 180.
36. See note 17.
37. *Ibid.*
38. *Ta-Ch'ing shih-lu* (Veritable records of successive reigns of the Ch'ing dynasty) (Taipei: 1964), chuan 291, p. 3.
39. *Li Wen-chung Kung ch'uan-chi* (Complete Works of Li Hung-chang) *I-shu han-kao* I. 19b-22.
40. *Ibid.*
41. *Ibid.*
42. *Ibid.*
43. *Ibid.*
44. *Ibid.*
45. *Ibid.*

46. *IWSM: TC,* chuan 82, pp. 46-50.

47. *Ibid.*

48. *Ibid.,* chuan 83, pp. la-2b.

49. *Ibid.*

50. *IWSM: TC,* chuan 85, pp. 14-15.

51. *Ibid.,* chuan 86, pp. 13-14.

52. *Ibid.,* chuan 86, p. 14b.

53. As quoted in Low to Fish, dated Feb. 5, 1872, *Papers related to the Foreign Relations of the United States* (1872), p. 131.

54. *The North China Herald and Supreme Court and Consular Gazette,* Shanghai, Feb. 22, 1 872 (microfilm).

55. *Ibid.,* August 31, 1872.

56. *Shen-pao (a* newspaper published in Shanghai), Aug. 5, 1872.

57. *Ibid.,* July 16, 1872; Hsu Jun, *Hsu Yu-chai tzu-hsu nien-p'u* (Autobiography of Hsu Jun) (Shanghai: 1927), pp. 17a-b.

58. To strengthen the Chinese teaching, a headquarters located at 400 Collins Street, Hartford, Conn., was later established, which had large classrooms for Chinese courses. The double three-story building was large enough to house the staff and seventy-five students. It was constructed at a cost of US $43,000.

59. Ku Tun-jou, "Pai-nien liu-Mei chiao-yu ti hui-ku yu chien-chan," (A hundred years of Chinese students studying in America: a Study) *Chiao-yu yu wen-hua* 8.1 (June 1955), pp. 4-14.

60. C.K. Yang's review of Y.C. Wang's *Chinese Intellectuals and the West, 1872-1949, in Journal of Asian Studies* XXVI.1 (Nov. 1960), pp. 115-117.

10

The First Chinese College Graduate in America: Yung Wing and His Educational Experiences

Naturalized in 1852 as an American citizen while a student at Yale, Yung Wing (Jung Hung 1828-1912) is known in history as the first Chinese who graduated from an American college, and later, as "father of the education of Chinese in the U.S." for his pioneer work in bringing Chinese students to America for education. As a Chinese American, he spent almost half of his eighty-three years of his life in America—as student (1847-1854), co-commissioner of the Chinese Educational Mission (1872-1881), Associate Minister of the Chinese legation (1878-1881), and ordinary American citizen. He died a frustrated man in Hartford, Connecticut, on April 21, 1912.

Yung Wing was born in China on November 17, 1828, into a peasant family of four children. In his childhood, he witnessed the invasion of China by Western Powers. Foreign influence also began penetrating into the economically backward Confucian society. Since Yung's native village Namping was not far from the Portuguese colony of Macao in South China, he was therefore exposed to Western ideas at a very young age. At seven, his father took him to Macao to study in Mrs. K.F. Gutzlaff's school, hoping that it could lead to a commercial career. But the school was disbanded soon, and Yung Wing found himself returning to his village to resume his Chinese studies. In the fall of 1840, because of his father's sudden death, Yung and one of his brothers had to go peddling candy to help support the family. When winter was over and when no candy was made, he went into the fields to glean rice after the reapers.[1]

When the Morrison Education Society School (founded in memory of the first Protestant missionary in China—Robert Morrison) was opened in Macao, Yung enrolled as a student and continued his schooling there in 1841. The school was run by Rev. Samuel Robbins Brown (1810-1880), a graduate of Yale of the class of 1832. In 1842, when Hong Kong was ceded to Britain after China's defeat in the Opium War, the school was moved to the British colony.[2] Yung did well in the school.

In 1847, Rev. Brown left Hong Kong to return to the U.S. because of ill health. He took three of his brilliant students with him—Yung Wing, Wong Shing (Huang Sheng) and Wong Foon (Huang K'uan)—to continue their education in America. According to Yung's autobiography, since the three boys had the financial backing of several Hong Kong and Canton benefactors who also promised to help support the three boys' families, there was no practical reason prohibiting their making the trip.[3]

Brown, with the three boys, arrived in America in April, 1847. The Chinese students were subsequently enrolled in the Monson Academy at Monson, Massachusetts, a school which Brown once attended. Yung was then eighteen years old.

Despite his already quite Westernized education in Macao and Hong Kong, it was in America, however, that Yung Wing's perspective began to shift Westward. During his stay at Monson, Yung became more and more attracted to American education. As he wrote: "I have a great inclination to get a liberal education, and there is great probability so much so that it amounts to almost certainty that I am going to stay (in America for further education)."[4]

Indeed, after Monson, he stayed to further his education at Yale College. His education at Yale (1850-54), no doubt had great intellectual impact and stimulation on his young mind. As he described his student life there: ". . . There is also great excitement among the students themselves. I mean mental excitement. . . I never was subject to such excitement. I enjoy its (Yale's) influence very much."[5] Later, in his last years, he recalled that: "(My American education) had unmistakenly enlarged my mental and moral horizon, and revealed to me responsibilities which the sealed eyes of ignorance can never see."[6]

So overwhelmed was Yung Wing into the American education, that while his English was making extremely good progress, (as evidenced by his winning the first prize in English composition two terms out of three during his sophomore year at Yale), at the same time, he was fast losing his Chinese language.[7] This achievement in English is a positive indication of his assimilation of Western culture.

Two other manifestations of Yung Wing's early leaning toward the West are his conversion to Christianity and his naturalization as an American citizen.[8] Doubtlessly, Yung's Christianity was at that juncture in Chinese history a definite step away from China, and especially his family, since his mother and uncle were "afraid that I (Yung) will embrace the new religion or the gospel."[9] His naturalization as an American citizen, though not mentioned in his autobiography, can also testify to his growing attachment to America.

In spite of the fact that Yung seemed to adapt so readily to Yale and America, he still was drawn to China by his family and the love for his fatherland; in fact, there is little doubt that he felt torn between China and America. All the time while he was studying at Yale, he was sorry to see the lamentable conditions of China—internal corruption and external aggression—and felt keenly the responsibility of redressing the wrongs in his fatherland. Finally, he came to the conclusion that only through Western education could the deteriorating and impotent China be saved. As he explained: "I was determined that the rising generation of China should enjoy the same educational advantages that I had enjoyed; that through Western education China might be regenerated, become enlightened and powerful."[10] And, in order to accomplish that goal, he decided to return to China upon his graduation from Yale in 1854, so that he could better promote American educational influence in China. He was particularly interested in persuading the Chinese government to send students to America for education.[11]

In China, around the mid-nineteenth century, the intellectual world was still dominated by Confucianism, despite the continuous challenges by the West. Although there was a government-led movement aimed at self-strengthening through Western learning, the Chinese officials were interested only in the technological aspects of Western culture. The establishment of arsenals, shipyards, language schools and other new projects in the name of "self-strengthening" all aimed at learning Western science and technology then mostly unavailable in China. These "innovations" were justified in terms of military defense without conflicting with orthodox Confucianism.[12] Even among the progressive Chinese leaders, there was no plan to send students to the West for education, as they feared that the Chinese students might also pick up some "undesirable" Western cultural elements. Therefore, at least during the 1860's, a deliberate effort was made to develop Western knowledge in China without sending Chinese students abroad.[13] Under these circumstances, Yung Wing's suggestion of sending Chinese students to America did not win acceptance in the government circle.

As time went on, however, it became increasingly obvious that if China were to master the secrets of Western science and technology, it would be necessary for the Chinese government to send young students to Western countries for direct training. Yung's suggestion also received impetus in 1868 when the Burlingame-Seward Treaty was signed between China and the United States, which provided a student exchange agreement.[14] But it was not until May 13, 1872, that the educational project—Yung's "brainchild"—finally received Imperial sanction from the Chinese court. The plan scheduled 120 students to be sent in four groups to the United States following in successive years. They were to be trained in Western sciences and technology, then mostly unavailable in China, for a period of fifteen years with the sponsorship of the Chinese government.[15]

The project had an office in Shanghai under Commissioner Liu Han-ch'ing, whose duty was to select and prepare students' studies abroad, and an office in America staffed by Commissioners Ch'en Lan-pin and Yung Wing, one interpreter and two Chinese instructors. The office in America was known as the Chinese Educational Mission.

A preparatory school was opened in Shanghai, where candidates received some preliminary training and were examined on their general fitness for study abroad. Few candidates came from central and northern provinces. Yung Wing literally combed the coastal cities of Kwangtung for youths who had received some Western education in the government schools of Hong Kong or in missionary schools along the China coast.[16] As a result, most candidates were Southern Chinese teenagers.

As co-commissioner of the Chinese Educational Mission, Yung preceded the first students to America to make arrangements for their arrival. When he arrived in New Haven, he consulted Noah Porter (1811-1892), then President of Yale College, for advice on the best method for achieving the students' education. There was in Connecticut, particularly at Hartford, a partiality toward the family approach.[17] Thus, President Porter strongly advised Yung Wing not to keep the young Chinese together in one group, but to place them by two and threes in American families.[18] Yung agreed, and with the cooperation of the faculty of Yale College and the Connecticut State Board of Education, he made the necessary arrangements. An observer recorded that: "The response to the call for homes and instruction for Chinese boys has been surprisingly prompt and cordial. One hundred and twenty-two families have offered to receive two each, so that homes are open for two hundred forty-four ... (this is) a desire (of the American people) to aid in promoting the progress of the largest nation on the globe."[19] The Chinese Educational Mission was regarded by the American government with "much interest" and "friendly feeling."[20] In response, the Chinese government expressed that "such acts of kindness tend to strengthen and make lasting the sympathy and friendship now so happily existing between your country and mine."[21] Indeed, Yung Wing's educational mission became a bond between the "oldest and newest nations" in the early 1870's, despite the gradually expanding forces of anti-Chinese feeling in the newly established Western states and territories.

In order to safeguard the students from being "enclosed by foreign learning" and to keep before them the Confucian ideal of loyalty to the Chinese Emperor, a staff of Chinese teachers was to accompany the Mission and instruct the students in the Chinese language and Confucian classics.[22] Specific provision was made for periodic assemblies of the students to hear the Chinese Imperial Edict and to enable them to make the proper ceremonial obeisance to the Emperor. To strengthen the Chinese teaching, a headquarters located at 400 Collins Street, Hartford, was later established, which had large classrooms for Chinese courses.[23] A recent recollection of the Mission students' Chinese school work reveals that these teenagers had to receive intensive and strict Chinese classical education given by the Mission.[24]

Yung Wing understood that the increase of Chinese teaching would create a certain cultural dilemma for the students. Yung himself, very frankly, desired to saturate the students with an American viewpoint, and in consequence, neglected their Chinese education, which according to the original plan was to parallel their American training.[25] When conflicts occurred, Yung always sided with the students.[26] Yung's liberal educational approach was at variance with his conservative colleagues'; conflict occurred within the Mission staff. The conservative staff members were dissatisfied with the very way Yung Wing educated the students. They sent to China a stream of unfavorable reports on the un-Chinese conduct of the students.[27] The clash between Yung Wing and his conservative colleagues was inevitable. A letter written by Li Hung-chang, a high Chinese official, to Co-commissioner Ch'en Lan-pin, dated May 10, 1880, reveals clearly this conflict: "(The Chinese instructor of the Mission) Jung Tseng-hsiang came to call and told me that the students had really neglected their Chinese studies and that this had arisen because Yung Wing held firmly the idea not to have the students spend too much time on Chinese learning... Yung Wing has also come to see me, saying it is true the students have neglected their Chinese studies. It is due to Yung Wing's obstinacy in not desiring these students to learning much Chinese."[28] This internal conflict within the Mission staff regarding the approach of educating the Chinese boys doubtlessly was a major factor leading to the eventual recall of the mission.

In 1880, the Chinese government finally ordered the teachers and students of the Chinese Educational Mission to return to China as soon as possible. This decision was received with deep disappointment by the Mission students who had to cut off their schooling in America. The disappointment was shared by many Americans who had come in contact with the students during their stay in the United States. An attempt was made to induce the Chinese government to rescind the order. This included a petition jointly written to the Chinese government by a number of noted American educators,[29] as well as a personal letter by former U.S. President Ulysses S. Grant.[30] These heartwarming efforts succeeded in temporarily postponing the recall of the Chinese Educational Mission. However, the Chinese government, alarmed by the reports on the Americanization of the Mission students and on the outraging anti-Chinese movement in America, insisted on its stand. The Mission was finally withdrawn on September 6, 1881.[31]

The recall of the Chinese Educational Mission shattered Yung Wing's dream of regenerating China through Western education. As Mark Twain recorded in his autobiography: "The order disbanding the schools was a great blow to Yung Wing, who had spent many years in working for their establishment. This order came upon him with the suddenness of a thunderclap. He did not know which way to turn."[32]

Indeed it was a blow to Yung Wing's confidence and aspiration, as he never again asked the Chinese government to send students to America. His dream vanished. He became a frustrated man. He was also heartbroken to see his fellow countrymen being maltreated in America. For example, in 1880 while simultaneously holding positions as co-commissioner of the Chinese Educational Mission and acting minister of the Chinese legation in Washington (he served concurrently as associate minister from 1878 to 1881), Yung complained several times to the U.S. Department of State that the condition of the Chinese, particularly in the Western states, was "so fraught with perplexity and danger" that he considered it imperative to lay the case before the Secretary of State and the U.S. government in the form of a strongly-worded letter of protest: "... at the present time ... tens of thousands of my countrymen are by law deprived of shelter and prohibited from earning a livelihood and are in hourly expectation of being driven from their homes to starve in the streets. Under such circumstances I could not acquit myself of my duty if I did not protest earnestly ... against the wrongs to which they have been subjected."[33]

Nevertheless, his protest did not produce any result, as the momentum of the anti-Chinese movement continued and even climaxed by the passage of the Chinese Exclusion Act in 1882. There was indeed no guarantee of the rights of the Chinese in America. Even Yung Wing's American citizenship was annulled in 1898, for no practical reason whatsoever, despite his naturalization in 1852, and marrying an American lady in 1875.[34] From the 1880's on to his death in 1912, except for some occasional travels back and forth between China and America, Yung Wing lived in retirement and despair.

Notes

1. Yung Wing, *My Life in China and America* (New York: reprinted 1978), pp. 8-9.
2. *Ibid.*, pp. 15-18.
3. *Ibid.*, p. 19.
4. Unpublished letter from Yung Wing to Samuel Wells Williams, April 15, 1849, as quoted in Edmund H. Worthy, Jr., "Yung Wing in America," *Pacific Historical Review* XXXIV. 3 (1965), p. 268.
5. Yung to Williams, Dec. 25, 1850, as quoted in *Ibid.*, p. 269.
6. Yung, *My Life in China and America*, pp. 40-1.
7. Worthy, *op. cit.*, p. 270.
8. New Haven City Court, Naturalization Records, Oct. 30, 1852.
9. Yung to Williams, Dec. 25, 1850.
10. Yung, *My Life...*, p. 41.
11. *Ibid.*, pp. 171-5.
12. Knight Biggerstaff, *The Earliest Modern Government Schools in China* (Ithaca, N.Y.: 1961), pp. 8, 74, 109-110.
13. *Ibid.*
14. See Article VII of the 1868 Treaty, in Frederick Wells *Williams, The Life and Letters of Samuel Wells Williams* (New York: 1889), Appendix I.
15. The original plan was that the expense would be taken from the income of the Shanghai customs.
16. Yung, *My Life* ... p. 186.
17. D.C. Gilman, "American Education, 1869-79," *Journal of Social Science, containing the Transactions of the American Association* X (Dec., 1879), p. 17.
18. It seems, too, according to one student's reminiscence, that the idea was to be able to give private English lessons to the Chinese boys until they were advanced enough in English before being sent to the schools, see Wen Ping-chung, "Reminiscence of a Pioneer Student," a lecture delivered to students at the Customs College at Peking, December 23, 1923. A copy of the lecture is in the LaFargue-Robinson Collection, Washington State University Library at Pullman.

19. Note of B.G. Northrop, Secretary of the Board of Education of the State of Connecticut, New Haven, dated October 1, 1872, U.S. *Foreign Relations* (1873-74), Vol. 1, pp. 141-2.
20. Frederick F. Low to Prince Kung, dated Jan. 10, 1873, *Ibid.,* p. 141.
21. Prince Kung to Low, Jan. 14, 1874, *Ibid.,* p. 143.
22. For more details about the Chinese Educational Mission, see Edwin Pak-wah Leung, "Education of the Early Chinese Students in America," *Proceedings of the 1980 National Conference on Chinese American Studies* (San Francisco: forthcoming).
23. The doubt three-story building was large enough to house the staff and seventy-five students. It was constructed at a cost of U.S. $43,000.
24. Ku Tun-jou, "Pai-nien Liu-mei chiao-yu ti hui-ku yu chien-chan" (A hundred years of Chinese students in America—the past and the future) *Chiao-yu yu wen-hua* 8.1 (June, 1955), pp. 4-14.
25. Yung Wing's Chinese education had been a little deficient. Li Hung-chang, in a letter to Kuo Sung-tao, dated Aug. 26, 1877, said, "Yung's proficiency in foreign languages and his familiarity with foreign conditions would make him a better diplomat than Ch'en Lan-pin. But even in him there is a defect - his Chinese education is insufficient, and he does not quite understand the basic proprieties in matters of government." *P'eng-liao han-kao,* 17.18a-b.
26. Thomas LaFargue, *China's First Hundred* (Pullman, W.A.: 1942), pp. 45-6.
27. For some of these reports, see *Ch'ing-chi wai-chiao shih-liao* (Historical materials of late Ch'ing Diplomacy) (Peking: 1932), 15.36b-37a.
28. Li to Ch'en, May 10, 1980, *P'eng-liao han-k ao* 19.20a.
29. For the text of the petition, see Arthur G. Robinson, *The Senior Returned Students* (Tientsin: 1932), pp. 17-18.
30. *Mark Twain's Autobiography I* (New York: 1924), pp. 21-24.
31. Hsueh Yu-fu's letter to Kate Pattee Aagin, from Amoy, China, dated Jan. 10, 1882, collected in LaFargue-Robinson Collection, Washington State University Library at Pullman.
32. Mark Twain's Autobiography 1, pp. 21-24.
33. Yung Wing to Secretary of State William M. Evarts, March 9, 1880. Notes from the Chinese legation to the Department of State, National Archives 98, Roll 1.
34. Worthy, *op. cit.*, p. 265, 283-4.

11

China's Quest from the West: The Chinese Educational Mission to the United States, 1872-1881

In early August 1872, a group of Chinese students made a historic visit to the United States legation in Peking. As it turned out, they came to say goodbye to the American Ambassador Frederick F. Low before they set sail to the United States for education. Low greeted the Chinese boys warmly and asserted that the American government would do everything possible to facilitate their studies in the United States.[1] Several days later, on August 12, these pioneer students left China for America.[2]

Between 1872 and 1875, four groups of such Chinese students totaling 120 arrived in America. Known as the Chinese Educational Mission students, they were sent to the United States by the Chinese imperial government, and it was indeed the first group of Chinese government students ever sent to the West.[3]

The Chinese Educational Mission would not have been sent to America without the effort of Yung Wing (Jung Hung), the first Chinese graduate of an American college (Yale, 1854) and later the co-commissioner of the Mission. Yung was regarded by many as the "father of the education of Chinese in the United States."[4] He was brought to America at the age of eighteen by a Yale-educated minister, Reverend Samuel R. Brown, who had once been the principal of the Morrison Educational Society school in Hong Kong.[5] In April 1847, Yung was enrolled at Monson Academy in Massachusetts. During his sojourn there, Yung became deeply interested in Western education. In a letter to Samuel Wells Williams, a friend whom he had met in Hong Kong, Yung indicated that he had "a great inclination to get a liberal education [in America]."[6]

His Yale education in subsequent years became the key to his intellectual orientation, as he wrote in his autobiography: "[My American education] has unmistakenly enlarged my mental and moral horizon, and revealed to me responsibilities which the sealed eye of ignorance can never see."[7] Indeed, this intellectual excitement gained during his youthful years in America later influenced his perspective on life, and, upon his return to China, his request to the Chinese government that students be sent to America for education. Yung explained:

> I was determined that the rising generation of China should enjoy the same educational advantages that I had enjoyed; that through Western education China might be regenerated, become enlightened and powerful. To accomplish that object became the guiding star of my ambition. Toward such a goal, I directed all my mental resources and energy. Through thick and thin, and the vicissitudes of a checkered life from 1854 to 1872, I labored and waited for its consumation.[8]

Yung's suggestion received impetus in 1868 when the Seward-Burlingame Treaty was signed between China and the United States, which provided a student exchange agreement.[9] But it was not until May 13, 1872, that the educational project—Yung's "brainchild"—finally received sanction from the Chinese Court. The plan scheduled 120 students to be sent in four groups to the United States in successive years. They were to be trained in Western sciences and technology then mostly unavailable in China, for a period of fifteen years with the sponsorship of the Chinese government.[10]

The project had an office in Shanghai under Commissioner Liu Han-ch'ing, whose duty was to select and prepare students' studies abroad, and an office in America staffed by commissioners Ch'en Lan-pin and Yung Wing, one interpreter and two Chinese instructors. The office in America was known as the Chinese Educational Mission.

A preparatory school was opened in Shanghai, where candidates received some preliminary training and were examined on their general fitness for study abroad. Few candidates came from central and northern provinces. Yung Wing literally combed the coastal cities of Kwangtung for youths who had received some Western education in government schools of Hong Kong or in missionary schools along the coast. Consequently about 70 percent of the students were Cantonese.[11]

Yung Wing, as co-commissioner of the Chinese Educational Mission, preceded the first students to America to make arrangements for their arrival. When he arrived in New Haven, he consulted Noah Porter, President of Yale College, for advice on the best method for achieving the students' education. There was in Connecticut, especially at Hartford, a partiality toward the family approach.[12] Thus President Porter strongly advised Yung Wing not to keep the young Chinese together in one group but to place them by twos and threes in American families.[13] Yung agreed, and with the cooperation of the faculty of Yale College and the Connecticut State Board of Education, he made the necessary arrangements. An observer recorded that: "The response to the call for homes and instruction for Chinese boys has been surprisingly prompt and cordial. One hundred and twenty-two families have offered to receive two each, so that homes are open for two hundred forty-four . . . [this is] a desire [of the American people] to aid in promoting the progress of the largest nation on the globe."[14] The Chinese Educational Mission was regarded by the American government with "much interest" and "friendly feeling."[15] In response, the Chinese government expressed that "such acts of kindness tend to strengthen and make lasting the sympathy and friendship now so happily existing between your country and mine."[16] Indeed, the Chinese Educational Mission became a bond between the "oldest and newest nations" in the early 1870s, despite the gradually expanding forces of anti-Chinese feeling in the newly established Western states and territories.

Within a short time after their arrival at Hartford, the Chinese students found themselves sharing the daily lives of the particular families to which they had been assigned in typical New England towns and villages. Since the boys were in their early teens,[17] their overall impressions of America were not sophisticated and scholarly; nevertheless, their attitudes reflected certain differences between the two cultures. For example, as one student recalled his meeting with the assigned host family:

> It was my good fortune to be placed into the hands of a most motherly lady in Springfield. She came after us in a hack. As I was pointed out to her, she put her arms around me and kissed me. This made the rest of the boys laugh, and perhaps I got rather red in the face; however, I would say nothing to show my embarrassment. But that was the first kiss I ever had had since my infancy.[18]

In their American homes the students were taught Western table manners and were introduced to the strict discipline of New England family life. Wu Yang-tseng, one of the boys who lived in the Bartlett home in Hartford, recounted some of his early experiences, "I remember Miss Mary Bartlett was a strict disciplinarian. When we held our knives and forks too low at meals, she would correct us. When she heard us talking in our rooms in the attic after nine or ten p.m., she would call from below, 'Boys, stop talking, it is time to sleep.' Old Mr. Bartlett used to have Prayer Meeting mornings and evenings each day."[19] The Bartletts had remarkably close relations with Yung Wing.[20] They were one of the many families who gradually became devoted friends and counsellors of the Chinese boys who came into their families. In the words of Louise Bartlett, the boys appeared:

> very youthful as I looked upon them as playmates, very bright and full of fun, generally winning in games as we taught them to them and picking up English so fast that I do not remember except at the very first any difficulty in communicating with them. They were soon favorites with their schoolmates and delighted their teachers by their progress after they began to attend a public school.[21]

Exact records about the students' life at Hartford are few, in both English and in Chinese. The most valuable one seems to be William Lyon Phelps' autobiography.[22] A renowned professor at Yale and a famous writer, Phelps was a schoolmate of some of the Chinese students in Hartford Public High School during the late 1870s (the rest of the Chinese students attending West Middle School, Hartford District School, Holyoke High School, New Haven High School, and Hopkins Grammar School).[23] Phelps reported that the "visitors" had been getting along with their American mates very well. The reason "may have been partly owing to the attractive qualities of these Orientals, and their genius for adaptation."[24]

Their high school days, the major portion of their sojourn in the United States, shaped their personalities. According to Phelps, "they had excellent manners, were splendid sportsmen, alert in mind, good in their studies, good at athletics; I do not think I have ever known a finer group of boys or young men."[25] One of the boys nicknamed Cho (Ts'ao Chia-hsiang?) had impressed Phelps most: "My most intimate friend at the high school was a splendid Chinese boy named Cho—dignified and serious, who even at that time was more a sophisticated man of the world than I shall ever be. To hear that young gentleman translate Caesar in the classroom was a liberal education."[26]

Another Chinese student then attending Hartford Public High was Liang Tun-yen who, some years after his return to China, became China's Foreign Minister. His interest in international politics and diplomacy can be traced back to his high school days. In 1878, for example, he completed his graduation essay entitled: "The Northern Bear." It was an interesting and remarkably well-written piece of work in which Liang described in detail the strife and turmoil that gripped the world of his day, particularly the role played by Russia.[27]

Hartford Public High School during that time was extremely strict: "There was a printed monthly report, which gave the exact standing of every pupil in the school. This report was public, was sent to all parents, so that the precise position in scholarship of every boy and girl in the school was known. If one's average fell below Five for three months, one was dropped into the lower classes; and if one was in the lowest class, one was dropped from the school."[28]

The social life of the Chinese Educational Mission youths was also attractive and exciting. In Phelps' memory:

> When the Chinese youth entered the social arena, none of us had any chance. Their manner to the girls had a deferential elegance far behind our possibilities. Whether it was the exotic pleasure of dancing with Orientals, or what is more probable, the real charm of their manners and talk, I do not know; certain it is that at dances and receptions, the fairest and most sought-out belles invariably gave the swains from the Orient the preference. I can remember the pained expressions on the faces of some of my American comrades when the girls deliberately passed them by and accepted the attentions of Chinese rivals with a more than yielding grace.[29]

The social life of the Mission students described above suggests that these young Chinese had undergone a considerable degree of Americanization. In sports, they also picked up American games. According to Phelps again, "they became excellent at baseball, football, hockey on ice, then known as `shinny', and in fancy skating they were supreme."[30] Hsueh Yu-fu, at the time when he was about to leave America in 1881, still did not fail to tell his American friend such words like: "How I long I could skate now for just a few hours."[31] Chung Wen-yao's reputation in boat-racing was especially well-known while he was a student at Yale:

> He was coxswain of the victorious Yale crews of 1880 and 1881; and at some Yale-Harvard meeting many years later, when a Harvard man expressed doubt as to whether Mun Yew Chung [Chung Wen-yao] had even seen a university race, much less taken part in it, the Chinese suavely confessed he had never seen a Harvard crew row; and after a pause, explained that they were always behind him.[32]

In 1876, an International Exhibition celebrating the 100th anniversary of the American Revolution was held in Philadelphia and the Chinese government was asked, as one of the thirty-seven countries, to participate in the exhibition. Li Kuei was sent by China as a representative. According to his diary, he met one hundred and thirteen Chinese Educational Mission students accompanied by Interpreter K'uang Ch'i-chao, Chinese Instructor Liu Ch'i (Tsung?) -chun, and six American teachers in the exhibition. Of his impression of the students, he recorded:

> The young boys appear to me very intelligent and are willing to learn. They care for one another and interact with Westerners in elegant manners. Some who have been to the States about one year can unbelievably speak pretty good English. I am sure they must have learned a great deal this time from the exhibition ... Through traveling around the exhibition among hundreds and thousands of other foreign visitors, the boys did not seem timid and shy. They dressed like Westerners; however, their Chinese jackets made them appear to be Oriental. They seemed to like

> me ... I singled out the older ones and asked them if the exhibition would serve any purpose ... their answers were simple and relevant, and appealed to me ... How far the Western studies will benefit us we cannot say for certain. What the young boys want to learn is technical knowledge. The universal obligations and universal virtues our sages have laid down, and the three relationships and the five constants of the Confucian ethnics are in-born, and these young boys have already learned and practised them, and their study of technical knowledge will not affect them.[33]

Li Kuei expected these students to maintain their Chinese cultural heritage during their process of Western learning in America. Nevertheless, the boys succumbed to the American environment so completely that, in time, it became increasingly difficult to keep them at their Chinese studies.

In order to safeguard the students from being "enclosed by foreign learning" and to keep before them the Confucian ideal of loyalty to the Chinese Emperor, Chinese teachers were to accompany the Mission and instruct the students in the Chinese language and Confucian classics. Specific provision was made for periodic assemblies of the students to hear the Chinese Imperial Edict and to enable them to make the proper ceremonial obeisance to the emperor.[34] To strengthen the Chinese teaching, a headquarters located at 400 Collins Street was later established, which had large classrooms for Chinese courses.[35] A recent recollection of the Mission students' Chinese school work reveals that these teenagers had to receive intensive and strict Chinese classical education by the Mission.[36]

Co-commissioner Yung Wing understood that the increase of Chinese teaching would create a certain cultural dilemma for the students. Yung himself desired to saturate the students with an American viewpoint and, in consequence, neglected their Chinese education,[37] which according to the original plan was to parallel their American training. When conflicts occurred, Yung always sided with the students.[38] Yung's liberal educational approach was at variance with his conservative colleagues; conflict occurred within the Mission staff. Commissioners Ch'en Lan-pin, Ou E-liang, and Wu Chia-shan, in particular, were dissatisfied with the way Yung Wing educated the students. They sent to Peking a stream of unfavorable reports on the un-Chinese conduct of the students. The clash between Yung Wing and these conservative colleagues was inevitable.[39] A letter written by Li Hung-chang, a high Chinese official, to Ch'en Lan-pin, dated May 10, 1880, reveals this conflict:

> (The Chinese Instructor of the Mission) Jung Tseng-hsiang came to call and told me that the students had really neglected their Chinese studies and that this had arisen because Yung Wing held firmly the idea not to have the students spend too much time on Chinese learning . . . Yung Wing has also come to see me, saying it is true the students have neglected their Chinese studies. It is due to Yung Wing's obstinacy in not desiring these students to learn much Chinese.[40]

This internal conflict within the Mission staff over the approach of educating the Chinese boys was a major factor leading to the eventual recall of the Mission.

In 1880 the Chinese government ordered the teachers and students of the Chinese Educational Mission to return to China as soon as possible. This decision was received with deep disappointment by the Mission students who had to cut off their schooling in America. The disappointment was shared by many Americans who had come in contact with the students during their stay in the United States. An attempt was made to induce the Chinese government to rescind the order.

A petition to the Tsungli Yamen [China's Foreign Office], drafted by President Porter, was signed by the heads of many institutions where the students had been placed. Chief among them were Reverend Joseph H. Twichell, Reverend John W. Lane, Laurenus Clark Seelye, Samuel L. Clemens (Mark Twain), T.F. Frelinghuysen, and John Russell Young.[41] In this petition, they urged that: "We deeply regret that the young men have been taken away just at the time when they were about to reap the most important advantages from their previous studies, and to gather in the rich harvest which their painful and laborious industry had been preparing for them reap . . . We would respectfully urge that the reasons for this sudden decision should be reconsidered."[42]

Former President Ulysses S. Grant, who had been to China in 1879 and had had acquaintance with the Chinese Court, was requested by Yung Wing, through the assistance of Mark Twain, to write a letter to Li Hung-chang to help save the life of the Chinese Educational Mission. Grant's letter, according to Mark Twain, was a "clear, compact, and admirably written statement of the case of the Chinese pupils, with some equally clear arguments to show that the breaking up of the schools would be a mistake."[43] These heartwarming efforts succeeded in postponing the recall of the Chinese Educational Mission. On March 29, 1881, Li Hung-chang suggested an alternative to the Tsungli Yamen of recalling only a portion of the students.[44] But the Yamen, alarmed by reports on the Americanization of the Mission students and on the anti-Chinese movement in America, insisted on their stand and, on June 8, memorialized the Chinese Emperor to request the abolition of the Chinese Educational Mission. The Mission was withdrawn on September 6, 1881.[45]

The Chinese Educational Mission affords an especially rewarding object of study as it sheds light on China's internal social and intellectual development toward modernization. One Sinologist has said, "The traumatic transformation of traditional China would not have been born without the modernization of her intellectuals led by the movement of Chinese studying abroad."[46] If we agree to this statement, then the American-educated Mission students were no doubt the pioneers of this movement. Not only had they rendered their service to China's modernization, but more profoundly, pushed China into the family of nation-states. It was during their sojourn in the United States at their impressionable ages that the seeds of their future values, various plans, and eventual frustration were sown. In these formative years America became the source of their idealism as well as the molder of their views toward China. Even Yung Wing himself, as the first Chinese graduate from an American college, provides an illuminating example for examination. Yung's proposal for Western-learning, as well as his career as co-commissionership in the Chinese Educational Mission, reveals a complex episode of China's transitional process to modernization through numerous attempts in the age of crisis.

If a traditional society is by definition bound by the cultural horizons set by its tradition, then a modern society is culturally dynamic and oriented to change and innovation. From this point of view, Yung Wing's contribution is his suggestion of an alternative for China's future—the introduction of Western education through a cross-cultural perspective. And indeed, most of the students of the Chinese Educational Mission were able to justify amply the inspiration and encouragement they had received from their American teachers and friends by subsequent decades of service of China's modernization.

But we must not exaggerate the role of these American-educated intellectuals in the task of China's modernization. Prior to 1901, only fifty-seven students of Chinese citizenship had entered American colleges and universities.[47] And within this handful, almost all studied science and technology rather than philosophy, social science or humanities. Furthermore, most of them did not complete their schooling, which handicapped their careers and consequently limited their contributions to China. Fortunately, their work was continued by a much larger number of American-trained Chinese returned students during the twentieth century.

Notes

1. *Shen-pao* (Shanghai), August 5, 1872.
2. Cf. an earlier version of this paper, to be published in the *Proceedings* of the 1980 National Conference on Chinese American Studies, San Francisco.

3. A major source of information on the Chinese Educational Mission is Yung Wing's autobiography *My Life in* China *and America* (New York: Henry Holt, 1909), which has Chinese and Japanese translated editions. But this book contains numerous mistakes, so does Thomas LaFargue's *China's First Hundred* (Pullman, WA: State College of Washington, 1942). A brief description of the Mission is Arthur G. Robinson's *The Senior Returned Students: A Brief Account* of Chinese *Educational Mission (1872-1881) under Dr. Yung Wing* (Tientsin: Tientsin Press, 1932).
4. See, for example, *American University Men in China* (Shanghai: Comacrib, 1934), p. 1.
5. Yung, *My Life in China and America* (hereinafter cited as *My Life)*, pp. 40-41.
6. Yung Wing's letter to Samuel Wells Williams, April 15, 1849, in Edmund H. Worthy, Jr. "Yung Wing in America," *Pacific Historical Review,* XXXIV, No. 3 (1965), p. 268.
7. *My Life,* pp. 40-41.
8. *Ibid.*
9. See Article VII of the 1868 Treaty, in Frederick Wells Williams, *The Life and Letters of Samuel Wells Williams* (New York: Putnam's, 1889), Appendix I.
10. The original plan was that the expense would be taken from the income of the Shanghai customs.
11. The ethnic composition of the 120 Mission students:

China	Province	Number	Percentage
South	Kwangtung	84	70.0
Central	Kiangsu	21	17.5
South	Chekiang	8	6.7
Central	Anhwei	4	3.3
South	Fukien	2	1.7
North	Shantung	1	0.8

Source: Hsu Jun, *Hsu yu-chai tzu-hsu nien-p'u* [Autobiographical Chronicle of Hsu Jun] (Shanghai, 1927), pp. 17-23.

12. D.C. Gilman, "American Education, 1869-1879," *Journal of Social Science, Containing the Transactions of the American Association,* X (December, 1879), p. 17.
13. It seems, too, according to one student's reminiscence, that the idea was to be able to give private English lessons to the Chinese boys until they were advanced enough in English before being sent to the schools, see Wen Ping-chung, "Reminiscence of a Pioneer Student"' a lecture deliv-

ered to students at the Customs College at Peking, December 23, 1923. A copy of the lecture is in the LaFargue-Robinson Collection, Washington State University Library, Pullman.

14. Note of B.G. Northrop, Secretary of the Board of Education of the State of Connecticut, New Haven, October I, 1872, in *Foreign Relations of the United States,* First Session, 43rd Congress, Executive Documents (Washington, D.C.: United States Government Printing Office, 1874), I, pp. 141-142.
15. Frederick F. Low to Prince Kung, January 10, 1873, *Ibid.,* p. 141.
16. Prince Kung to Low, January 14, 1874, *Ibid.,* p. 143.
17. A review of the age of the Mission students reveals that the average age ranges from 13 to 15.
18. This student was Yen Fu-lee, quoted from LaFargue, *China's First Hundred,* pp. 37-38.
19. *Ibid.,* p. 35.
20. Rev. Samuel R. Brown, Yung Wing's former teacher in China, was related with the Bartlett family by marriage. His wife was Elizabeth Bartlett. *Ibid.,* p. 40.
21. *Ibid.,* pp. 39-40.
22. William Lyon Phelps, *Autobiography with Letters* (New York: Oxford University Press, 1939).
23. *Ibid.,* pp. 83, 100; Kate Pattee Again's letter to LaFargue, from Reading, Mass., March 8, 1946, in LaFargue-Robinson Collection; Charles F. Thwing, "Japanese and Chinese Students in America," *Scribner's Monthly* 20 (July 1880), p. 451.
24. Phelps, *Autobiography,* p. 83.
25. *Ibid.*
26. *Ibid.,* p. 85.
27. The essay was reprinted in full in *The Hartford Times,* May 31, 1938.
28. Phelps, *Autobiography,* p. 100.
29. *Ibid.,* p. 85.
30. *Ibid.,* pp. 83-84.
31. Hsueh Yu-fu's letter to Kit (Kate Pattee Again) from San Francisco, September 1, 1881, in LaFargue-Robinson Collection.
32. Phelps, *Autobiography, p.* 84.

33. Li Kuei, *Huan-yu ti-ch'iu hsin-lu* [The Trip Around the World] (Shanghai, 1887), ch. 3, pp. 25a-b.

34. For the text of the Sixteen Maxims of the Sacred Edict, see: *The Sacred Edict, containing 16 Maxims of the Emperor Kang-hi, amplified by his son, the Emperor Young-ching; together with a paraphrase on the whole,* translated from the Chinese original, and illustrated with notes, by Rev. William Milne (Shanghai, 1870).

35. The double three-story building was large enough to house the staff and seventy-five students. It was constructed at a cost of US $43,000.

36. Ku Tun-jou, "Pai-nien liu-Mei chiao-yu ti hui-ku yu Chien-chan" (A hundred years of Chinese students studying in America—a study), *Chiao-yu yu wen-hua* 8.1 (June 1955), pp. 4-14.

37. Yung Wing's Chinese education had been a little deficient. Li Hung-chang, in a letter to Kuo Sung-tao, August 26, 1877, said, "Yung's proficiency in foreign languages and his familiarity with foreign conditions would make him a better diplomat than Ch'en Lan-pin. But even in him there is the defect—his Chinese education is insufficient, and he does not quite understand the basic proprieties in matters of government," *P'eng-liao han-k'ao,* in *Li Wen-chung Kung ch'uan-chi* [Complete Works of Li Hung-chang] (Shanghai: Commercial Press, 1922), ch. 17, pp. 18a-b; Jung Tseng-hsiang, a Chinese instructor of the Mission, reported to Li in 1880 (?) that the students had neglected their Chinese studies because of Yung Wing, see Li's letter to Ch'en Lan-pin, May 10, 1880, *Ibid.*, ch. 19, p. 20a.

38. According to LaFargue, *China's First Hundred,* pp. 45-46, Jung K'uei (Yung Kwai) was one of the Mission students who had become a Christian and was deprived of his place in the Mission just as he was ready to enter Harvard College. Yung Wing saved him and maintained his stay in the States. However, LaFargue was mistaken in stating that Jung Kuei was to enter Harvard. Instead, he was accepted by Yale; see *Catalogue of the Officers and Students of Yale College with a Statement of the Course of Instruction in the various Departments, 1881-1882* (New Haven: Yale University Press, 1881), p. 33.

39. For some of the memorials by Ch'en Lan-pin and Wu Chia-shan, see *Ch'ing-chi wai-chiao shi-liao* [Historical materials of late Ch'ing diplomacy] (reprint; Taipei: Wen-hai, 1963), ch. 15, pp. 36b-37a.

40. Li's letter to Ch'en, May 10, 1880, see note 37.

41. *My Life,* p. 211.

42. For the text of the petition, see Robinson, *Senior Returned Students,* pp. 17-18.
43. *Mark Twain's Autobiography,* Vol. I (New York: Harper & Brothers, 1924), p. 23.
44. *I-shu han-kao, in Li Wen-chung Kung ch'uan-chi,* ch. 12, pp. 7-9.
45. Hsueh Yu-fu's letter to Kate Pattee Aagin from Amoy, January 10, 1882, in the LaFargue-Robinson Collection.
46. C.K. Yang's book review on Y.C. Wang, *Chinese Intellectuals and the West,* in *Journal of Asian Studies* XXVI, No. 1 (November 1960), pp. 115-117.
47. K.C. Liu, *Americans and Chinese* (Cambridge, Mass.: Harvard University Press, 1963), p. 30.

12

The Making of the Chinese Yankees: School Life of the Chinese Educational Mission Students in New England

Introduction

Before the 19th-century, China stood unchallenged in Asia. The Chinese believed that it was their culture of Confucianism which made them "civilized" and distinguished them from the Western "barbarians." Hence, there was no need for the Chinese to leave their homeland to learn outside China.

In the early 19th-century, however, some Chinese were brought to the West by the missionaries, as in the case of the five Chinese students in the Foreign Mission School in Cornwal, Connecticut.[1] In 1847, the Yale-educated Reverend Samuel R. Brown, at his retirement in Hong Kong and return to the United States, brought three Chinese students along with him. One of the three students—Yung Wing—later became the first Chinese to have graduated from an American college (Yale, 1854).[2]

Impressed by his American education, Yung Wing returned to China after college and urged the Chinese government to send students to America for Western training. By the 1860's, some

Confucian officials had also finally realized that China must learn the Western "barbarian" way of how to be strong and powerful, since China had been suffering from serious Western invasions. The more progressive leaders reasoned that sending students abroad would be a shortcut for China to acquire the Western secrets of wealth and power, and thus they found Yung Wing's proposed educational project of sending Chinese students to America acceptable. In 1870, the project was approved and finalized, which stipulated that four groups of young Chinese students totaling 120 would be sent to America between 1872 and 1875. The project also stipulated to set up an office in Shanghai under Commissioner Liu Han-ch'ing, whose duty was to select and prepare students' studies abroad, and an office in America staffed by Commissioners Ch'en Lan-pin and Yung Wing, one interpreter and two Chinese instructors. The office in America is known as the Chinese Educational Mission.[3]

A preparatory school was opened in Shanghai, where candidates received some preliminary training and were examined on their general fitness for study abroad. According to one student's recollection: "the curriculum [of the preparatory school] contained few subjects, which had, however, to be learned well and thoroughly. Memorizing the classics was compulsory. Science was not taught. Shouting one's lessons at the top of the voice was considered the proper way to learn."[4] This marks a significant difference with the American system of education.

Another student also recalled his English-learning experience in the preparatory school: "The teacher of this brance was a Chinese gentleman who learned his English at Hong Kong. The first thing to be done was to teach me the alphabet. When the teacher grew tired he set some advanced pupils to teach me. The letters sounded rather funny, I must say. It took me two days to learn them. The letter *R* was the hardest one to pronounce, but I soon learned to give it, with a peculiar roll of the tongue even. We were taught to read and write English and managed by means of primers and phrase-books to pick up a limited knowledge of the language. A year thus passed in study and pastime."[5]

Preliminary Instruction in America

Yung Wing, as co-commissioner of the Chinese Educational Mission, preceded the first students to America to make arrangements for their arrival. When he arrived in New Haven, he consulted B.G. Northrop, Commissioner of Education for Connecticut, for advice on the best method for achieving the students' education. There was in Connecticut, especially at Hartford, a partiality toward the family approach.[6] Thus Northrop strongly advised Yung Wing not to keep the young Chinese together in one group but to place them by twos and threes in American families.[7] Yung agreed, and with the cooperation of the faculty of Yale College and the Connecticut State Board of Education, he made the necessary arrangements. An observer recorded that: "The response to the call for homes and instruction for Chinese boys has been surprisingly prompt and cordial. One hundred and twenty-two families have offered to receive two each, so that homes are open for two hundred forty-four."[8]

List of Preliminary Instructors and Students

	Instructor Name	Location of Home	Student Name
1	A.G. Loomis	Greenfield, Mass.	Teng Kuei-t'ing
			Chuo Jen-chih
			Liang Chin-jung
2	Lizzie Clark	Greenfield, Mass.	Tang Chi-yao
			Huang Chi-liang
			Yang Chang-ling
			Lin P'ei-ch'uan
3	N.L. Dickerman	Holyoke, Mass.	Ting Ch'ung-chi
			Wang Liang-teng
			K'uang Kuo-kuang
			K'uang Ping-kuang
4	E.R. Kagwin	Holyoke, Mass.	Chou Wan-peng
5	A. Worswick	Holyoke, Mass.	Hsueh Yu-fu
6	E.A. Moore	S. Hadley Falls, Mass.	Chu Pao-k'uei
			Chi Tsu-i
7	J.M. Harrington	Amherst, Mass.	Liang Pi-hsu
			Ch'en Shao-ch'ang
8	M.W. (E.W.?) Kellogg	N. Amherst, Mass.	Ts'ao Chia-chueh
			Lo Tsu-hua
9	J.H. Herrick	N. Amherst and Gardner, Mass.	Li Kuei-p'an
			Wu Chung-hsien
10	M.E. (Lamson) Phillips	?	Chin Ta-t'ing
			Ch'en Chin-k'uei
11	Clara Potter Hopkins	Enfield, Mass.	Lin Lien-huei
			Lin Lien-sheng
12	A.S. Moody	Belchertown, Mass.	Ts'ao Mao-hsiang
			Chu Hsi-shou
13	A.E. Burt	Oakham, Mass.	T'an Yao-hsun
			Liu Chia-chao
14	Deacon A. and Mary R. Hyde	Lee, Mass.	Wu Chin-dung
			Sun Kuang-ming
15	Maria D.S. Longley	Belchertown, Mass.	Tang Jung-chun
16	John W. Lane	S. Hadley, Mass.	Yang Chao-nan

	Instructor Name	Location of Home	Student Name
17	M.H. Lane	Whateley, Mass.	Ts'ao Chia-hsiang
18	D.C. Miller	Easthampton, Mass.	K'uang Hsien-chou K'uang Ching-yang
19	M.L. Paseo	Hadley, Mass.	Cheng T'ing-hsiang Hsu Chen-peng Lo Tsu-hua
20	H.M. and J.G. Clarke	Northampton, Mass.	Liang Pu-chao Liang Pu-shih
21	M.E. Matthews	Northampton, Mass.	Chang Kang-jen Ho T ing-lian K'uang Jung-kuang Su Jui-chao K'uang Ching-huan Tang Kuo-an
22	A.S. McClean	Springfield, Mass.	Chung Wen-yao Tang Yuan-chan Ts'ai T'ing-kan
23	E.C. Gardner	Springfield, Mass.	Tang Shao-yi Liang Ju-hao Huang Yu-chang Sheng Wen-yang
24	H.R. Vaille	Springfield, Mass.	Li En-fu Niu Shang-chou
25	William H. Foote	Westfield, Mass.	Tang Chih-yao Lin P'ei-chuan Huang Chi-liang Yang Ch'ang-ling
26	David (Charles?) E. Bartlett	Hartford, Conn.	Liang Tun-yen Ts'ai Shao-chi Huang K'ai-chia Wu Yang-tseng
27	C. Goldthwaite (Goldwait?)	Hartford, Conn.	Ch'en Chu-yung
28	J. Goldthwaite (Goldwait?)	Hartford, Conn.	Teng Shih-ts'ung
29	Helen E. Blakeslee	Hartford, Conn.	Wu Chi-tsao Pan Ssu-ch'ih Tang Chih-yao Teng Shih-ts'ung
30	J.B. Burbank	Hartford, Conn.	Jung Shang-ch'ien

	Instructor Name	**Location of Home**	**Student Name**
31	Katherine Burbank	Hartford, Conn.	Ts'ao Chia-hsiang
32	H.A. Kellogg	Hartford, Conn.	Lu Tsu-hua
33	H.O. Barber	Hartford, Conn.	Ch'ien Wen-k'uei
34	J.S.R. Stevens	Hartford, Conn.	Shih Chin-yung
35	C.J. Stevens	Hartford, Conn.	Lu Hsi-kuei
36	John B. Woodforth	Hartford, Conn.	Wu Chung-hsien Li Kuei-pan
37	Delight Twichell Hall	Plantsville, Conn.	Tang Kuo-an Chang Yu-kung
38	C.J. Alford	Farms Village, Conn.	Chang Hsiang-h'u Wang Feng-chieh Ts'ao Mao-hsiang
39	H. Carrington	Colebrook (Colchester?), Conn.	Liu Chia-chao
40	C.F. Weitzel	?	Huang Chung-liang
41	Geo. H. Martin	?	Ch'en Pei-hu Ts'ai Chin-chang
42	Wm. R. Potter	?	Ch'en Pei-hu
43	J.L. Richard	Washington, Conn.	Lu Yung-chuan Ts'ai Chin-chang
44	Guy B. Day	Bridgeport, Conn.	Ou-yang Keng Lo Kuo-jui Chang Kang-jen
45	M .J. Post	Clinton, Conn.	Lu Hsi-kuei Huan Wei-cheng Ch'eng Ta-yeh
46	L.A. Garett	Norwich, Conn.	Li Kuei-p'an Wu Chung-hsien Ts'ai Chin-chang Ch'en Pei-hu
47	R.S. Beston	Norwich, Conn.	Chou Chuan-chieh Chou Chuan-e Chu Pao-k'uei
48	C.E. Rogers	Norwich, Conn.	Lu Te-chang Shen Shou-ch'ang Huang Chung-liang Chung Chin-cheng
49	Edward Howard	Norwich, Conn.	Ts'ai Chin-chang Ch'en Pei-hu
50	M.W. Hakes	Norwich, Conn.	Huang Yao-ch'ang

	Instructor Name	Location of Home	Student Name
			Ch'en Pei-hu
51	W.S. Phillips	W. Winsted, Conn.	Chou Ch'ang-ling
			Lo Tsu-hua
52	J.N. Bartlett	New Britain, Conn.	Tang Jung-hao
			Ts'ai T'ing-kan
			Shih Chin-tang
			Jung Yao-huan
53	Henry E. Sawyer	New Britain, Conn.	Yuan Ch'ang-k'un
			Ts'ai T'ing-kan
54	Virginia T. Smith	Hartford, Conn. (?)	Huang Chung-liang
			Chung Wen-yao
			Chang Kang-jen
			Tang Shao-yi
			Liang Pi-hsu
			Huang Yao-ch'ang
55	Brownell	Hartford, Conn.	Tang Shao-yi

Source: This list is compiled from various materials and student memoirs now in the LaFargue Collection, Washington State University Library, Pullman, Washington; see also Fred Gilbert Blakeslee, "Chinese Came here to Study Western Ideas: Hartford Was Home of First Chinese Educational Mission to the United States," *The Hartford Daily Times*, Feb. 16, 1929; and Fu Wei-ling, "Tsao-ch'i liu-Mei shih-hua—wei chi-nien Chung-kuo shou-p'i kuan-fei yu-t'ung fu-Mei i-pai-chou-nien tso" (Historical notes on early Chinese students studying in America—written in commemoration of the 100th anniversary of China's first group of government students sending to the U.S.) *Chung-wai tsa-chih*, Part I, 12.2 (Aug. 1972), pp. 6-12; Part II, 12.3 (Sept. 1972), pp. 86-91; Part III, 12.4 (Oct. 1972), pp. 54-59.

"Yung Wing assigned the students to their respective teachers who had come to take the students away to their own homes in the various parts of the states and who were to have the guardianship over them during their term in America," recalled Mission student Wen Ping-chung. "The students were distributed in twos and fours and placed under the care of their guardians. Those students who were advanced enough in English were sent to schools while the others were given private lessons at home."[9]

In their initial encounters in American homes, the Chinese students found themselves sharing the daily lives of the particular families to which they had been assigned in typical New England towns and villages. Since the boys were in their early teens,[10] their overall impressions of America were not sophisticated and scholarly; nevertheless, their attitudes reflected certain differences between the two cultures. For example, as Li En-fu recalled his meeting with the assigned host family:

> It was my good fortune to be placed into the hands of a most motherly lady in Springfield. She came after us in a hack. As I was pointed out to her, she put her arms around me and kissed me. This made the rest of the boys laugh, and perhaps I got rather red in the face; however, I would say nothing to show my embarrassment. But that was the first kiss I ever had had since my infancy.[11]

In their American homes the students were taught Western table manners and were introduced to the strict discipline of New England family life. Wu Yang-tseng, one of the boys who lived in the Bartlett home in Hartford, recounted some of his early experiences, "I remember Miss Marry Bartlett was a strict disciplinarian. When we held our knives and forks too low at meals, she would correct us. When she heard us talking in our rooms in the attic after nine or ten p.m., she would call from below, 'Boys, stop talking, it is time to sleep.' Old Mr. Bartlett used to have Prayer Meeting mornings and evenings each day."[12] The Bartletts had remarkably close relations with Yung Wing.[13] They were one of the many families who gradually became devoted friends and counsellors of the Chinese boys who came into their families. In the words of Louise Bartlett, the boys appeared:

> Very youthful as I looked upon them as playmates, very bright and full of fun, generally winning in games as we taught them to them and picking up English so fast that I do not remember except at the very first any difficulty in communicating with them. They were soon favorites with their schoolmates and delighted their teachers by their progress after they began to attend a public school.[14]

Many of the Chinese students were making good progress in English since the family method provided favorable circumstances for cultural re-orientation and language acquisition. Li En-fu explained: "We learned English by object-lessons. At table we were always told the names of certain dishes, and then assured that if we could not remember the name we were not to partake of that article of food. Taught by this method, our progress was rapid and surprising."[15] However, not all of them were making progress in learning English. Sun Kuang-ming, for example, complained that after three years he still had not improved his English and asked Yung Wing for a transfer to another home.[16]

Elementary and Secondary Education

The following is a tentative list of the Chinese Educational Mission students attending elementary and secondary schools in America (See next page):

Extant records about the students' school life in New England are few. The most valuable one seems to be William Lyon Phelps' autobiography.[17] A renown professor at Yale and a famous writer, Phelps was a schoolmate of some of the Chinese students in Hartford Public High School during the late 1870s. Phelps reported that the "visitors" had been getting along with their American mates very well. The reason "may have been partly owing to the attractive qualities of these Orientals, and their genius for adaptation."[18]

Elementary, Junior, and High Schools Attended by Mission Students

School Name	Student Name
1. Hartford Public High School	Liang Tun-yen
	Ch'eng Ta-yeh
	Kang Keng-ling
	Ts'ao Chia-hsiang
	Wu Ching-jung
	Chang Hsiang-h'u
	Tang Shao-yi
	Huang Yao-ch'ang
	Liang Ju-hao
	Teng Kuei-t'ing
	Lo Tsu-hua
	Hsu Chen-peng
	Cheng T'ing-hsiang
	Wu Chi-tsao
	Ts'ai Shao-chi
	Huang K'ai-chia
	Ch'en Chu-yung
	Chang Kang-jen
	Huang Chung-liang
	Chung Wen-yao
	Teng Shih-ts'ung
	Ch'en Jung-kuei
	Lu Hsi-hui

School Name	Student Name
	Wu Yang-tseng
	Jung Shang-chin
	Chuo Jen-chih
	Ts'ao Chi-fu
	Tseng Tu-kung
2. New Haven High School	Ou-yang Keng
3. Holyoke High School	Hsueh Yu-fu
4. New Britain High School	Ts'ai Ting-kan
5. Hillhouse High School	Chan T'ien-yu
6. Springfield High School	Jung K'uei
7. Phillips Exeter Academy	Tang Kuo-an
(Exeter, New Hampshire)	Chang Yu-kung
	Niu Shang-chou
	Ch'en Chin-k'uei
	Chin Ta-t'ing
	Li Ju-chin
	Huang Tsu-lin
8. Phillips Academy (Andover, Mass.)	Chou Ch'ang-ling
	Liang Pi-hsu
	Liu Yu-lin
9. Seaside Institute (West Haven, Conn.)	Chan T'ien-yu
	Ou-yang Keng
10. West Middle Grammar School	Liang Tun-yen
11. Hopkins Grammar School	Chou Chuan-chien (?)
12. Hartford Grammar School	Ts'ai Ting-kan

Source: Information provided to Arthur G. Robinson by Jung Shang-chin and Chung Wen-yao, from Shanghai, dated August 26, 1938; autobiographies of some of the Mission students, now deposited in the LaFargue Collection, Washington State University Library, Pullman, Washington; Kate Patte Aagin's letter to Thomas LaFargue, March 8,1946; William Lyon Phelps, *Autobiography with Letters* (New York: 1939), passim; Edouard L. Desrochers, periodicals librarian and archivist of the Phillips Exeter Academy, to Peter New, dated Nov. 15, 1984; Peter New's letter to the present author, October 7, 1985.

Their high school days, the major portion of their sojourn in the United States, shaped their personalities. According to Phelps, "they had excellent manners, were splendid sportsmen, alert in mind, good in their studies, good at athletics; I do not think I have ever known a finer group of boys or young men."[19] One of the boys nicknamed Cho (Ts'ao Chia-hsiang?) impressed Phelps most: "My most intimate friend at the high school was a splendid Chinese boy named Cho—dignified and serious, who even at that time was more a sophisticated man of the world than I shall ever be. To hear that young gentleman translate Caesar in the classroom was a liberal education."[20]

Another Chinese student then attending Hartford Public High was Liang Tun-yen who became China's Foreign Minister some years after his return. His interest in international politics and diplomacy can be traced back to his high school days. In 1878, for example, he completed his graduation essay entitled: "The Northern Bear." It was an interesting and remarkably well-written piece of work in which Liang described in detail the strife and turmoil that gripped the world of his day, particularly the role played by Russia.[21]

Hartford Public High School during that time, like many New England secondary schools, was extremely strict: "There was a printed monthly report, which gave the exact standing of every pupil in the school. This report was public, was sent to all parents, so that the precise position in scholarship of every boy and girl in the school was known. If one's average fell below Five for three months, one was dropped into the lower classes; and if one was in the lowest class, one was dropped from the school."[22]

The social life of the Chinese Educational Mission youths also deserves our attention here. In Phelps' memory:

> When the Chinese youth entered the social arena, none of us had any chance. Their manner to the girls had a deferential elegance far behind our possibilities. Whether it was the exotic pleasure of dancing with Orientals, or what is more probable, the real charm of their manners and talk, I do not know; certain it is that at dances and receptions, the fairest and most sought-out belles invariably gave the swains from the Orient the preference. I can remember the pained expressions on the faces of my American comrades when the girls deliberately passed them by and accepted the attentions of Chinese rivals with a more than yielding grace.[23]

In sports, they also picked up American games. According to Phelps again, "they became excellent at baseball, football, hockey on ice, then known as 'shinny', and in fancy skating they were supreme."[24] Hsueh Yu-fu, at the time when he was about to leave America in 1881, still did not fail to tell his American friend such words like: "How I long I could skate now for just a few hours."[25] Such descriptions of the social life of the Chinese Educational Mission students indicate that they were considerably Americanized.

College Education

List Showing Those Mission Students Who Had Entered American Colleges before the Time of Their Recall in 1881

Institution	Name of Student	Graduated by 1881?
Yale College	Chan T'ien-yu	Yes
	Ou-yang Keng	Yes
	Liang Tun-yen	No
	Chung Wen-yao	No
	Tang Kuo-an	No

Institution	Name of Student	Graduated by 1881?
	Jung K'uei	No
	Ts'ai Shao-chi	No
	Huang K'ai-chia	No
	T'an Yao-hsun	No
	Li En-fu	No
	Wu Chung-hsien	No
	Ch'en Pei-hu	No
	Liu Chia-chao	No
	Jung Yao-huan	No
	Tang Kuo-kuang	No
	Tseng P'u	No
	Chang Kang-jen	No
	Chi Tsu-i	No
Columbia College	Chou Ch'ang-ling	No
	Tang Shao-yi	No
	Wu Yang-tseng	No
Massachusetts Institute of Technology	Hsueh Yu-fu	No
	Fang Po-liang	No
	K'uang Ching-yang	No
Worcester Institute of Technology	Wen Ping-chung	No
Rensselaer Polytechnic Institute	Su Jui-chao	No
	Wu Ying-k'o	No
	Lo Kuo-jui	No
Stevens School of Technology	Liang Ju-hao	No
Amherst College	Ho T'ing-liang	No
Harvard College	Ting Ch'ung-chi	No
Lafayette College	K'uang Jung-kuang	No
Lehigh College	Huang Chung-liang	No
Hopkins University	Shen Chia-shu	No

Source: Miscellaneous materials in the LaFargue Collection, Washington State University Library, Pullman, Washington; *Catalogue of the Officers and Students of Yale College, with a Statement of the Course of Instruction in the Various Departments, 1881-1883* (New Haven: 1881); Arthur G. Robinson, "China's Pioneers in Western Education," *Peking and Tientsin Sunday Times,* July 30, 1933; Charles F. Thwing, "Japanese and Chinese Students in America," *Scribner's Monthly* 20 (July 1880), pp. 450-453; Knight Biggerstaff, *The Earliest Modern Government Schools in China* (Ithaca, N.Y.: 1961), p. 70; Fu Wei-ling, "Tsao-ch'i liu-Mei shih-hua—wei chi-nien Chung-kuo shou-p'i kuan-fei yu-t'ung fu-Mei i-pai-chou-nien tso" (Historical notes on early Chinese students studying in America—written in commemoration of the 100th anniversary of China's first group of government students sending to the United States) *Chung-wai tsa-chih* 12.4 (October 1972), pp. 54-59.

The above list indicates that at the time of the sudden recall of the Mission in 1881, only two students (Chan T'ien-yu and Ou-yang Keng) had graduated from college, the rest were either still in college or in high school. However, several of them decided not to return to China and secretly stayed behind to continue their education. These included: Jung K'uei, Li En-fu, Tan Yao-hsun, and Wu Chung-hsien.[26]

Chan T'ien-yu was admitted to the Sheffield Scientific School of Yale College in 1878. Because of his aptitude for science and mathematics, he studied civil engineering. He graduated from Yale in the class of 1881 at the age of 20, receiving a Ph.B. degree in civil engineering. He became a leading Chinese engineer after his return to China.[27]

Another Chinese student Chung Wen-yao earned his reputation in boat-racing while at Yale:

> He was coxswain of the victorious Yale crews of 1880 and 1881; and at some Yale-Harvard meeting many years later, when a Harvard men expressed doubt as to whether Mun Yew Chung [Chung Wen-yao] had even seen a university race, much less taken part in it, the Chinese suavely confessed he had never seen a Harvard crew row; and after a pause, explained that they were always behind him.[28]

Another Yale student, Tang Kuo-an of the class of 1884, won second prize in Latin composition in his freshman year. Later in

China, Tang became the first president of the Tsing Hua College.[29]

Another outstanding Yale student was Liang Tun-yen who later became China's Minister of Foreign affairs. He earned his reputation as a "southpaw" pitcher on his freshman baseball nine at Yale. Liang stayed with the Bartlett family while at Hartford. In 1910, the Bartletts were invited by Liang to spend a whole year in China. These New Englanders accepted the invitation and for one year they lived like Chinese aristocrats amidst the luxurious surroundings of the family of a wealthy and prominent Chinese official.[30]

Chinese Education

While the Chinese students were receiving American education, they were at the same time continuing their Chinese studies. In order to safeguard the students from being "enclosed by foreign learning" and to keep before them the Confucian ideal of loyalty to the Chinese emperor, Chinese teachers accompanied the Mission to instruct the students in the Chinese language and Confucian classics. Specific provision was made for periodic assemblies of the students to hear the Chinese Imperial Edict and to enable them to make the proper ceremonial obeisance to the emperor.[31] To strengthen the Chinese teaching, a headquarters located at 400 Collins Street, Hartford, Connecticut, was later established, which had large classrooms for Chinese courses.[32] A recent discovery of the Mission students' Chinese school work reveals that these teenagers received intensive and strict Chinese classical education while in America.[33] Some students resented their Chinese education, and they even called the Chinese school the "hell house"![34]

Co-commissioner Yung Wing understood that the increase of Chinese learning would create a certain cultural dilemma for the students. Yung, himself Americanized and even married an American wife in 1875, desired to saturate the students with an American viewpoint and, in consequence, neglected their Chinese education,[35] which according to the original plan was to parallel their American training. When conflicts occurred, Yung always sided with the students.[36]

Yung's liberal educational approach was at variance with his conservative Chinese colleagues, resulting in conflicts within the Mission staff. Co-commissioner Ch'en Lan-pin and his successors Ou E-liang and Wu Chia-shan, in particular, were dissatisfied with the way Yung Wing was educating the students. They sent a stream of unfavorable reports on the un-Chinese conduct of the students to Peking. The clash between Yung Wing and these conservative colleagues was inevitable and eventually led to the recall of the Mission.[37]

Conclusion

It is obvious that the American education that the Chinese Educational Mission students received must have had significant impact on the minds of these youngsters. It was during their sojourn in the United States at their impressionable ages that the seeds of their future values and various plans were sown. In these formative years America became the source of their idealism as well as the molder of their views toward China. In retrospect, most of the students of the Chinese Educational Mission were able to justify amply the inspiration and encouragement they had received from their American teachers and friends by subsequent decades of service of China's modernization.

The Mission students' stay in America also provided an opportunity for some Americans for the first time to observe and interact with the Chinese people. This constituted the first impetus for the later revision of the American perception of the culture and ability of the Chinese. A quote from those American educators and families acquainted with the Mission students provides evidence of this image revision: "As a result of their good conduct, many of the prejudices of ignorant and wicked men toward the Chinese have been removed, and more favorable sentiments have taken place."[38] William Phelps' impression of his Chinese schoolmates, as noted previously, is particularly noteworthy. These Chinese youngsters had unintentionally carried out the work of what we now call *Kuo-min wai-chiao* (people-to-people diplomacy), or, in the words of the contemporary Americans, the "unofficial ambassadors."[39] This certainly adds an interesting and important footnote to the history of Chinese-American relations.

Notes

1. Information obtained from the LaFargue-Robinson Collection in the Library of the Washington State University, Pullman.

2. Edwin Pak-wah Leung, "To Americanize China: the Career of Yung Wing," *Proceedings of the Sixth International Symposium on Asian Studies* (1984), Vol. I, 257-267; and Edwin Pak-wah Leung, "China's Decision to Send Students to the West: the Making of a 'Revolutionary' Policy," paper presented at the "International Conference on the History of the Ming-Ch'ing Periods," University of Hong Kong, December 11-15, 1985, Hong Kong.
3. Edwin Pak-wah Leung, "China's Quest from the West: the Chinese Educational Mission to the United States, 1872-1881," *Asian Profile* 11.6 (December 1983), 527-534. See also Yung Wing, *My Life in China and America* (New York: Henry Holt, 1909); Thomas LaFargue, *China's First Hundred* (Pullman, WA: Washington State College Press, 1942); and Arthur G. Robinson, *The Senior Returned Students: A Brief Account of the Chinese Educational Mission (1872-1881) under Dr. Yung Wing* (Tientsin: Tientsin Press, 1932.)
4. Wen Ping-chung, "Reminiscence of a Pioneer Student," a lecture delivered at the Customs College, Peking, China, on Dec. 23, 1923. A copy of the lecture is now in the LaFargue Collection, Washington State University Library, Pullman, Washington.
5. Yan Phou Lee (Li En-fu), *When I was a Boy in China* (Boston: D Lothrop Co. 1887), 99-104.
6. D.C. Gilma, "American Education, 1869-18'79," *Journal of Social Science, Containing the Transactions of the American* X (Dec. 1879), 17.
7. It seems, too, according to Li En-fu's reminiscence, that the idea was to be able to give private English lessons to the Chinese boys until they were advanced enough in English before being sent to the schools.
8. Note of B.G. Northrop, Secretary of the Board of Education of the State of Connecticut, New Haven, Oct. 1, 1872, in *Foreign Relations of the United States,* First Session, 43rd Congress, Executive Documents (Washington, D.C.: United States Government Printing Office, 1874), I:141-142.
9. See note 4.
10. A review of the age of the Mission students reveals that the average age ranges from 13 to 15.
11. Lee, *op. cit.,* pp. 109-111.
12. LaFarge, *op. cit.,* p. 35.
13. Rev. Samuel R. Brown, Yung Wing's former teacher in China, was related with the Bartlett family by marriage. His wife was Elizabeth Bartlett. *Ibid,* p. 40.

14. *Ibid.*, pp. 39-40.
15. Lee, *op. cit.*, p. 111.
16. Sun Kuang-ming's autobiography, now in the LaFargue Collection.
17. William Lyon Phelps, *Autobiography with Letters* (New York: Oxford University Press, 1939).
18. *Ibid.*, p. 83.
19. *Ibid.*
20. *Ibid.*, p. 85.
21. The essay was reprinted in full in the *Hartford Times*, May 31, 1938.
22. Phelps, *op. cit.*, p. 100.
23. *Ibid.*, p. 85.
24. *Ibid.*, pp. 83-84.
25. Hsueh Yu-fu's letter to Kit (Kate Pattee Again) from San Francisco, September 1, 1881, in LaFargue Collection.
26. LaFargue, *op. cit.*, pp. 45-46.
27. Cf. Ling Hung-hsun and Kao Tsung-lu, *Chan Tien-yu yu Chung-kuo t'i-lu* (Chan T'ien-yu and the Chinese Railway) (Taipei: The Modern History Institute, Academia Sinica, 1977).
28. Phelps, *op. cit., p.* 84.
29. Lo Hsiang-lin, "Jung Hung yu Chung-kuo hsin wen-hua yun-tung chih ch'i-fa," (Yung Wing's influence in the Chinese New Cultural Movement) *Hsin-ya hsueh-pao* 1.2 (Feb. 1956), pp. 367-417.
30. LaFargue, *op. cit.*, p. 40.
31. For the text of the Sixteen Maxims of the Sacred Edict, see: *The Sacred Edict, containing 16 Maxims of the Emperor* Kang-*hi,* translated from the Chinese original, and illustrated with notes, by Rev. William Milne, (Shanghai: 1970).
32. The double three-story building was large enough to house the staff and seventy-five students. It was constructed at a cost of US $43,000.
33. Ku Tun-jou, "Pai-nien liu-Mei chiao-yu ti hui-ku yu chien-chan" (A hundred years of Chinese students studying in America—a study), *Chiao-yu yu wen-hua* 8.1 (June 1955), pp. 4-14.
34. Yung Shang-him, "The Chinese Educational Mission and Its Influence," *Tien Hsia Monthly* 9.3 (Oct. 1939), p. 232.
35. Yung Wing's Chinese education had been deficient. Li Hung-chang, in a letter to Kuo Sung-t'ao, August 26, 1877, said, "Yung's proficiency in

foreign languages and his familiarity with foreign conditions would make him a better diplomat than Ch'en Lan-pin. But even in him there is the defect—his Chinese education is insufficient, and he does not quite understand the basic proprieties in matters of government." *P'eng-liao han-k'ao in Li Wen-chung Kung ch'uan-chi* (Complete Works of Li Hung-chang) (Shanghai: Commercial Press, 1922), ch. 17:18a-b. Jung Tseng-hsiang, a Chinese instructor of the Mission, reported to Li in 1880 (?) that the students had neglected their Chinese studies because of Yung Wing, see Li's letter to Ch'en Lan-pin, May *10*, 1880, *Ibid*, ch. 19:20a.

36. LaFargue, *op. cit.*, pp. 45-46.

37. For some of the memorials by Ch'en Lan-pin and Wu Chia-shan, see *Ch'ing-chi wai-chiao shih-liao* (Historical materials of late Ch'ing diplomacy) (Taipei: Wen-hai, 1963), ch. 15:36b-37a.

38. This paragraph is taken from a letter written by the American educators, appeared in A.G. Robinson, *op. cit.*, p. 17.

39. Since 1928 the Committee on Friendly Relations among Foreign Students has published annually a pamphlet called *The Unofficial Ambassadors,* which includes a census of foreign students in America, see Robert S. Schwantes, *Japanese and Americans: A Century of Cultural Relations* (New York: 1955), p. 359.

13

The Quest for an Education in America: Chinese Students' Legal Battle and the Supreme Court's Decision

In the United States, bilingual-bicultural education is a matter of rapidly growing interest.[1] It has become particularly marked in the past decade.[2] Yet, as of the present, many educators still consider bilingual schooling nothing more than a "compensation" to those language minority students whose English is deficient. Few of them look at bilingual teaching from the perspective of providing an equal educational opportunity to the linguistically disadvantaged students, as demanded by their human rights and, as American citizens, their civil rights.

Article 26 of the Universal Declaration of Human Rights, adopted by the United Nations on December 10, 1948, states that: "Everyone has the right to an education," and that: "Education shall be directed to the full development of the human personality and to the strengthening of respect for human rights and fundamental freedoms."[3] The question naturally arises: Does the teaching of limited-English proficiency (LEP) students solely in English in America constitute an education? In other words, are these students being denied an education because they cannot comprehend the language in which they are being taught?

A report by the Human Rights Commission of San Francisco, for example, shows that, as of April 1973, there were 3,457 Chinese students in the San Francisco school system who spoke little or no English. But no more than 1,707 of these students needing bilingual instruction were receiving it.[4] The other half of them were simply excluded from an equal educational opportunity, even though they were physically present in the schools.[5] Yet, strangely, no effort was made by the San Francisco Unified School District (SFUSD) to improve this unfortunate condition. It was not until the U.S. Supreme Court's favorable decision in the *Lau vs. Nichols* case in early 1974 that the Asian students in San Francisco as well as elsewhere in America began to find better educational opportunity in the public schools.

The *Lau* decision is, undoubtedly, a major landmark in the development of Asian bilingual-bicultural education in the United States. The Supreme Court judges, in making this historic decision, expressed that:

> We know that those who do not understand English are certain to find their classroom experiences wholly incomprehensible and in no way meaningful.[6]

The subsequent decision has produced far-reaching consequences. To many people, educators or otherwise, the *Lau* decision is a "legal mandate" to provide the LEP students with bilingual instruction. This paper will discuss the legal aspect of the *Lau* case and its implications for the education of the Asian immigrant students in America.

The *Lau vs. Nichols* case began on March 25, 1970, when Kinney Kinmon Lau[7] and twelve others, on behalf of 2,856 Chinese-speaking LEP students, filed a lawsuit in the United States District Court in San Francisco against Alan Nichols, president of the San Francisco Board of Education.[8] These students alleged that they were being effectively denied an education because they could not comprehend the language in which they were being taught. It was further claimed that this deprivation of an education was "dooming these children to become dropouts and to join the rolls of the unemployed."[9] They argued that the failure to teach them bilingually should be prohibited on two legal grounds: first, that not to do so was a violation of their constitutional right to "equal protection under the law"[10]; second, that it was a violation of the Civil Rights Act of 1964.[11]

Like so many lawsuits, the *Lau* case was brought because of a deep sense of frustration; it was the Chinese community's last resort after all other avenues had been exhausted in hopes of overcoming the serious educational harms suffered by non-English-speaking children.[12] The law of the state of California required that these children attend school; thus, they went. Yet, while they were unable to speak or understand the English language, all the instruction they received—for six hours a day, five days a week, thirty-six weeks a year—was in English, as were all books and all the visual materials that were used. However, from an educational point of view, children can profit from education only when they are able to understand the instruction, ask and answer questions, do their homework, and speak with their classmates and teachers. For children who do not understand English, there can be no educational opportunity.

Indeed the seriousness of the students' position was admitted by the San Francisco Unified School District (SFUSD). During the trial of the *Lau* case, the school district stipulated that in 1970 there were 2,856 Chinese-speaking students in the district who needed special instruction in English, but that 1,790 of these children received no special help or instruction at all. The SFUSD further stipulated that of the 1,066 Chinese-speaking students who did receive some special help, nearly two-thirds received such help on a part-time, 50-minute-a-day basis. Finally, only 260 of those 1,066 Chinese-speaking students receiving special instruction in English were taught by bilingual, Chinese-speaking teachers.[13]

When confronted in District Court, the SFUSD argued that these students were not being discriminated against. The reasoning used was that they were being taught in the same facilities and by the same teachers at the same time as everyone else. Thus, since everything was the same for all students, there was no discrimination, and therefore, no violation of anyone's right to equal protection. In effect, their position was that the schools had no obligation to recognize and respond to the demonstrable communications difficulties encountered by the LEP students.[14]

In its decision, the United States District Court agreed with the SFUSD and denied the Chinese-speaking students any relief. The court expressed sympathy for the plight of the students, but concluded that their rights to an education and to equal educational opportunities had been satisfied as "they received the same education made available on the same terms and conditions to the other tens of thousands of students in the San Francisco Unified School District."[15] Though the plaintiffs contended that the "surface" equality of identical textbooks, teachers, and classrooms afforded no education to LEP children, the District Court ruled the SFUSD had no legal duty to rectify this situation.

Dissatisfied, the Chinese students appealed to the United States Circuit Court of Appeals for the Ninth Circuit. They made the same arguments, offered the same justifications and asked for the same relief. The Circuit Court chose to affirm the decision of the District Court. This decision was handed down on January 8, 1973.[16]

By this time, the problem of the Chinese students' education in the SFUSD had grown tremendously due to the constant influx of Chinese immigrants into San Francisco. In the 1973-1974 school years, the SFUSD had a total student enrollment of 78,023, kindergarten through twelfth grade, and its racial distribution was as follows:[17]

Ethnic Composition of the SFUSD, 1973-1974

	Number	**% of Total**
White	21,000	26.9
Asian American	19,728	25.3
Chinese	12,315	15.8
Filipino	5,715	7.3
Japanese	1,304	1.7
Korean	394	0.5

	Number	% of Total
Black	23,794	30.5
Hispanic	11,131	14.3
Other non-White	2,103	2.7
Native American	266	0.3

From this table, it is clear that the Circuit Court decision was made in negligence of the mounting need of the Chinese students for bilingual schooling. Faced with the devastating Circuit Court decision, the Chinese-speaking students took the last step and petitioned the United States Supreme Court to take their case and reverse the Circuit Court decision. On June 12, 1973, the Supreme Court granted the petition to hear the case, and oral arguments were heard on December 10, 1973. The United States government supported the children at the Supreme Court level by filing an *amicus curiae* brief recommending the reversal of the lower court opinion.[18] In addition, *amicus curiae* briefs in support of the NESA Chinese-American students were also filed by numerous organizations throughout the country, including the National Education Association, the Harvard University Center for Law and Education, the Lawyers' Committee for Civil Rights under Law, the Mexican-American Legal Defense and Education Fund, and the Puerto Rican Legal Defense and Education Fund.

Finally, on January 21, 1974, after nearly four long years of litigation, the Supreme Court delivered its *unanimous* decision which directly refuted both the position and language of the lower courts:

> There is no equality of treatment merely by providing students with the same facilities, textbooks, teachers and curriculum; for

> students who do not understand English are effectively foreclosed from any meaningful education.[19]

The Supreme Court was openly astonished that a school district would even suggest that requiring LEP children to sit and languish in regular English-language classrooms amounts to an "education." Viewing the evidence as a whole, the Court said:

> Basic English skills are at the very core of what these public schools teach. Imposition of a requirement that before a child can effectively participate in the educational program he must have already required those basic skills is to make a mockery of public education.[20]

Casting itself directly into the plight confronting LEP children, the Court concluded that:

> We know that those who do not understand English are certain to find their classroom experiences wholly incomprehensible and in no way meaningful.[21]

But the Supreme Court decision was not based on a constitutional requirement. The entire rationale was provided by Section 601 of the Civil Rights Act of 1964.[22] That section reads as follows:

> No person in the United States shall, on the ground of race, color, or national origin be excluded from participation in, be denied the benefits of, or be subjected to discrimination under any program or activity receiving Federal financial assistance.

This section was a mandate by Congress to make sure that Federal monies were spent in a non-discriminatory fashion.

The reasoning was perfectly applicable in the Lau case since the school district was the recipient of a large sum of Federal funds. By accepting these funds, the school district had contractually agreed to all the regulations of the United States Department of Health, Education and Welfare, which were issued pursuant to Sections 601 and 602 of Title VI of the Civil Rights Act of 1964. They also had agreed to take any measure necessary to implement the agreement. The SFUSD was clearly not complying with a validly imposed regulation.

Interestingly, the Lau decision does not require any specific program. Bilingual-bicultural education has not been specifically mandated by the Supreme Court. However, every court which has approached the problem of providing "a meaningful education" to the LEP students has concluded that some form of bilingual-bicultural education is necessary.

Notes

1. Bilingual-bicultural education in America, broadly defined, is "the use of two languages, one of them English, for instructional purposes." The definition used by the U.S. Commission on Civil Rights is "instruction using the native language and culture as a basis for learning subjects until second language skills have been developed sufficiently: it is the most widely discussed of approaches to providing language minority children with an equal educational opportunity." *A Better Chance to Learn: Bilingual-Bicultural Education* (Washington, D.C.: 1975), 3.
2. The Bilingual Education Act was signed into law by President Johnson in 1968.
3. Office of Public Information, United Nations. *The United Nations and Human Rights* (N.Y.: 1968), 33.
4. Report of the Human Rights Commission of San Francisco, Bilingual Education in San Francisco Public Schools, August 9, 1973: see also: "Supreme Court Rules in Lau vs. Nichols Case." *The Linguistic Reporter* 16.3 (March 1974), 6-7.
5. *The Third Annual Report of the National Advisory Council on Bilingual Education* (Washington, D.C.: November 1977), 90.

6. Supreme Court of the United States, Slip Op. No. 76-6520. The full text of the Supreme Court opinion is reprinted in *A Better Change to Learn,* Appendix B-4.
7. Kinney Kinmon Lau, a minor, was represented by his guardian Mrs. Kan Wai Lau.
8. Cf. L. Ling-chi Wang, "Lau vs. Nichols: the Right of Limited-English-Speaking Students," *Amerasia Journal* 11.2 (Fall 1974), 16-45; the same author's "Lau vs. Nichols: History of a Struggle for Equal and Quality Education," *Counterpoint: Perspectives on Asian Americans* (Asian American Studies Center, UCLA: 1976). 240-263; Dexter Waugh, "Lau vs. Nichols: the Legal Struggle for Bilingual Education," *San Francisco Examiner,* May 27, 1974.
9. Press Statement of the Plaintiffs, March 25, 1970.
10. Referring to the 14th Amendment of the Constitution.
11. As will be seen later, Section 601 of Title VI of the Civil Rights Act of 1964 provides that: "No person shall, on the ground of race, color, or national origin be excluded from participation in, be denied the benefits of, or be subjected to discrimination under any program or activity receiving Federal financial assistance."
12. Wang, "Lau vs. Nichols: History of a Struggle for Equal and Quality Education," 241.
13. SFUSD, *Pilot Program: Chinese Bilingual* (San Francisco: May 5, 1969), 3 A.
14. U.S. District Court for the Northern District of California, Civil No. C-70627 LHB Order, May 26, 1970.
15. An important passage of the order reads as follows: "....To provide such special instruction would be a desirable and commendable approach to take. Yet, this court cannot say that such an approach is legally required. On the contrary, plaintiffs herein seek relief for a special need—which they allege is necessary if their rights to an education and equal educational opportunities are to be received—that does not constitute a rights which would create a duty on defendants' part to act."
16. The Circuit Court further observed that the problems suffered by the children were "not the result of law enacted by the state ... but the result of the deficiencies created by the (children) themselves in failing to learn the English language." As Edward Steinman, attorney for the plaintiffs, correctly pointed out, "Such a statement ... not only suggests that the 'sins' of the fathers be visited upon the children; it further labels the child 'sinful' for not absorbing on his own, the language of the society into which he has been cast." "Testimony of Edward Steinman before the Committee on Ways and Means of the California State Assembly," December 10, 1974.

17. SFUSD, "Selected Data for Study in the Challenge to Effect a Better Racial Balance in the San Francisco Public Schools, 1973-1974."
18. For the legal brief of the United States before the Supreme Court in the *Lau* case, see: *Bilingual Education Act: Hearings before the General Subcommittee on Education of the Committee on Education and Labor, U.S. House of Representatives,* 10-19. 93rd Congress, 2nd Session, 1974.
19. See note 6.
20. *Ibid.*
21. *Ibid.*
22. Bureau of National Affairs, Washington D.C., *The Civil Rights Act of 1964: Text, Analyses, Legislative History, What it means to Employers, Businessmen, Unions, Employees, Minority Groups.* (Washington, D.C.: 1964).

PART IV

ETHNICITY AND NATIONAL INTEGRATION

14

Regional Autonomy versus Central Authority: The Inner Mongolian Autonomous Movement and the Chinese Response, 1925-1947

Introduction

Today, Inner Mongolia is one of the five ethnic autonomous regions in the People's Republic of China (PRC).[1] The Inner Mongolian Autonomous Government (IMAG) was established by the Chinese Communists in 1947, two years before the founding of the PRC.[2] For two decades prior to 1947, however, Inner Mongolia had been in a state of chaos and crises, as many of the Mongol nationalists, reformists, revolutionaries, as well as the princes and lamas, faced by the uncertainty of their future in the changing times, were actively involved in movements for possible political solutions. The major goal of these movements was autonomy for Inner Mongolia.[3]

This paper deals with the different types of autonomous movement in Inner Mongolia during the period from the 1920s to the 1940s. The Inner Mongols' aspirations and revolutionary plans, their expectations and demands from the Han-dominated Chinese Nationalists and Communists, as well as their dealings with the

Japanese, Soviets and Outer Mongols will be discussed. An attempt will also be made in this paper to highlight the Chinese Nationalist government's response to the Inner Mongols' demands during the Nanjing decade, as the autonomous movement reached its peak in the early 1930s.

Inner Mongolia in Flux: Development of the Autonomous Movement

Inner Mongolia in the early twentieth century was beset by a series of external and internal crises unprecedented in Mongol history. The collapse of the Manchu Qing Empire in China proper after the 1911 Republican Revolution upset the previous political equilibrium in China's frontier regions. The instability in Inner Mongolia was further stirred by the 1917 Bolshevik Revolution in Russia, and by the subsequent detachment of Outer Mongolia from the Chinese state in 1924.[4]

Internally, the Inner Mongolian society was rent by serious conflicts of interest among all walks of life. The traditional and rigid society was ruled by the privileged princes and lamas, and the Mongol people were subject to their oppression and exploitation. The burden of feeding the princes and lamas, and in addition sometimes supplying officials from China proper with all sorts of comforts, lay increasingly on the shoulders of the Mongol herdsmen.[5] Conscripted labour, compulsory military service and hosts of requisitions were making their lives more and more miserable.

But the most serious conflict was perhaps the general hostility that existed between the Mongols and the Han settlers.

Relations between the Mongols and the Hans in Inner Mongolia, to be sure, had been deteriorating since the late nineteenth century. The root cause was Han colonization, which had been steadily increasing, and which limited the nomads' pastoral movements and reduced their pasture. The ever-growing Han presence in Inner Mongolia at a time when the Inner Mongols were politically becoming increasingly aware of themselves as a separate ethnic group, therefore, directly or indirectly encouraged separatist inclinations among ordinary rank-and-file Mongols.[6]

Among the privileged princes and lamas, however, fear of Outer Mongolia's influence was growing. The threat of revolution and possible Soviet domination prompted many Inner Mongolian princes and lamas to cling to China and so ironically to encourage Han settlements in their domains. For them, inclusion in the Soviet-protected Outer Mongolia would have meant the loss of princely and monastic privileges.[7]

Some princes and lamas, and many of the commoners and lesser nobility, were nonetheless attracted to separatist ideas and to moderate programmes for social change; they were encouraged by the example of Outer Mongolia which had succeeded, in all but name, in winning independence from China. Others were discouraged by Republican China's assimilation policy in Inner Mongolia, a policy which went contradictory to Dr. Sun Yat-sen's earlier pronouncements of racial equality.

It should be noted that, by the 1920s, especially after Dr. Sun's death in 1925, the official ideology of the Chinese Nationalist Party (Guomindang or GMD) had gradually changed: the long-term solution to the problem of the ethnic minority peoples, such as the Mongols and Tibetans, was that they should be assimilated into the Han culture. If they would abandon their own languages and customs, there would be no discrimination against them.[8]

In carrying out this official GMD minority policy, therefore, a certain amount of money was spent on schools at the edges of Mongol and Tibetan territory to teach Chinese language and the principles of the GMD, but no money was spent to educate them in their own languages. The only exception was a Mongol-Tibetan School *(Meng-Zang Xue-xiao)* in Beijing, but the purpose of this school was to provide the Chinese authorities with minor bureaucrats who could translate Chinese orders and regulations into these minority peoples' languages.[9] Yet, ironically, this school later turned into the cradle of the Inner Mongolian Communist movement for there were a number of Mongolian students in the school who were destined to play significant roles in the later Inner Mongolian revolutionary movement: Ulanhu, Jiyadai, Kuibi and Li Zhiyu among others.[10] Ulanhu, Jiyadai and Kuibi all rose to power in the Communist Inner Mongolian Autonomous Government after 1947. Ulanhu was particularly instrumental in organizing the Chinese Communist movement in Inner Mongolia before 1947.

Chinese Communist sources, particularly Jiyadai's memoir, indicate that Ulanhu and several other Mongol students then in the

Mongol-Tibetan School joined the Chinese Communist Party (CCP) in the winter of 1923-24.[11] By then, it should be noted, the CCP and the GMD had joined hands to form the First United Front against warlordism and imperialism, thus allowing the Communist elements to penetrate into the student circle in Beijing. It was reported that Li Dazhao, co-founder of the CCP, had visited the Mongol-Tibetan School and on many occasions had talked to the Inner Mongolian students there.[12] This was the first link between the CCP and the Inner Mongols.

Meanwhile, in the mid-1920s, two political parties favouring Inner Mongolian autonomy and social reform had taken shape. One was the Young Mongols, whose main leader was Prince Demchugdonggrub, known as Prince De. The Young Mongols advocated modification of princely privileges and desired Inner Mongolian autonomy within the political system of the Republic of China. They were particularly active in the 1930s.[13]

The other party was the Inner Mongolian People's Revolutionary Party (IMPRP, or in Mongolian, *Totugadu Mongol-in Arad-in Hubisgaltu Nam),* headed by a partially sinicized and pro-GMD Mongol named Buyantai, who espoused the China-oriented revolutionism of the GMD.[14] Unlike Prince De and the Young Mongols, the IMPRP wanted to replace the rule of the princes with a more representative democratic structure and advocated political autonomy within a federated Republic of China.

According to Japanese intelligence sources, the first Congress of the IMPRP took place in Kalgan on October 12, 1925.[15] This meeting, attended by 125 delegates, adopted a line calling for opposition to imperialism; full implementation of the GMD constitutional provision for equality; an end to warlordism; internal reform in the Inner Mongolian banner and princely system; and full self-determination of nationalities within China.

There are indications in the manifesto of the Congress that an autonomous government of Inner Mongolia was contemplated, which would have been federated to the Chinese Republic rather than made part of the provincial system. The manifesto, adopted on October 20, stated: "When the Chinese wipe out imperialism and establish a real democratic government by uprooting the cruel military clans, we people in Inner Mongolia shall establish a similar democratic government."[16] Furthermore, "the land controlled by the princes and chieftains shall be handed over to a popularly elected organ," and "the popularly elected organ shall look after the protection of the interests of the country, and all the tyrannical administration now practised in Mongolia shall be abolished."[17] And finally, "colleges, middle schools and primary schools for common people as well as various technical schools shall be established at state expense ... and a People's Sanitation Office and various kinds of charity organs shall be established."[18]

Clearly, the programme was directed at the old princely system and at domination by warlords and provincial authorities. To support the struggle for this programme, Buyantai planned the organization of a volunteer corps in Inner Mongolia. A brigade was to be set up in each of the Special Administrative Areas of Suiyuan, Rehe and Chahar (established in 1914 by the Chinese Nationalist government in Inner Mongolia). It is interesting to note that Communist sources at present credit this organization to Ulanhu.[19] It is possible that Ulanhu was active in the Congress and perhaps also in the organization of the Suiyuan brigade, but he did not appear to have been so prominent as Buyantai during this period.

At this time, the GMD, due to the United Front policy, was allied with the Chinese Communists and the Soviet Union and was on cordial—although not fully defined—terms with Outer Mongolia (or Mongolian People's Republic, MPR), so the pro-GMD Buyantai also desired a close relationship with the MPR. In consequence, the IMPRP sent a number of young Inner Mongols to study in the MPR and at Sun Yixian (Sun Yat-sen) University in Moscow. Among those sent to Moscow was Ulanhu.[20]

Upon his arrival in Moscow in late 1925, Ulanhu enrolled in Sun Yixian University and received training in orthodox Marxism-Leninism. He also made a careful study of the industrial construction then blossoming throughout the Soviet Union. Some sources indicate that Ulanhu joined the CCP in 1927 in Moscow, rather than in 1923-24. At any rate, by 1927 Ulanhu seems to have become dedicated to the Communist cause and to the movement of liberating Inner Mongolia.[21]

In 1929, a number of Mongolian students who had been studying in the Soviet Union graduated and were dispatched to Ulan Bator, capital of MPR, where they were given special training, apparently in espionage and revolutionary activities. Subsequently, a group of the students gathered at the city of Choibolsan (formerly Bointomen), which became the base for planning and carrying out an independence movement for the Holonbier region of Eastern Mongolia. An uprising was fomented and the movement reached a peak in August of 1929 in Holonbier but was suppressed by Zhang Xue-liang, the warlord of Manchuria. Japanese experts feel that Ulanhu was involved in this abortive scheme or "independence movement", and that it is this event that is meant when the Communists refer to Ulanhu's two years of training following graduation from a Soviet university and his involvement in the independence movement in Outer Mongolia.[22] By 1930, however, Ulanhu had returned to Inner Mongolia to engage in underground Communist activities.

The Chinese Nationalist Government's Response to the Inner Mongolian Autonomous Movement

By 1930, also, the Inner Mongolian revolutionary movement led by the IMPRP had come to an abrupt end. When Jiang Jieshi (Chiang Kai-shek) broke with the Chinese Communists in 1927, captured Beijing (renaming it Beiping), and in 1928 established a right-wing GMD government at Nanjing, the pro-GMD Buyantai quickly terminated the IMPRP's relations with the MPR and merged his party with Jiang's GMD. But in 1928, the Nanjing government officially abolished Inner Mongolia, creating in its place four Chinese provinces—Rehe, Chahar, Suiyuan and Ningxia. These provinces formalized the former Special Administrative Areas established in 1914.[23] This facilitated the national policy of colonization in these areas. The Inner Mongols were therefore ethnically submerged in a "sea" of Han settlers.

At the same time, the Nanjing government also established a Commission on Mongolian and Tibetan Affairs *(Meng-Zang Wei Yuan Hui)* with the status of a ministry directly responsible to the Executive Yuan.[24] As one study has pointed out, if this Commission had any real function, it was merely to carry out the official solution of the minority problem, namely, a complete assimilation of the non-Han peoples into the Chinese state.[25] The Inner Mongols felt that Buyantai had betrayed them, so he and the short-lived IMPRP lost all effectiveness. Throughout his life, Buyantai remained loyal to the GMD until his recent death in Taiwan in late 1980.[26]

By 1930, therefore, Prince De's Young Mongols had become the only indigenous mobilizers of Inner Mongolian national sentiment. They in fact became more influential because many ex-members of the IMPRP—such as Merse, Fumingtai, Zhu Shifu and others—had joined them.[27]

With his support widened, Prince De was anxious to strike a bargain with the Nanjing government for self-autonomy. His most important demand on Jiang Jieshi was that Inner Mongolia should no longer be divided into sectors, each attached and subordinated to a Chinese province, which prevented unity of Mongol action. He maintained that Inner Mongolia was a flank position on which China was highly vulnerable in face of the menace of Japan, because the Mongols could not be expected to resist Japan solely in the interests of China. They must have interests of their own to defend. He therefore demanded autonomy for Inner Mongolia, under a government chosen by the Mongols, not appointed by the Chinese.[28]

To allay the anxieties of Prince De and the Inner Mongols, the Nanjing government in 1930 called a Mongolian Affairs Conference.[29] The declared aim of the conference was to "deliberate and formulate measures to facilitate enforcement of various administrative policies for Mongolia during the period of political tutelage," and also to "determine a number of practical reconstruction schemes and other improvements which will prove beneficial to the general Mongol public."[30] The policy of the central government was ostensibly to improve the economic and social position of the Mongols under the direction of the Nanjing government, without altering the political structure or giving the Mongols a separate autonomous regime.

It was proposed that certain internal reforms, such as the abolition of slavery and nationalization of Lamaist temples, be introduced, as well as the improvement of transportation, livestock, health and education. On paper the plan offered promise, and might have had much appeal if it had not been for the delay in implementing it. Critics of the time accused the Nanjing government of giving the Inner Mongols a "blank check."[31] During the period of delay, the example of Outer Mongolia and the increasing Japanese propaganda for an "autonomous" Inner Mongolia built up nationalistic pressures. The Chinese government attempted to counter these forces with propaganda through the establishment of newspapers, a singularly inept method for a highly illiterate group. Meanwhile, feeling for Mongolian autonomy grew steadily.

It should be noted that during this time, the Chinese Communists also promised "autonomy" to the Inner Mongols. The constitution of the Jiangxi Soviet Republic of 1931, for example, called for equality of nationalities, freedom of religion, and, most of all, recognition of:

> ... the right of self-determination of the minorities in China, their right to complete separation from China, and to the formation of an independent state for each minority. All Mongolians, Tibetans, Miao, Yao, Koreans and others living on the territory of China shall enjoy the full right to self-determination, i.e. they may either join the Union of Chinese Soviets or secede from it and form their own state as they may prefer. The Soviet regime of China will do its utmost to assist the minorities in liberating themselves from the yoke of imperialists, the GMD militarists, local chieftains, the princes, lamas, and others, and in achieving complete freedom and autonomy. The Soviet regime must encourage the development of the cultures and of the respective languages of these peoples.[32]

This promise, in retrospect, had had at least psychological appeal to some nationalistic Inner Mongols, which in turn facilitated the Chinese Communist movement then fresh in Inner Mongolia. But at this time, in comparison with the activities of the Young Mongols, the Chinese Communist movement in Inner Mongolia was relatively weak. This situation did not change significantly until after the Japanese full-scale invasion of China.

The Japanese invasion of China was precipitated by the invasion of Manchuria. In 1931 the Japanese invaded the three eastern provinces of Liaoning (formerly Fengtian), Jilin and Heilongjiang, and in 1932 declared them independent of China under the name of Manzhouguo. In 1933 Manzhouguo annexed Rehe province—a region of what had formerly been part of Inner Mongolia—and created an autonomous Mongolian province, named Xingan, out of the Mongolian areas of the former Rehe, Liaoning and Heilongjiang, banning all Han settlement in the new province. This gained an important propaganda advantage for the Japanese against the Nanjing government in Inner Mongolia.

The Japanese were trying to utilize the desire of the Mongols for autonomy and to convince the Mongols that it was the Japanese who would deliver them from "extermination" by the Han Chinese. An effort was even made by the Japanese to establish Mongols in the higher posts in the Japanese-controlled Xingan "autonomous" government.[33] To some Inner Mongols, at least initially, Japan offered an illusion of new and real autonomy.

Before 1933-34, Prince De and his followers still hoped that Inner Mongolia would remain part of the Chinese realm, but enjoy a high degree of self-autonomy. To achieve that goal, the prince in mid-1933 called a conference of princes at the temple of Bailingmiao in Suiyuan to discuss the advance toward autonomy.[34] By this time, Prince De had become the most powerful symbol representing the Inner Mongolian autonomous movement. Though he was a prince, and thus a representative of the traditional aristocracy, he was also symbolic of a new emerging generation which was aggressive and nationalistic.

The Bailingmiao Conference declared itself firmly for a Mongolian Inner Mongolia, and telegraphed the central government in Nanjing demanding full autonomy. The Nationalist government responded by dispatching a delegation headed by Huang Shaoxiong, newly appointed Chief Commissioner for Inner Mongolia.[35] Prince De met with Huang at Bailingmiao in October 1933 in an attempt to find a solution. The conference produced no concrete result, for Huang guaranteed the Inner Mongols no immediate and full autonomy. Prince De reacted by forming a western Inner Mongolian government (the eastern Inner Mongols being those in Manzhouguo). It is clear that the GMD policy towards the Inner Mongols backfired this time, because Prince De, out of desperation, would turn to others like the Japanese who could guarantee him and the Inner Mongols self-autonomy. And the Japanese were an alternative. Despairing of winning anything from the GMD, Prince De formed a larger Inner Mongolian government in 1936 with secret Japanese aid.[36] This created a split within the Mongolian leadership. A China-oriented coalition withdrew from Prince De's nationalist movement, but the prince held his ground and joined Manzhouguo in an unsuccessful attempt to invade Suiyuan.

Suiyuan had by now been exposed to much greater Chinese Communist influence, largely due to Ulanhu's underground work there since his return from the Soviet Union. One Communist account reveals an incident of Ulanhu's underground work in Inner Mongolia.[37] In 1931 Ulanhu met with Wang Ruofei, his former classmate at Sun Yixian University and now a comrade, in Baotou, west of Guisui (now Hohhot). Ulanhu is alleged to have given

Wang a report on the party's "organization in the [Guisui-Baotou] region, its nationalities work, its military work, etc.,"[38] and he also gave Wang a list of aliases used by Communist agents in the area. While working as an undercover CCP agent, Ulanhu also worked with warlord elements in Suiyuan, probably for the sake of collecting intelligence regarding Chinese Nationalist activities.

To be sure, the Chinese Nationalist control over the border provinces was weak in the 1930s. In fact, in northern China, a coalition of warlords Feng Yuxiang and Yan Xishan from Shanxi (next to Suiyuan) was supported by GMD dissident Wang Jingwei and by Li Zongren from Guangxi. This group was feuding with the Jiang government in Nanjing. In these circumstances, Ulanhu was able, in the early 1930s, to find a position as personal secretary to Fu Zuoyi, a lieutenant of Yan Xishan. At about this same time he was also a section chief in the Political Department of Fu's Third Cavalry Regiment.[39] When Fu became chairman of the Suiyuan provincial government, Ulanhu followed him into the administration there. For the next several years he and Fu were associated from time to time both in administering Suiyuan and in fighting the Japanese.

Ulanhu was also reported to be working in 1933 with the anti-Japanese Mongol resistance and, in 1934, teaching in a school in his native Tumet Banner.[40] The next year, he was north-west of Guisui on the outskirts of Bailingmiao where he took part in an uprising of Mongol troops against the Japanese, until the Chinese Communists arrived in North China after the Long March.

The Chinese Communists and the Inner Mongolian Autonomous Movement

The Long March of the Chinese Communists from Jiangxi to Yenan, and the subsequent Xi'an Incident of December 1936, drastically changed the situation in Inner Mongolia as in China proper itself. The terms of the settlement of the Incident committed the Nationalist government to outright opposition to Japanese expansion and to relaxing its pressure on the Chinese Communists who, because of geographical proximity, took advantage of the shift of events to move further into Inner Mongolia and to establish a stronger underground movement there.

Japan, now becoming more belligerent, occupied North China in the summer of 1937. Following their seizure of the province of Suiyuan, the Japanese set up the Mongolian Federated Autonomous Government at Guisui, which, shortly after, was enlarged into the Autonomous Government of Mengjiang with Prince De as chairman.[41] However, it was to all intents and purposes a Japanese-dominated regime.

During the war years, Prince De suffered disappointments under the Japanese occupation akin to those suffered under the GMD. The Japanese kept Prince De's western Inner Mongols separate from the eastern Inner Mongols of Manzhouguo, and in 1940 they even reaffirmed the western Inner Mongols' subordination to China by placing them under Japan's puppet Chinese government at Nanjing.

Toward the mid-1940s, when Japan's military forces began to collapse, Prince De's nationalists tried to forestall the danger of being considered Japanese collaborators by coordinating their efforts in 1945 to expel the Japanese activists before Japan's defeat.[42] At the encouragement of Outer Mongolia (and probably the Soviet Union), the Inner Mongolian nationalists created a provincial government.[43] But later in that year, the Chinese Communist Eighth Route Army entered Inner Mongolia, disbanded the provincial government, and replaced it with the more revolutionary Inner Mongolian Autonomy Movement Association (IMAMA) under Ulanhu.[44]

The situation in Inner Mongolia continued to remain fluid. Nationalistic followers of Prince De, pro-GMD followers of Buyantai, a rival China-oriented faction known as the Suiyuan group, and another coalition representing the interests of nobility vied with one another for power.[45] All these groups were composed of people who wanted, in one form or another, an autonomous Inner Mongolia that would comprise all of China's Mongolian areas, from Ningxia to Heilongjiang. But, as it turned out, none of these groups succeeded in materializing their dreams. It remained for the Chinese Communists and Ulanhu to gradually gain control over the entire area of Inner Mongolia.

To be sure, Ulanhu experienced tremendous difficulty for his Communist movement in Inner Mongolia. The eastern Mongolian nationalist group, for example, had organized a movement of their own within days of Japan's fall, and by 1946 it had established an Eastern Mongolian People's Autonomous Government at Wangyemiao (now Ulanhot), apparently through Soviet and MPR assistance.[46] The president of this government was Boyanmando, former governor of the Japanese-controlled Xingan regime. The secretary-general was Hafengga, who in 1947 became the vice-chairman of the IMAG.[47] It was reported that the Wangyemiao group was dedicated to the notion of a union of Eastern Mongolia, Inner Mongolia and Outer Mongolia into a Great Mongolian Republic.[48] Nevertheless, prior to 1946, Boyanmando's government failed in reaching its avowed goal, largely due to GMD obscurity and Soviet-MPR default. By March 1946, therefore, the Wangyemiao group could find in Ulanhu its only possible ally.

In March 1946, Ulanhu, representing the IMAMA, called a meeting at Chengde, Rehe.[49] The meeting brought together representatives from both western and eastern Inner Mongolia, and Ulanhu succeeded in effecting a merger of the two groups in a new joint committee under Chinese Communist direction. The Chengde meeting reflected this direction by denouncing the Chinese Nationalists and by announcing support for the creation of a new democratic autonomous government in Inner Mongolia.[50] These pronouncements were premature, however, for during the latter part of 1946 the Nationalists made significant military advances in Suiyuan and Rehe, as well as in North China and Manchuria.

When the Chinese Nationalists took Kalgan in October, Ulanhu and the IMAMA moved to Wangyemiao where the strong forces of Lin Biao could give them protection. It was at Wangyemiao and under these circumstances that the Chinese Communists on May 1, 1947, called a session of the Inner Mongolian People's Congress and the Inner Mongolian Autonomous Government was formally proclaimed.[51] Initially, the IMAG controlled only the predominantly Mongol areas of Western Manchuria, plus the northern portions of Rehe and Chahar. In retrospect, however, it was long before the Communists established a government for China proper and it was obviously a bid for Mongol support. Ulanhu was made chairman of the government and was also appointed secretary of the Inner Mongolian sub-bureau of the CCP's Central Committee. Hafengga was appointed vice-chairman, thus reflecting the coalition nature of the government.[52]

Ulanhu was also appointed concurrently to the posts of director of the Commission for Economic and Financial Affairs and commander and political commissar of the Inner Mongolian People's Protection Army.[53] In this latter role, Ulanhu was particularly useful to the Chinese Communists when they went over to the offensive in the late summer and autumn of 1947 in Manchuria. Mongolian troops under Ulanhu campaigned with the Chinese People's Liberation Army, and as operations expanded westward into Mongolian territory, the area controlled by the IMAG was expanded accordingly.

Conclusion

In summing up the protracted and diversified Inner Mongolian autonomous movement from the 1920s to the 1940s, a typology of autonomy can be constructed as follows:

1. The Inner Mongolian People's Revolutionary Party, led by Buyantai, desired the type of autonomous government based on the GMD model federated to, yet separated from, the Republic of China. Naturally, they advocated the abolition of the princely and lamaist feudal-like system and favoured a democratic representative government by the Inner Mongols themselves.
2. The Young Mongols led by Prince De, on the other hand, because of their aristocratic and vested interests, favoured social reforms but not any major change in the political structure. They desired Inner Mongolian autonomy within Republican China's political system, or within any other system that could guarantee them security and protection.
3. The Chinese Nationalist government denied any form of political autonomy to the Inner Mongols. Rather, it held the view that Inner Mongolia, as a provincial part of China like any other province, must not have a separate autonomous government. Ethnic interests and sentiments, in other words, could find no place in the political structure of the Chinese Nationalist government.
4. The Chinese Communist position on the Inner Mongolian question changed from that of the earlier support of separation and independence to that of the new policy of ethnic regional autonomy within the Chinese Communist system, as will be discussed later.

In retrospect, when the Inner Mongolia autonomous movement reached its peak during the Nanjing Decade, the Chinese Nationalist government was obviously disturbed by the development, as it related not only to the problem of national integration but also the problem of frontier security. The Nanjing government, however, appeared to have little understanding or consideration of the burning question of autonomy which the Inner Mongols deemed so important. Although Buyantai and Prince De both had interests in common with the GMD, the lack of sensitivity (and certainly sincerity, in the eyes of the Inner Mongols) on the part of the Nanjing government contributed to the failure of the negotiations in the early 1930s. The subsequent Japanese penetration into Inner Mongolia after Manchuria only further complicated the problem.

On the other hand, many of the demands made by the Inner Mongols of the Nanjing government were either too vague or unrealistic. The Chinese Nationalist and Mongol leaders never really saw eye-to-eye on the question of "autonomy". The Nanjing leaders never wished to grant Inner Mongolia a high degree of autonomy, since it would amount to separation of that region from the Chinese system, thereby exposing the vulnerability of the Chinese security along the sensitive and strategically important frontier.

Interestingly enough, the Chinese Communists later shared this view with the Nationalists. This is evidenced by the fact that the Chinese Communist leaders changed their position on the Inner Mongolia issue over a short period of time during the 1930s. As has been noted previously, the Jiangxi Constitution of 1931 promised the Mongols and other minorities the rights of self-determination and secession. However, the experience of the Inner Mongols in their struggle for autonomy at any cost (even colluding with foreign powers) worried the Chinese Communists and finally led to their change of position. This change became known in 1938 when Mao Zedong made a speech at the Sixth Plenary Session of the Sixth Central Committee on November 6. In this speech, Mao stated that all nationalities, including the Mongols, "shall have the right to handle their own affairs and at the same time to unite with the Hans in building a unified country."[54] The previously guaranteed rights of self-determination and secession were dropped, and the new idea of ethnic regional autonomy emerged, which promised only the appointment of minorities in their local self-government as well as the respect of ethnic culture and languages.[55] When the Chinese Communists overpowered Inner Mongolia in 1947, the protracted autonomous movement to all intents and purposes came to an abrupt end. Since then, Inner Mongolia has been a part of the Chinese Communist system.

Notes

1. The other four autonomous regions are: Xinjiang Uygur Autonomous Region, Ningxia Hui Autonomous Region, Tibet Autonomous Region, and Guangxi Zhuang Autonomous Region.
2. The IMAG was established on May 1, 1947. See *Meng-Zang yuebao (The Mongolian-Tibetan Monthly),* 19.5:13 (May 1947).
3. For more recent discussion on this subject, see Karen E. Rawling, "The political socialization of Inner Mongol elites," unpublished PhD dissertation (University of North Carolina, Chapel Hill, 1972); Owen Lattimore, "Inner Mongolian nationalism and the Pan-Mongolian idea: recollections and reflections," *Journal of the AngloMongolian Society,* 6.1:5-21 (April 1980); Lao Minghui, *Menggu "zizhi yundong" shimo* (A Detailed Account of the Mongolian "Autonomous Movement") (Beijing: Zhonghua, 1980).
4. For more details, see S. Sandag, *The Mongolian People's Struggle for National Independence and the Building of a New Life* (Ulan Bator: State Publishing House, 1966).
5. Chen Han-seng, "A critical survey of Chinese policy in Inner Mongolia," *Pacific Affairs,* IX.4:557-9 (December 1936).
6. Fang Fanjiu, *Menggu gaikuang yu Nei-Meng zizhi yundong* (Situation in Mongolia and the Inner Mongolian Autonomous Movement) (Shang-

hai: Shangwu, 1934), pp. 57-60; Owen Lattimore, "Chinese colonization in Inner Mongolia: its history and present development," in W.L.G. Joerg (ed.), *Pioneer Settlement: Cooperative Studies by 26 Authors* (New York: American Geographical Society, 1932), pp. 288-312.

7. Fang, *Mengu*, pp. 60-1.
8. For a study of the GMD policy towards the minorities, see June T. Dreyer, *China's Forty Million: Minority Nationalities and National Integration in the People's Republic of China* (Cambridge, Mass.: Harvard University Press, 1976), pp. 15-41.
9. Owen Lattimore, *Nationalism and Revolution in Mongolia* (New York: Oxford University Press, 1955), p. 27.
10. Ji-yia-tai, "Li Dazhao tongzhi he Nei Menggu cuqi de geming hudong" (Comrade Li Dazhao and the early Inner Mongolian revolutionary activities), *Minzu tuanjie* (National Solidarity) 7:11 (1961).
11. *Ibid.*
12. *Ibid.*, pp. 11-2.
13. *Nei-Meng jiufen jingguo (jimi)* (Confidential Report on the Course of the Inner Mongolian Conflict) (n.p.: n.d.), passim, esp. pp. 2-10; Huang Fensheng, *Nei-Meng mengqizizhi yundong jishi* (A True Record of the Autonomous Movement in Inner Mongolia) (Shanghai: Zhonghua, 1935), pp. 67-73.
14. For studies on Buyantai, see Huang Fensheng, *Bianjiang renwu zhi* (Biographies of Frontier Leaders) (Shanghai: Zhengzhong, 1946), pp. 57-8; Howard Boorman (ed.), *Biographic Dictionary of Republican China* (New York: Columbia University Press, 1970), vol. I, pp. 6-9.
15. The most detailed study on the IMPRP is "Uchimoko ni okeru sekishoku undo no hensen" (Changes in the Communist Movement in Inner Mongolia), *Koain chosa geppo* (Monthly Investigation Reports of the Koain), 3.10:1-65 (October 1942).
16. *Ibid.*, pp. 11-2.
17. *Ibid.*
18. *Ibid.*
19. *A Regional Handbook on the Inner Mongolian Autonomous Region* (New Haven: Human Relations Area Files, 1956), p. 52.
20. Mary E. Alonso (ed.), *China's Inner Asian Frontier* (Cambridge, Mass.: Harvard University Press, 1979), p. 45.
21. Boorman, *Biographic Dictionary*, vol. III, p. 350.

22. Paul Hyer, "Ulanfu and Inner Mongolian autonomy under the Chinese People's Republic," *The Mongolia Society Bulletin,* VIII: 30-1 (1969).

23. Huang, *Nei-Meng*, pp. 61-2.

24. *Nei Menggu zizhi yundong ji qi cankao wenjian* (The Inner Mongolian Autonomous Movement and its Reference Materials) (Taipei: Meng-Zang Wei Yuan Hui, 1953), pp. 7-8.

25. Frank J. Pezzano, "Sino-Mongolian relations in the 20th century," unpublished M.A. thesis (Asian Studies, Seton Hall University, 1974), p. 77.

26. Chen Jiying, "Dao yidai juren de jushi—Mengzu guo zhi dalao Baiyunti zhi yisheng" (In memory of a Mongol hero: the life of Buyantai), *Zhongwai zazhi* (Sino-Foreign Magazine), 28.4:8-9 (October 1980).

27. Koain, "Uchimoko", pp. 53-4.

28. Lattimore, *Nationalism and Revolution,* p. 28.

29. *Menggu huiyihuibian* (Collected Documents of the Mongolian Conference) (Nanjing: Meng-Zang Wei Yuan Hui, 1930); and *Menggu Huiyi jueyian* (Resolutions in the Mongolian Conference) (Nanjing: Meng-Zang Wei Yuan Hui, 1930).

30. Huang, *Nei-Meng,* p. 64.

31. Chen, "A critical survey."

32. Conrad Brandt, Benjamin Schwartz and John K. Fairbank, *A Documentary History of Chinese Communism* (Cambridge, Mass.: Harvard University Press, 1952), pp. 220-4.

33. Alonso, *China's Inner Asian Frontier,* p. 46.

34. For details, see Huang, *Nei-Meng,* pp. 67-95; Fang, *Menggu,* pp. 63-77.

35. Huang, *Nei-Meng,* pp. 108-77.

36. Alonso, *China's Inner Asian Frontier,* p. 46.

37. Yang Zhilin and Qiao Mingfu, *Wang Ruofei zai yuzhong* (Wang Ruofei in Prison) (Hong Kong: Sanlian, 1965).

38. *Ibid.*

39. Donald W. Klein and Anne B. Clark (eds.), *Biographic Dictionary of Chinese Communism, 1921-1965* (Cambridge, Mass.: Harvard University Press, 1971), p. 882.

40. *Ibid.*

41. *A Regional Handbook,* p. 398.

42. Alonso, *China's Inner Asian Frontier,* p. 46.

43. Also known as the Inner Mongolian Republican Temporary Government. See *Documents on Inner Mongolia: Selected U.S. Intelligence Reports (Declassified) on Leaders and Factions in Inner Mongolia, 1946-1949* (Washington D.C.: Center for Chinese Research Materials, Association of Research Libraries, 1972), p. 13.

44. For more details, see Ulanhu's own account: "Nei Meng zizhi yundong zhong de liangtiao daolu," (The Two Roads in Inner Mongolia's Autonomous Movement) in *Xinsheng de Nei-Meng* (The Newly-born Inner Mongolia) (n.p.: Liaonan, 1948), pp. 1-4.

45. *Documents on Inner Mongolia,* pp. 16-7.

46. For an eyewitness account, see Frank B. Bessac, "Revolution and government in Inner Mongolia, 1945-50," *Michigan Academy of Science, Arts and Letters Papers,* 50:421-2 (1964).

47. *Documents on Inner Mongolia,* pp. 29-30.

48. Bessac, "Revolution," pp. 421-2.

49. Klein and Clark, *Biographic Dictionary,* p. 882

50. *Ibid.*

51. *Documents on Inner Mongolia,* pp. 49-50.

52. *Ibid.*, pp. 29-30.

53. *Ibid.*, p. 9.

54. Extracted in Xie Hechou, "Weida di minzu quyu zizhi zhengce" (The great policy of ethnic regiona autonomy), *Minzu tuanjie* (National Solidarity), 1:3 (January 1960).

55. See Edwin Pak-wah Leung (ed.), *Ethnic Compartmentalization and Regional Autonomy in the People Republic of China,* special volume of *Chinese Law and Government,* XIV.4 (Winter 1981-82).

15

China's Minority Nationalities under Communism

Ethnic minorities in China constitute only 6.7 percent of that nation's one-billion population. However, the approximately 67 million members of that minority population are divided into no fewer than 55 ethnic groups, scattered over the vast frontier land.

Two-thirds belong to fifteen nationalities with over one million members each, such as the Zhuang (12.09 million), Uygurs (5.48), Miao (3.92), Tibetans (3.45) and Mongols (2.66). The others range from the tiny group of 800 Hezhe in the far northeast to groups like the Yao, Dong and Li, each with several hundred thousand members dispersed in small communities throughout the southwestern provinces.

The minorities are highly diversified in their languages, customs and cultural sophistication. Over the long history of China, they had been regarded by the Han majority as the "barbarians" unable to live up to Han cultural expectations. A Han policy of assimilation further reinforced and aggravated the problems of ethnic tension, suspicion and even mutual hatred between the Han and the non-Han peoples over the centuries.

The establishment of the People's Republic in 1949 resulted in a new policy for dealing with the minorities. Since then, the minority nationalities have been compartmentalized along the lines of ethnicity. Within the ethnic "compartments" (which are regarded by the minority residents as their "homes" or, technically, as "autonomous areas") the non-Han peoples are said to enjoy their own ethnic "regional autonomy" *(quyu zizhi)* as prescribed by the state constitution and other laws and regulations.

In theory, the minority nationalities are the masters of their own "compartments." Their regional affairs are administered by elected representatives of their ethnic background; minority languages are used officially in the autonomous governments.

However, the central authorities have repeatedly emphasized that the ethnic "compartments" or autonomous governments are but parts of the People's Republic along the frontier; they may enjoy self-government in their respective areas, but never independence. And in fact, despite the promised regional autonomy, the central government still maintains considerable control over the autonomous areas inhabited by the minority nationalities.

Thus, the ethnic compartmentalization policy has not yet fully resolved the minorities problems of China—a fact perhaps attested to by the recent increased recognition of minority groups as playing roles in both the Chinese Communist Party and in the central government.

16

Ethnic Compartmentalization and Regional Autonomy in the People's Republic of China

Ethnic compartmentalization is a unique phenomenon in the People's Republic of China (PRC). The 55 ethnic minority groups, while constituting only 6 percent of China's population of 980 million, nonetheless occupy over half the land of China.[1] Since the early years of the PRC, the minority nationalities (*shaoshu minzu*) have been compartmentalized along the lines of ethnicity. Within the ethnic "compartments," which are regarded by the minority residents as their "homes,"[2] the non-Han peoples are said to have enjoyed their own "regional autonomy" (*quyu zizhi*) as prescribed by the constitution and other rules and regulations (some of which are included in this volume). In theory, as shown in the following pages, the minority nationalities are the masters of their own "compartments," since they are in charge of their own regional affairs. At the same time, however, the ethnic "compartments" are but parts of the PRC along the frontier; the minority nationalities can at best enjoy self-government in their respective areas, but never independence.

The official Chinese definition of the policy of "ethnic regional autonomy" is that in China, "any area where a minority nationality lives in a compact community or where a number of minority nationalities live together can exercise regional autonomy and set up organs of self-government as long as it constitutes an administrative unit—autonomous region, autonomous prefecture and autonomous county (or banner). All the national autonomous areas are inalienable parts of the People's Republic of China. The organs of self-government of national autonomous areas are people's congress and revolutionary committees (replaced by local governments by 1980) and they are all Chinese local state organs."[3] As a result of this ethnic compartmentalization policy, China today has established five autonomous regions, twenty-nine autonomous prefectures, and seventy-five autonomous counties (or banners).[4]

The nature of China's minority policy has been a subject of much controversy in the academic world. Some scholars, George Moseley for one, believe that the implementation of the ethnic regional autonomy policy in China "made it possible for the Han Chinese revolution to proceed while the non-Han revolution lagged behind."[5] As Moseley concludes: "'Regional autonomy' is the opposite of what its name implies: 'regional detention' would be more descriptive."[6] Other scholars, however, do not seem to agree with this interpretation. Harold C. Hinton, for example, contends that the PRC's minority policy is "one of assimilation,"[7] a view which is shared by a number of scholars outside China.[8]

The purpose of this volume is not to evaluate the PRC's ethnic regional autonomy policy, however. Rather, as a documentary study, it is to document the formation of the official policy (Part I), its implementation (Part II), the problems and issues arisen from its implementation (Part III), as well as the most recent developments (Part IV). It is hoped that by examining the major original policy documents through translation, the readers can acquire a more direct understanding of the Chinese administrative experience in the ethnic areas and with the minority nationalities.

Notes

1. "China's Minority Peoples," *Beijing Review* (February 9, 1979), 17.
2. Zhang Zhiyi, *Zhongguo geming de minzu wenti he minzu zhengce jianghua (tigang)* [A Discussion of the National Question in the Chinese Revolution and of Nationalities Policy (Draft)] (Beijing, 1956), pp. 33-41.
3. "China's Minority Peoples," p. 18.
4. Information obtained by the guest editor during his visit to China in the summer of 1981.
5. George Moseley, ed. and trans., *The Party and the National Question in China* (Cambridge, Mass., 1966), p. 16.
6. *Ibid.*, p. 17.
7. Harold C. Hinton, *An Introduction to Chinese Politics,* 2nd edition (New York, 1979), p. 272.
8. See, for example, Amrit Lal, "Sinification of Ethnic Minorities in China," *Current Scene* VIII. 4 (February 15, 1970), 1-23; Hung-mao Tien, "Sinicization of National Minorities in China," *Current Scene* XIL. 11 (November 1974), 1-14.

17

Educating China's Minority Nationalities: Integration through Ethnicization

I. Introduction

Although the Han Chinese constitute 93.3 percent of China's one-billion population, there are at least 55 non-Han ethnic groups scattered over the vast frontier land.[1] Among the minority nationalities (*shaoshu minzu*), there is enormous diversity in terms of language, size, customs, and cultural sophistication.

Of the approximately 67-million minority population, two thirds belong to the 13 nationalities with over one million members such as the Zhuang (12.09 million), Uygurs (5.48), Miao (3.92), Tibetans (3.45), and Mongols (2.66). The others range from the tiny group of 800 Hezhe in the far northeast, to those like the Yao, Dong, and Li each with several hundred thousand members living in groups dispersed throughout the southwestern provinces.[2]

The minorities are highly diversified in their languages. According to one study,[3] 74 percent of them speak Sino-Tibetan languages (divided into Sino-Thai, Tibeto-Burmese and Miao-Yao language branches), and 21 percent belong to the Altaic family of languages (Turkic, Mongolian, and Tunguzic). A remaining 4 percent speak Korean, while some 1 percent belong to the Indo-European and Austroasiatic language families. Among these minority groups, 21 had their own written languages before 1949.[4]

Over the long history of China, the minorities had been regarded by the Han majority as "barbarians" for not being able to live up to the Han cultural expectations. Their languages and cultures were not respected. The Han policy of assimilation further reinforced and aggravated the problems of ethnic tension, mutual hatred and suspicion between the Han and the non-Han peoples.[5]

When the Chinese Communists took control over the Mainland in 1949, they also inherited these historical problems. The new government's policy towards the minority nationalities is of great interest in the academic circle, as it has been a subject of much controversy for a number of years.[6] The controversy lies in whether or not the minority policy of the People's Republic of China (PRC) is of assimilative nature. Unfortunately, most studies on the subject have emphasized on the political aspect of the minority policy in the PRC, and very few research has been done on the language and educational aspects.

Language has been called "the most important factor in modern nationalism,"[7] and "a strong bastion against assimilation."[8] Have the minority nationalities in China been given freedom by the Communist authorities to learn their own ethnic languages through the schools? How has this affected local nationalism *vis-a-vis* national integration? Has the minority policy of the PRC been of assimilative nature, as has been suggested by some scholars? Obviously, the answer cannot be sought without examining the language and educational aspects of the Chinese Communist minority policy.

This paper concerns only with the language and educational aspects of the minority policy in the PRC, as well as their developments since 1949. In studying the subject, it is necessary to understand the Chinese Communist concept of "ethnicization" (*minzu-hua*). In fact, the idea of "ethnicization" has been said to have become the guiding principle in minority language and educational developments since 1949.[9]

II. Ethnicization: The Theory

The term "ethnicization" was originally used to refer to the political arrangements in the PRC for the minority nationalities in terms of administration, using the minorities' languages and personnel for "regional autonomy" in ethnic areas.[10] According to Chinese Premier Zhou Enlai: "In places where minority nationalities exercise autonomy, the language of the majority nationality should be used as the first language. Since it is autonomy by the minority nationalities, we have to train minority nationalities, we must respect their customs and habits. All these mean ethnicization."[11]

Actually, prior to 1949, the Chinese Communists had already made themselves clear about their concept of "ethnicization": to encourage the development of all aspects of ethnic minorities' language and culture. Mao Zedong in 1938, for instance, spoke openly that: "The culture, religion and customs of the minority nationalities shall be respected. They must be helped to *develop their culture and education in their own languages.*"[12]

Similar ideas were expressed at the Chinese People's Political Consultative Conference in 1949. Article 53 of the Common Program of the conference reads: "All minority nationalities shall have freedom to develop their dialects and languages, to preserve or reform their traditions, customs, and religious beliefs. The People's government shall assist the masses of the people of all minority nationalities to develop their political, economic, cultural, and educational construction work."[13]

The State Constitution of the PRC, promulgated in 1954, has several articles dealing with the rights of the minority nationalities. Article 3, for example, says: "All the nationalities have freedom to use and foster the growth of their spoken and written languages, and to preserve or reform their own customs or ways."[14] Article 71 furthermore stipulates that: "In performing their duties, organs of self-government of all autonomous regions, autonomous prefectures and autonomous counties employ the spoken and written languages commonly used by the nationality or nationalities in a given area."[15] Similar provisions can also be found in the later versions of the Constitution.[16]

In theory, therefore, the spoken and written languages of the minority nationalities are to be respected. All minority nationalities have the right to use and develop their languages. No discrimination against minority nationalities and their languages is allowed. Furthermore, as promised by Mao himself, the minority nationalities can even develop their culture and education in their own languages.

The "ethnicization" theory appears to be a Utopia to the minority nationalities in China—something unprecedented in Chinese history. Yet the theory at the same time appears also in total contradiction with the Chinese Communist goal to create a new Socialist culture for *all* Chinese people. How could the Chinese Communists in practice be able to reconcile this seeming contradiction?

III. Ethnicization: The Practice

It appears that the Chinese Communists would have to face two inevitable and yet important problems if they were to put the ethnicization policy into practice: (1.) Should the minority nationalities be included in the new universal Socialist culture at the expense of the ethnic cultures? (2.) How could national integration be achieved through the linguistic and cultural autonomy of the minority nationalities? With this in mind, let us examine the ethnicization policy in practice.

In September 1951, the First All-China Minorities Education Conference advocated that all minorities having their own written languages be taught in those languages at the primary and secondary school levels. Those who did not have a written language, or whose written languages were "imperfect", should be helped to develop and reform their written languages; and could be taught with Han language or minority-language textbooks where the latter existed. The conference also however voted unanimously to establish Han language classes in various grades of minorities schools "in accordance with the needs of the minorities concerned."[17] The decisions of the conference had far-reaching consequences on the subsequent development of minority language policy and education.

A. Minority Language Policy

Partly in order to effect the Communist promises to the minority nationalities, and partly because the new government wished to create a better basis for understanding the minority peoples in order to consolidate its rule over them, there was a good deal of interest in minority languages.[18] In the 1950's, the government even went so far as to try to provide each minority language with a script of its own. The rationale for this is fairly obvious: the Chinese Communists sought to make the minority nationalities literate by creating scripts for their own languages.[19]

The creation of scripts for minority languages was a difficult task. Some minority groups were scattered throughout several provinces or autonomous regions and spoke a variety of dialects. In 1950 a script using the Latin alphabet was devised for the Yi to replace their former "imperfect" writing system. With this new script it was claimed that an adult, by studying six hours a day, could learn to read in three months. By late 1952 the first newspaper in Yi language appeared.[20] A Zhuang script was in use in 1955 and in July 1957, the first Zhuang language newspaper began publication. Eight additional ethnic minorities in the southwest had new scripts reformed.[21]

In 1958 a conference on ethnic minority languages adopted certain criteria for deciding whether or not to create new scripts for minorities. The conference decided that a single script would be created for those minorities speaking the same language living in compact areas and for different minorities who spoke similar languages. If there were several widely different minority languages used in a single area three alternatives were possible: (1.) the adoption of the written language of another nationality; (2.) the establishment of a language alliance "between different languages; (3.) the creation of additional written languages. If a nationality had been using Mandarin-Chinese or some other language, either partially or fully, there was to be no further work on creation a script for their spoken language.[22]

Unfortunately, the early enthusiasm in minority languages was short-lived, for investigatory work into minority languages was cut back or halted entirely in the late 1950's.[23] After 1958, in conjunction with the political movements of the Great Leap Forward and the rectification campaign, emphasis was placed on the learning of Mandarin-Chinese rather than on the preservation of minority languages. At the fifth session of the 1958 National People's Congress (NPC), for example, the delegates were told that one use of the Chinese language phoneticization scheme was to enable minority languages to absorb the vocabulary of the Mandarin-Chinese language more readily.[24] Two members of the NPC pointed out that phoneticization would enable the minority nationalities to learn Mandarin-Chinese with less difficulty. A later directive warned that they must "grasp the tendency for spoken and written languages to draw closer to the Chinese languages. Any plea for the preservation or purity of the existing minority languages must be resolutely attacked."[25] Clearly, this was in violation of the right promised to the minorities by the Chinese Communist leaders and by the Constitution.

The 1960's and early 1970's witnessed the discontinuation of the minority language policy and the strong emphasis on Mandarin-Chinese learning. Minority languages were attacked because they were associated with the idea of "promoting national splitism."[26] Many minority leaders were accused of "seeking to exploit the nationalities to establish an independent kingdom,"[27] thereby putting national integration in great jeopardy. Minority languages became the symbol of regional or local nationalism and were suppressed.

The inconsistency of the minority language policy, as can be imagined, had devastating impact on minority educational development. The languages were switched back and forth in the minorities schools in terms of instruction and curriculum materials, resulting in confusion and chaos. Although the minority language policy has been revived today, it is obvious that it will take a long time before the wounds be recovered and confidence restored.

B. Curriculum Materials and Translation

In accordance with the ethnicization policy, the minority students are supposed not only to be taught in their own languages but also to be using minority language or bilingual materials. One convenient and less expensive method to provide minority-language or bilingual curriculum materials has been to translate them from the Han. However, the problem of translation has been very serious.

One problem involved the translator's use of words which gave minority readers misleading impressions likely to lead to future problems—for example, translating "central people's government" as "the imperial house" and "capital" as "the palace in Peking,"[28] or using the same term for both the "liberation" of Shanghai city by the Chinese Communists in 1949 and for the independence of Ghana from a decade later.[29]

A second problem concerned resistance to borrowing Han vocabulary, on grounds that it was structurally inappropriate to the minority language concerned. Where the minority language did not have a term for a new concept, translators were found to go to unacceptable lengths to coin a new word from existing elements of their language or, worst yet, would adopt a word from a foreign language.[30]

In the late 1950's, minority language specialists were criticized for their slogan "one dig, two create, three borrow." This slogan meant that in translating works from Han-Chinese into a minority language, translators would "dig out" old words from their own classical language, "create" new words, or "borrow" words from a foreign language rather than use loan words from Chinese.[31] For example, Miao would translate "cooperatives" as "bound together by a rope," and "China" as "the state's interior."[32]

In addition to the refusal of some minorities to borrow Chinese terms, there were other problems in minority publications work. The Tibetans were criticized for describing the Potala Palace in the first lesson of primary school textbooks and Beijing in the last lessons, a clear expression, in the eyes of the Chinese Communists, of local nationalism.[33] Minority publications also had difficulty keeping up with the shifting political scene. The nationalities presses were still publishing books on mutual-aid teams when cooperative were organized in minority areas, and books on cooperatives when communes were being formed! Too few books were published on class struggle and the importance of agricultural and industrial production, and too many were published on traditional literary themes, and on the virtues of religion. Quantitatively speaking, existing minority-language teaching materials for primary and secondary schools are far from adequate. While there are seven minority-language publishing agencies in the minority areas responsible for putting out the curriculum materials, only the one in Inner Mongolia is reportedly doing a fairly satisfactory job in terms of meeting the needs.[34]

To be sure, there are a lot of books published in the minority languages. For example, between 1953 and 1963, the Nationalities Publishing House alone published over 2,900 books in 24,700,000 volumes.[35] But most of the works published were politically-oriented materials such as Mao's *Selected Works*, translations of Marxist-Leninist classics, policy statements, writings of leaders of the Chinese Communist Party, as well as some scientific and technical books.

Obviously, the spread of publications in minority languages has been geared toward promoting the growth of a Socialist culture in the minority areas, than toward meeting the educational needs of the minority students. This situation has not been changed even after the death of Mao in 1976.

C. Minority Teacher Education

In line with the ethnicization policy, minority teachers are supposed to be employed in the minorities schools so that they cannot only instruct in the minority language, but can also promote ethnic interests and are able to communicate these concerns to the students with whom they will come in contact. In this respect most minorities were clearly in a difficult position in the 1950's, with very few primary- and secondary-level minority teachers.

As a result, teacher-recruitment and education efforts during the 1950's concentrated on training minority teacher educators. Han specialists were sent from the interior to minority teacher educators. Han specialists were sent from the interior to minority areas to establish teacher-education courses both of a formal nature (e.g. at Xinjiang University and Xinjiang Teachers College) and a non-formal nature (e.g. on site, short-term, intensive classes).[36]

By 1960 considerable advances had been made, but the government still found it necessary to re-state its initial position regarding the training of minority teachers—"Only by active fostering and training of teachers of minority nationalities can there be a strong foundation for a continue Leap Forward in the education of minority nationalities,"[37] indicating that there had not been satisfactory achievement in this area.

A major difficulty lay in the fact that teacher education instructional materials were primarily in the Chinese language. While translation efforts were under way, the currently vacillating language policy made this effort even more difficult and sluggish. The convenient solution to this problem, at least from the Chinese point of view, was to require all minority teacher-education students first to learn Chinese; and indeed this stipulation coincided with language policy during the 1960's.[38] The emphasis on Chinese as the medium of teacher-education instruction obviously influenced other aspects of teacher education and caused the feeling, among at least some minorities, that even though some minority teachers were entering the schools they had lost touch with their own language and possibly with their ethnic identity as well. This concern was reinforced by the nature of the teacher-education curriculum which emphasized Chinese language, literature, history and geography at the middle school level.[39]

It appears that the recent more pluralistic policy of training minority teachers in their own area has had the effect of providing more minority teachers and teacher educators trained in their own language (with Han study as well) and increasingly in control of local educational enterprises. In one significant minority region (Xinjiang), minority teachers at all levels are up 70 percent over 1965, and in some regions 90 percent of the teacher force are minorities.[40] It appears, then, that the locus and content of teacher education in many minority areas reflects the needs and aspirations of minorities more than at any time in the past.

D. Higher Education for the Minorities

Before the founding of the PRC, the Chinese Communist Party had already established special institutes for training minority cadres and providing higher education for the minority nationalities. After 1949, the Communists continued this practice. The November 1950 "Provisional Plan for Fostering Minority Nationality Cadres" provided that a Central Nationalities Institute be established in Beijing, with branches in the Northwest, Southwest, and Central-South, and that additional branches could be established as necessary. Since then, ten such institutes have been established across the country. According to Lu Bi, "these institutes are neither political cadre schools, nor universities in general for the minority nationalities. They are institutions of higher learning for these people, that have the advantages of both."[41]

The Central Nationalities Institute, established in Beijing on June 11, 1951, was designed primarily to provide ethnic minority languages. Under the presidency of a Mongol named Ulanhu, the Institute originally enrolled 262 students from 25 nationalities. A department of minority languages, added in February, 1952, enrolled 65 Chinese students transferred from other universities. Tibetan, Uygar, Miao,Yi, Naxi, Long, and Yao languages were taught.[42]

Within two years, 200 students had graduated from this institute, and eight additional minority languages were offered. By 1957, the institute offered a liberalized, full four-year course in two departments, language and literature and history. In the following year, however, as part of the rectification campaign being waged in ethnic minority areas against local nationalism, the students were once again exposed more to political training, In 1961, after ten years of operation, the Institute enrolled 2,784 students in six departments, had graduated a total of 3,931 students from 46 nationalities, and offered 26 minority languages.

The establishment of special nationalities institutes was a more effective means of minority education in several ways. Political training could be directly slanted to the needs of the minorities, research could be conducted into ethnic minority customs and languages, and the minority students need not travel great distances to attend one of the ten institutes scattered throughout China. The principal drawback, from the viewpoint of the minority student, was that one obtained a great deal of political training and very little higher education.

Because of the limited nature of education available at the special institutes for nationalities, enrollment in one of China's ordinary universities offered a minority student the best opportunity for sound academic training.

In 1963, fifty thousand national minority students graduated from minority institutes where as only 7,000 graduated from ordinary colleges and universities. This situation however has been reversed. According to the 1980 statistics released by the Chinese Ministry of Education, of the 40,000 ministry college enrollment during that year, only 10,000 were students of the ten nationalities institutes. In other words, the majority of minority college students study in the regular institutions of higher learning rather than in the special nationalities institutes.[43]

To encourage the pursuit of education by minority nationalities, the Chinese government granted them special considerations in the entrance examinations leading to higher education. In certain cases minority students did not need to take the exam in classical Chinese or in a foreign language; they were given special financial aid; they were allowed to enroll in preparatory classes if they had inadequate preparation for higher education; and translators were assigned to aid them to overcome their language difficulties. Some of these measures were incorporated into the "Regulations of Recruitment of Minority College Students" promulgated by the Chinese government in 1980.[44]

IV. Conclusion

In reviewing the ethnicization policy in China in terms of language policy and educational development over the past three decades or so, one striking feature emerges from our analyses: that is, the Chinese Communists are using ethnicity only as a vehicle to advance the assimilation of minority nationalities and the promotion of a new Socialist culture. Ethnicization, therefore, has become the means, and not the end.

In this light, therefore, the swings from toleration to repression of minority languages do not represent a significant divergence in the views of the Communist leaders on what the content of the message should be, but only on the medium through which it is expressed. The Uygur author of *At the Foot of Kyzyl Mountain* may have used Uygur proverbs and the Uygur language, but what was produced was a standard work on the struggle to build a model commune. Similarly, Korean folk tunes and Korean language were used to present a Han-socialist opera.

The present policy of encouraging the use of minority languages may, if it continues for any length of time, have the unintended result of reinforcing interest in nationalities' cultures and their uniqueness rather than the desired result of consolidating and integrating all ethnic groups into a unified and mutually tolerant supra-ethnic state. However, the former alternative is clearly not the intent of the leaders now backing policies of toleration toward minority languages.

On balance, however, the ethnicization policy has made a remarkable achievement at least on one aspect: the spread of literacy among the minorities through education. Since the 1950's, the Chinese Communists have established an impressive number of primary and middle schools in the minority areas. The number of elementary school students of elementary school students of minority background increased from that of 943,300 in 1951, to that of 7,685,000 in 1978.[45] The number of middle school students increased even more dramatically, from 45,600 (1951) to 2,526,000 (1978).[46] And the Chinese Communist government has claimed that, as of 1978, 85 percent of the school-age students in the minority areas actually attending schools.[47] This represents a significant progress in combating against mass illiteracy among the minority nationalities. Nevertheless, it is also cleat that the rapid increase in the rate of literacy among the minorities serves the function of hastening the spread of Socialist ideology and quickening the pace of national integration.

Notes

1. For more details, see: Edwin Pak-wah Leung (ed.) *Ethnic Conpartmentalization in the People's Republic of China*, special volume of *Chinese Law and Government* XIV.4 (Winter 1981-82), Introduction.
2. *Beijing Review* 9 (March 3, 1980), p. 17.
3. Josef Kolmas, "The Minority Nationalities," in Ruth Adams (ed.) *Contemporary China* (N.Y.: 1966), p. 53.
4. *Zhongguo shaoshu minzu* (China's Minority Nationalities) (Beijing: 1981), p. 3.
5. See Leung, *op. cit.*, Introduction; also June T. Dreyer, *China's Forty Millions: Minority Nationalities and National Integration in the People's Republic of China* (Cambridge, Maas.: 1976), pp. 7-14.
6. George Mosley (ed. and trans.) *The Party and the National Question in China* (Cambridge, Mass: 1966); Amrit Lai, "Signification of Ethnic Minorities in China," *Current Scene* (Feb. 15, 1970), pp. 1-23; Hung-mao Tien, "Signification of National Minorities in China," *Current Scene* XII. 11 (Nov. 1973), pp. 1-14.
7. Quoted in David M. Deal, "National Minority Policy in Southwest China, 1911-1965," (unpublished Ph.D. dissertation, University of Washington, 1971), p. 198.

8. *Ibid.*
9. "Flourishing Development of the Minority Education," *Renmin jiaoyu* (People's Education) 208 (1981), p. 6.
10. Leung, *op. cit.*, Introduction.
11. Zhou Enlai, "Some Questions on Policy towards Nationalities," a speech delivered at a forum held in Qingdao, Shandong, on August 4, 1957, in *Beijing Review* 10 (March 10, 1980), pp. 21-23.
12. Mao Zedong's speech delivered at the Sixth Plenary Session of the Sixth Chinese Communist Party Central Committee, Nov. 6, 1928: extracted in Xie Hechou, "The Great Policy of National Regional Autonomy," *Minzu tuanjie* (National Solidarity) 1 (Jan. 1960), p. 3.
13. Leung, *op. cit.*, p. 12.
14. Adopted on Sept. 20, 1954, by the first National People's Congress of the PRC at its First Session; in *Documents of the First Session of the First People's Congress* (Beijing: 1955).
15. Leung, *op. cit.*, p. 51.
16. *Ibid.*, pp. 70-71, 76-78.
17. U.S. Consulate General, Hong Kong, *Current Background*, no. 152, pp. 11-15.
18. For more details, see: June T. Dryer, "Language Planning for China's Ethnic Minorities," *Pacific Affairs* 51.3 (Fall 1978), pp. 369-383.
19. Deal, *op. cit.*, p. 199.
20. *Ibid.*; and *Zhongguo shaoshu minzu*, p. 17.
21. *Ibid.*
22. Henry Schwarz, "Policies and Administration of Minority Areas in Northwest China and Inner Mongolia, 1949-1959," (unpublished Ph.D. dissertation, University of Wisconsin, 1963), p. 382.
23. Dreyer, "Language Planning," p. 374
24. John F. DeFrancis, *Nationalism and Language Reform in China* (N.Y.: 1972), pp. 53-54.
25. Henry Schwarz, "Communist Language Policies for China's Ethnic Minorities: the First Decade," *China Quarterly* 12 (Oct.-Dec., 1962), p. 174.
26. Edwin Pak-wah Leung, "Ethnicity and Political Articulation in the PRC," paper presented at the 21st Annual Conference of the American Association for Chinese Studies, California State University, Long Beach (Nov. 1979), p. 5.
27. *Ibid*, p. 6.

28. *Minzu yanjiu* (Nationalities Research) (June 1959), p. 5.
29. *Renmin ribao* (People's Daily), Feb. 15, 1958.
30. *Minzu yanjiu* (June 1959), p. 5.
31. *Ibid.* 4 (1958), p. 6.
32. *Ibid.*
33. Deal, *op. cit.*, p. 201.
34. "Flourishing Development of the Minority Education," *Remin jiaoyu* 208 (1981), p. 6.
35. "Strengthening Minority Nationality Publication Activities," *Minzu tuanjie* 1 (Jan. 1963), as quoted in Deal, *op. cit.*, p. 20
36. John N. Hawkins, "National Minority Education in the PRC," *Comparative Educational Review* 22.1 (Feb. 1978), p. 157.
37. "Actively Foster Teachers of Minority Nationalities," *Survey of Mainland China Press* (SCMP), no.2263 (May 9, 1960), pp. 29-30.
38. *Renmin ribao* (People's Daily), Feb. 17, 1962; *Guangming ribao* (The Bright Daily), August 25, 1960 and May 19, 1961.
39. Hawkins, *op. cit.*, p. 157.
40. "More Schools for Minority People in Northwest China Region," *SCMP*, no.5347 (April 6, 1973), p. 65; and "More Teachers of Minority Nationality for Xinjiang," *SCMP*, no.5598 (April 9, 1974), pp. 27-28.
41. Bi Lu, "Brief Description of the Spoken and Written Languages of China's Minority Nationalities and China's Educational Policy concerning the Institutes of Nationalities," (Paris: UNESCO Paper, 1980), p. 21.
42. Deal, *op. cit.*, p. 190-91.
43. *Beijing Review* (Nov. 17, 1980), p. 8.
44. *Minzu Tuanjie* 6 (1980), p. 11.
45. *Zhongguo shaoshu minzu*, pp. 24 -25.
46. *Ibid.*
47. *Zhongguo baike nianjian* (The Encyclopedia of China, 1980), (Beijing and Shanghai: 1980), p. 547.

18

Transition from De-ethnicization to Re-ethnicization: The Re-emergence of Chinese Ethnic Identity and the Birth of a New Culture in Macao since the Handover

1. Introduction

Anyone engaged in serious studies on the "Macao Handover" issue has un-mistakenly found that the existing research on the subject is focusing primarily on the political and economic aspects. While it is important that the political and economic issues be studied thoroughly, these issues alone however cannot lead to a full understanding of Macao's transition after the Handover. More specifically, while we see a new political superstructure being set up in post-1999 Macao, we also need to deal with the problems associated with the subsequent changes in the infrastructure, particularly with regard to the Macao people's problem of identification, education, and cultural changes as a result of the Handover.

The problem of identification among the Macao Chinese is a serious matter since many of them had been de-ethnicized following the over-400 years of Portuguese colonial rule there, and the Portuguese language was the only official language until as late as 1991. What happened to these Chinese people after the Portuguese departure and the return of Macao's sovereignty to China after 1999?

Unlike some former colonies in other parts of the world, and according to the "One-Nation, Two-System formula", Macao after 1999 has become a Special Administrative Region under the Chinese Central Government. As such, Macao is not having a brand new identity as a new nation like many other former colonies such as India, Malaysia and Singapore (Macao is too small to be independent anyway). Thus, the question of the Macao people's identification will pose a serious problem if not being addressed and handled properly.

2. From De-ethnicization to Re-ethnicization

De-ethnicization occurs in one form or another in any society colonized by others. In the case of Macao, Portuguese had been used for so many years as the only official language, thus having had a great deal of impact on the educational and cultural system. For example, in the schools before 1999, students did not learn much about China, particularly about modern Chinese history and other developments. Students knew very little about the nature of Western imperialism in China, nor did they know the details of the developments in China during the 20th century such as the Revolution of 1911, the Nationalist government, the Communist movement, the Great Leap Forward, the Cultural Revolution, and the Open Door Policy. In other words, the China components were not focused in the Macao school curriculum which, I believe, was a device used by the Portuguese colonial government in Macao to de-ethnicize the Macao Chinese people. Should this situation continue after 1999, it could certainly pose a serious identification problem of the Macao Chinese people to the government of the Macao Special Administrative Region. The solution to the problem is—"re-ethnicization"!

"Re-ethnicization" must include the more popular use of the Chinese language as the medium of instruction in all subjects in the school. Furthermore, there is a need to teach Putonghua or Mandarin Chinese to the Chinese students, so that the people in Macao can communicate with the mainland Chinese after 1999.

"Re-ethnicization" naturally also includes the expansion of the China components in the school curriculum, so that the Chinese students in Macao can learn and get to know more about their motherland's geography, culture, and history. They must be taught that their ethnic roots are in China, not anywhere else. This will definitely foster their sense of identification with China. But I think a major part of "re-ethnicization" is that of fostering and cultivating the sense of Macao's unique identity among the Macao Chinese.

Over the years, the Macao Chinese have developed their own brand of local culture which is an interesting mixture of a lot of cultural elements from South China, from Portugal, from other parts of the world, and most importantly, from their own experiences. This so-called Macao local culture must be respected by the new government after 1999. In fact, I believe the Macao local culture must be vigorously preserved and even promoted in order to win the support of the Macao Chinese. The preservation of local or indigenous culture is a major aspect in terms of ethnic identification. This is quite similar to that of the minority nationalities in China since their languages and cultures have been, according to the Chinese state constitution, legally protected and allowed to stay while accepting the Greater Chinese Culture. Almost in the same fashion, ethnic minorities in the United States of America—including the Chinese Americans—have been included in the recent quest for cultural pluralism across the nation. If a people is not thinking positive about themselves (including their language and culture), we simply cannot talk of any ethnic identity at all.

3. The Birth of a New Macao Culture

The years after 1999 witness the withdrawal of the Portuguese and their influence in Macao, the increase of the Chinese presence and influence there, and the promotion of the Macao ethnicity and identity. These developments have un-mistakenly and collectively helped shape a New Macao Culture. While this New Macao Culture is still in the process of taking shape and is therefore not definitive and conclusive as yet, it appears however that it should contain the following elements:

1. Gradual decline of the Portuguese political as well as cultural influence in Macao;
2. Gradual increase of China's presence and influence in Macao;

3. Preserving and even promoting Macao's local ethnic heritage, including Macao literature and writings with ethnic and local characteristics. This can be seen by the sudden increase in the number of publications on the subject;
4. Discovering the roots of Macao, particularly the local history and folklores of Macao, and that universities (such as the University of Macao and Macao Polytechnic Institute) and high schools must teach this subject; developing a more China-centered Social Studies curriculum in schools;
5. Promoting the use of Chinese as the medium of instruction in school, including the teaching of Putonghua or Mandarin Chinese to students; and
6. A new political culture with more political articulation and participation by the Macao Chinese in the local government, with the new political parties and organizations with new identifications.

4. The Role of Globalization

The discussion of the rise of Macao's New Culture after the Handover is not completed without mentioning the role of globalization and its impact. Globalization in Macao comes with many modern transformations before and after 1999. Over the last twenty years, the city has experienced dramatic transformations in its landscape. These transformations include the burgeoning creation of "modern" space such as glittering high rises with heavy surveillances, Vegas-style resort hotels and casinos, shopping malls, and other types of modern sites and infrastructures.

Many would like to believe that in order for cities to complete under today's global environment, they have to produce iconic architectures and modern infrastructures. Undoubtedly the government of Macao put much effort in the past twenty years to brand the city as modern and global by building various infrastructures. In 1993, a new ferry terminal that was budgeted at 100 million US dollars to attract tourists from Hong Kong commenced operation. In addition, the first international airport in Macao, costing 1.2 billion US dollars, completed its construction in 1995. And the Macao Culture Center, which costs 100 million US dollars, was built in 1999 to provide venue for conferences, exhibitions, and events. Most importantly, after 1999 when Macao was officially handed over to China, the government decided to release gaming licenses to the foreign companies. The idea is to prevent monopoly and globalize Macao as a city.

Macao after 1999, therefore, has thrived to develop and become global and modern by making itself more attractive. While the new modern sites and infrastructures are imagined by Macao locals to provide an entry ticket for Macao into today's global world, the school system and the school curricula must also respond by providing more multi-cultural and multi-lingual methods in educating and producing Macao's new citizens. English as a global language must be taught at least as a subject in all the schools in Macao and should be promoted even more vigorously. Universities in Macao must also engage in more international exchanges with other global universities in order to interact with other cultures and peoples. And the government of Macao must also take the initiative of further promoting cultural activities with other governments of the world while continuing to have interactions with the Chinese motherland.

5. Conclusion

As a former colony of Portugal for over 400 years, Macao has been viewed as one of the first places where West meets East. Today, Macao, with the size of only eleven square miles, strives to become "the other Hong Kong" with the focus of gaming and tourism. The plan to build a Hong Kong-Macao-Zhuhai Bridge, once completed, will definitely help to further enhance the prosperity in the region as well as Macao's global image.

As discussed in this paper, in order to ensure Macao's future development to be on the right track after the Handover, the educational and cultural authorities must follow two directions in order to develop a New Macao Culture supportive of the new political change after 1999. These two directions are as follows:

(I) Re-ethnicization:

(a) Nationalization: China's history, culture, and language must be taught vigorously in school, following the "One-Nation, Two-systems" formula for the people in Macao to identify with the Greater Chinese culture on the national level.

(b) Localization: Macao's local history, heritage, folklores, etc, must be preserved and promoted also in order to generate people's grass-root identification with Macao on the local level.

(II) Globalization:

Re-ethnicization does not conflict with the trend of globalization in Macao. On the contrary, it only enhances the uniqueness of Macao in its role in Sino-Western cultural exchanges by presenting and consolidating the China element/component after the 1999 Handover. The emergence of a new identity and culture will help Macao to advance on the global level in the world arena while furthering its integration with China internally.

We have discussed conceptually the transition of de-ethnicization to re-ethnicization of the Macao Chinese following the Handover. Re-ethnicization is no doubt a necessity since the return of Macao's sovereignty to China in 1999 does not automatically bring an end to the "identification problem" of Macao Chinese and to readily and psychologically accepting China.

However, re-ethnicization must accompany the preservation of the local Macao culture and heritage in order to ensure a smooth and stable transition. The result is that of the emergence of a New Macao Culture, one which reflects the new changes, needs, and realities in Macao while preserving the local heritage.

The emerging New Macao Culture will provide a convenient vehicle in achieving the success of a smooth and stable transition, which will also serve as a new symbol of identity to the Macao Chinese following the Portuguese departure. Expectedly, the transformation will result in producing a new infrastructure and people supportive of the new superstructure as created by the Macao Special Administrative Region.

The New Macao Culture is a powerful force which will pull the Macao people together. This is something China as the motherland should acknowledge and encourage. After all China has initiated the "One-Nation, Two-Systems formula", she should also endorse a more culturally pluralistic and realistic approach in the integration of the Macao Chinese into the mainstream of China.

This paper has attempted to tackle only the conceptual framework of an important subject by providing some guiding principles for future directions. Hopefully my remarks will form the basis of further and larger studies in the near future.

References

1. Arjun Appadurai. *Modernity at Large: Cultural Dimensions of Globalization.* (London: 1996).
2. Joao De Pina-Cabral. *Between China and Europe: Person, Culture and Emotion in Macao.* (London: 2002).
3. Government Information Bureau, Macao SAR, 2008. "Modern Infrastructures." (Dec. 2008).
4. *Macao Daily*
5. Jill McGivering. *Macao Remembers.* (Oxford: 1999).
6. Nicholas Appleton. *Cultural Pluralism in Education: Theoretical Foundations.* (New York: 1983).
7. Andrew Cohen. *A Sociological Approach to Bilingual Education.* (Rowley, MA: 1975).

8. Francesco Cordasco. *Bilingual Schooling in the U.S.: A Source Book for Educational Personnel.* (New York: 1976).
9. *Curriculum Guidelines for Multiethnic Education: Positional Statement.* (National Council for the Social Studies, 1976).
10. Joshua A. Fishman. *Bilingual Education: An International Sociological Perspective.* (Rowley, MA: 1976).
11. Nathan Glazer and Daniel Moynihan. *Beyond the Melting Pot.* (Cambridge, MA: 1964).
12. Milton Gordon. *Assimilation in American Life.* (New York: 1964).
13. William T. Liu. *Methodological Problems in Minority Research.* (Chicago: 1982).

PART V

BOOK REVIEWS

19

Wei Yuan and China's Rediscovery of the Maritime World. By Jane Kate Leonard. [Cambridge, Mass. and London: Harvard University Press, 1984. 276 pp. £17.50.]

In recent years, there has been a growing trend among China scholars to discredit the "western-impact" theory in interpreting modern Chinese history. Some of these China scholars, like Jane Kate Leonard, seek "to understand the Chinese perspective from within" (Wang Gungwu's Foreword, p. xiv). The focus of Leonard's book is on Wei Yuan (1794-1856) and his famous *Treatise of the Sea Kingdoms (Hai-kuo t'u-chih; Haiguo tuzhi).* Challenging the previously accepted view that Wei was one of China's first western-inspired modernizers, Leonard contends that "the *Treatise* was traditionally inspired and conceived," and therefore "Eurocentric interpretive ideals have been inappropriate in assessing Wei and his text" (p. 7).

After careful reading of the *Treatise,* Leonard concludes that Wei Yuan was very much a traditional reformer who sought to restore the underlying strengths in China's historical policies towards Maritime Asia. "Wei's ... appeal for innovative change in the Ch'ing military-naval system," according to Leonard, "were not veiled suggestions to emulate the western approach to maritime relations. They were, on the contrary, purposeful attempts to bring Ch'ing

(Qing) practices more fully into line with traditions in the history of Chinese relations with Maritime Asia—traditions that seemed appropriate to nineteenth-century conditions" (p. 204).

While the book succeeds in presenting Wei Yuan's Nanyang-centered geopolitical perspective of the Maritime World, it fails to show how his views actually affected the reshaping of Ch'ing policies towards South-east Asia. In point of fact, it is doubtful that there was any significant impact that the *Treatise* had brought on the policy-making level. Chapter 8: "Wei Yuan's revision of Ch'ing maritime policy" hardly explains the extent of Wei's influence on the Ch'ing policy decision. Thus, the title of the book under review is misleading; a more accurate title should be: *Wei Yuan's Rediscovery of Maritime Asia.*

Those who are familiar with the history of the Chinese in South-east Asia are quick to point out that one of the key factors contributing to the reshaping of Ch'ing policies towards South-east Asia is that of the influx of Chinese nationals into that region throughout the 19th century. Unfortunately, Leonard's book totally ignores that important aspect.

Nor is the book a biography of Wei Yuan. The description of Wei's life and career is at best sketchy. The book would have been more attractive had there been more details on Wei Yuan, since such a biography in English is still not yet available.

The book however is solidly and painstakingly researched, with major Chinese sources included. Leonard's thesis is both challenging and refreshing—it leads one to think of Wei Yuan more along traditional Chinese lines. As such, the book is an important contribution to the understanding of Chinese history from a Chinese perspective (Paul Cohen labels it the "China-centered" Chinese history).

20

Americans and Chinese Reform and Revolution, 1898-1922: The Role of Private Citizens in Diplomacy. By Key Ray Chong. (Lanham, Md.: University Press of America, 1984. xiii + 308 pp. $24.75 cloth, $13.75 paper)

Recently, a number of scholarly works on early Chinese-American relations have been published. Key Ray Chong's book deals with the involvement of private US citizens in the Chinese reform and revolutionary movements during the period between 1898 and 1922. Original sources, largely from the Joshua B. Powers Collection at the Hoover Institution, have been extensively utilized. The book is carefully researched and solidly documented, even though many relevant Chinese materials have not been consulted. Unfortunately, *Americans and Chinese Reform and Revolution* is more a chronicle of facts than it is an analytical or interpretive study.

The book suffers from several conceptual problems. First, the term "Americans" is not clearly defined by the author. It is obvious that Chinese Americans fall into this category and should have been included in the study. Yung Wing and Sun Yat-sen, while active in the Chinese reform and revolutionary movements, were actually naturalized U.S. citizens. Should they be considered as Chinese or American citizens? A clarification of the meaning of the term "Americans" is therefore needed in order to avoid confusion. Secondly, the book's focus is on Homer Lea, yet Chong includes several other American citizens involved in the Chinese reform and revolutionary movements. The organization of the book would have been considerably improved had the author restricted his focus to Lea alone and provided greater interpretation of Lea's activities. Finally, as the subtitle of the book suggests, this is a study of the role of private citizens in diplomacy. But from an American legal point of view, private citizens involved in diplomacy without authorization from the US government are in violation of the Logan Act (1799). This legal obstacle must be dealt with in order to illustrate the theme of the book.

Although the volume is not especially readable and contains numerous typographical errors, it nonetheless fills an important gap in the historiography of relations between the Chinese and Americans.

21

The Making of a Special Relationship: The United States and China to 1914. By Michael H. Hunt. [New York: Columbia University Press, 1983. 416 pp. $36.00.]

Two hundred years have passed since the First American clipper, *Empress of China,* set sail to China in 1784, and yet the history of Sino-American relations still remains obscure. Tyler Dennett's work (1922) has proved to be unsatisfactory, and despite numerous monographic studies, few successful attempts have been made in treating the history between China and America in a comprehensive and scholarly manner.

Therefore, Michael Hunt's new book is a welcome addition to the field, as it is based firmly on American and Chinese sources. Indeed, many original Chinese materials, such as: *Chung-Mei kuan-hsi shih-liao; Ch'ing-chi wai-chiao shih-liao;* and *Wai-chiao-pu tang-an,* have been used. American sources have been used to even greater effect, as evidenced by the recounting of many hitherto unknown and interesting stories connected with Sino-American relations.

Ending at the outbreak of the First World War, Hunt's book claims to be a research survey which "is a history that rests exclusively on original research at some points, that relies substantially on standard monographs at others, and that at times mixes the two" (p. xi). It appears that reliance on available scholarship outweighs original research, as the book dwells on many already familiar themes: early American trade in China (Chapter 1); Chinese migration and the later American exclusion (Chapters 2, 3, 7); and the Open-Door policy (Chapter 6). The discussion on the Chinese migration to America constitutes a major part of the book, but, as compared with a recent book by Shih-shan Henry Tsai *(China and the Overseas Chinese in the United States, 1868-1911)*, Hunt apparently fails to keep up with the latest works produced by scholars in the field of Asian American studies.

Chapter 4, on "The United States in Li Hung-chang's Foreign Policy, 1879-1895," is original and refreshing, describing how Li tried to use the United States in defending China's tributary states—such as Liu-ch'iu (Ryukyu), Korea and Vietnam—from being annexed by other powers. According to Hunt, Ulysses S. Grant made a three-way split proposal during his mediation in the Sino-Japanese dispute over the Liu-ch'iu Islands (pp. 121-23). It is doubtful, however, that Grant had made such an official and concrete proposal. A check of the sources cited by Hunt (as well as relevant Japanese and Liu-ch'iuan sources) does not seem to support that view.

The major weakness of the book is that it does not pay adequate attention to the cultural and educational interactions between the Chinese and Americans during the period under study. For example, the first group of Chinese government students to America (known as the Chinese Educational Mission led by Yung Wing and Chen Lan-pin), as well as the later Boxer Indemnity

Scholarship students, which could have been used as good cases to illustrate Sino-American cultural relations, are only alluded to in the book without further analysis or interpretation.

The book on the whole is well written. Apart from the "epilogue" (which seems to be out of place), each chapter is painstakingly researched. Each chapter also recounts entertaining and factual stories. But the chapters together fall short in convincing readers that there was indeed a "special relationship" between China and America before 1914. Perhaps there was, but such a view needs to be further elaborated and substantiated.

22

Breaking the Iron Rice Bowl: Prospects for Socialism in China's Countryside. By Pat Howard (Armonk, N. Y.: An East Gate Book of M. E. Sharpe, Inc., 1988. 245 pp.)

China's post-Mao economic reform has been a subject of much interest among scholars. Dorothy Solinger, Gordon White, Christine P.W. Wong and others have provided different interpretations of this new Chinese phenomenon. However, in the words of Pat Howard, since "extensive field research and statistical work .... (have) barely begun ...., it is too early to make definitive judgments or even to draw tentative conclusions." (p. 176)

As such, Howard's book *Breaking the Iron Rice Bowl* is a welcome attempt: it recounts the many controversial interpretations about China's economic reforms (pp. 6-8); it provides a comprehensive coverage on the subject, even though focusing on the period between 1978 and 1985 (Chapters 3-7); and it also provides a new and interesting interpretation on where the Chinese society is heading (Chapter 8).

Based on numerous interviews and research conducted in Yunnan, Sichuan, Fujian, Shanghai and Inner Mongolia, the book questions a common assumption that there is an inherent incompatibility between commodity relations and communal or cooperative values and relations. It seeks to uncover how the reforms may improve the prospects for development of autonomous self-managing producers' collectives.

The interpretation that emerges from the book is that China is heading toward a "Society of Associated Producers," a development which the author believes is "feasible" (p. 175) and "realistic" (p. 176). "In such a society," Howard describes, "urban and rural freely associated producers could include individuals, families, small cooperatives, and larger collectives allied through a range of possible types of cooperation much the same as what has been emerging in China's countryside in recent years." (p. 175)

One must however caution this interpretation, for even Howard admits that "the producers' associations in a society of associated producers *must* have a certain degree of autonomy to freely associate and manage their own affairs *without state interference ....*" (pp. 190-191). If such a condition can not be met by the state, how valid, then, can Howard's interpretation be?

Breaking the Iron Rice Bowl has not properly addressed the political issues involved in China's recent economic reforms. However, the political framework is an essential factor shaping recent as well as future Chinese developments. If the "iron rice bowl" is broken, what about the "rice cooker" (political framework)? Are the new economic policies just like "new wine" in an "old bottle," as in the case of the Self-Strengthening Movement which took place in China a century ago? Clearly, Pat Howard should have paid more attention to the political issues in her treatment of China's recent economic reforms.

A List of Publications by Professor Edwin Pak-wah Leung

I. Publications in English

A. Books/Monographs:

1. (Editor), *Political Leaders of Modern China: A Biographical Dictionary* (Westport, CT: Greenwood Press, 2002)
2. (Author), *Historical Dictionary of the Chinese Civil War* (Lanham, MD: Scarecrow Press, 2002)
3. (Author), *Essentials of Modern Chinese History* (Piscataway, NJ: Research and Education Association, 2006)
4. (Editor), *Historical Dictionary of Revolutionary China, 1839-1976* (Westport, CT: Greenwood Press, 1992)
5. (Editor and Translator), *Ethnic Compartmentalization and Regional Autonomy in the People's Republic of China*, Special Volume of *Chinese Law and Government* XIV. 4 (Winter 1981-1982)
6. (Editor and Contributor), *China and the West: Studies in Education, Nationalism, and Diplomacy,* Special Volume of *Asian Profile* 16.5 (October 1988)
7. (Author), *Adaptability of the Chinese in America: Issues in Culture and Language* (Montclair, NJ: Global Learning Inc., 1989)
8. (Co-editor), *Modern China in Transition: Studies in Honor of Immanuel C. Y. Hsu* (Claremont, CA: Regina Books, 1995)
9. (Co-editor), *Papers of the International Conference on the 50th Anniversary of the War of Resistance* (Chinese-English edition) (Taipei: Academia Historica, 1997)
10. (Author), *The A to Z of the Chinese Civil War* (Lanham, MD: Scarecrow Press, 2010)

11. (Author), *Managing China's Modernization* (Paramus, NJ: Homa & Sekey Books, 2011)

B. Articles:

1. "Li Hung-chang and the Liu-ch'iu (Ryukyu) Controversy, 1871-1881," in Samuel C. Chu and Kwang-ching Liu (eds.) *Li Hung-chang and China's Early Modernization* (Armonk, NY: M.E. Sharpe, 1994), pp. 162-175.
2. "Introduction--Political Leaders of Modern China," in Edwin Pak-wah Leung (ed.) *Political Leaders of Modern China: A Biographical Dictionary* (Westport, CT: Greenwood Press, 2002), pp. xiii-xviii.
3. "Introduction--The Chinese Civil War," in Edwin Pak-wah Leung, *Historical Dictionary of the Chinese Civil War* (Lanham, MD: Scarecrow Press, 2002), pp. xxxi-xli.
4. (Co-author), "Observing a Nation in Transition: Professor Immanuel C.Y. Hsu as a Modern China Observer," in Philip Yuen-sang Leung and Edwin Pak-wah Leung (eds.) *Modern China in Transition: Studies in Honor of Immanuel C.Y. Hsu,* (Claremont, CA: Regina Books, 1995), pp. 1-6.
5. "Jiang Jieshi," in Edwin Pak-wah Leung (ed.) *Political Leaders of Modern China: A Biographical Dictionary* (Westport, CT: Greenwood Press, 2002), pp. 65-67.
6. "The Quasi-war in East Asia: Japan's Expedition to Taiwan and the Ryukyu Controversy," *Modern Asian Studies* (Cambridge University) 17.2 (April 1983), pp. 257-281.
7. "Central Authority vs. Regional Autonomy: The Inner Mongolian Autonomous Movement and the Chinese Response, 1925-1947," *Journal of Oriental Studies* XXV.1 (1987), pp. 49-62.
8. "General Ulysses S. Grant and the Sino-Japanese Dispute over the Ryukyu Islands," *Proceedings of the First International Symposium on Asian Studies*, Vol. II (1979), pp. 421-449.

9. "Chiang Kai-shek, 1887-1975," in *Read More About It: An Encyclopedia of Information Sources on Historical Figures and Events* (Ann Arbor: The Pierian Press, 1989), pp. 111-113.
10. (Co-author) "Chiang Kai-shek," *Funk and Wagnall's New Encyclopedia* Vol. 6 (New York: 1983), pp. 110-111.
11. "China's National Minorities," *Endeavors* (Seton Hall University), I.1 (Spring 1983), pp. 19-20.
12. "Educating China's Minority Nationalities: Integration through Ethnicization," *Proceedings of the 8th International Symposium on Asian Studies,* Vol. II (1986), pp. 309-319.
13. "Education of the Early Chinese Students in America," in Jenny Lim (ed.) *The Chinese American Experience: Proceedings of the 1980 National Conference on Chinese American Studies* (San Francisco: 1984), pp. 203-210.
14. "China's Quest from the West: the Chinese Educational Mission to the United States, 1872-1881," *Asian Profile* 11.6 (December 1983), pp. 527-534.
15. "To Americanize China: the Career of Yung Wing," *Proceedings of the 6th International Symposium on Asian Studies* (1984), pp. 257-267.
16. "The First Chinese College Graduate in America: Yung Wing and his Educational Experiences," in Edwin Pak-wah Leung (ed.) *China and the West: Studies in Education, Nationalism, and Diplomacy,* Special Volume of *Asian Profile* 16.5 (October 1988), pp. 453-458.
17. "The Making of the Chinese Yankees: School Life of the Chinese Educational Mission Studies in New England," in Edwin Pak-wah Leung (ed.) *China and the West: Studies in Education, Nationalism, and Diplomacy,* Special Volume of *Asian Profile* 16.5 (October 1988), pp. 401-412.
18. "China's Decision to send Students to the West: the Making of a 'Revolutionary' Policy," in Edwin Pak-wah Leung (ed.) *China and the West: Studies in Education, Nationalism, and Diplomacy,* Special Volume of *Asian Profile* 16.5 (October 1988), pp. 391-400.

19. "From Prohibition to Protection: Ch'ing Government's Changing Policy toward Chinese Emigration," *Asian Profile* 14.6 (December 1986), pp. 485-491.
20. "The Quest for an Education in America: Chinese Students' Legal Battle and the Supreme Court's Decision," *The Courier: Journal of International Affairs* 11.2 (Spring 1983), pp. 22-26.
21. "Transition from De-ethnicization to Re-ethnicization: The Reemergence of Chinese Ethnic Identity and the Birth of a New Culture in Hong Kong prior to 1997," *Hong Kong in Transition* (Hong Kong: One Country Two Systems Economic Research Institute, 1993), pp. 594-603.
22. "Review Article: the Politics of Chinese Communism during the Kiangsi Period," *Asian Profile* 7.4 (August 1979), pp. 389-393.
23. (Co-author), "Developing China's Market Economy," *Business Opportunities Journal* (Fall/Winter 1994), p. 50.
24. "Paris and the Revolution in France, 1815-1830," *Historical Studies* (Hong Kong), 7 (October 1971), pp. 36-45.
25. "An Organizational Approach to the Study of the English Privy Council, 1540-1630," *Historical Studies* (Hong Kong), 8 (Jan. 1973), pp. 24-30.
26. "Teaching Chinese History and Culture: A Bilingual Method," *Proceedings of the 17th Annual Conference of the Association of Chinese Schools* (December 1990), p. 31.
27. (Abstract) "The Quasi-war in East Asia: Japan's Expedition to Taiwan and the Ryukyu Controversy," *The Ryukyuanist* (Newsletter of the International Society for Ryukyuan Studies), 11 (Winter 1991), pp. 5-6.
28. "Book Review: Jane Leonard, Wei Yuan and China's Rediscovery of the Maritime World," *China Quarterly* 108 (December 1986), pp. 736-737.
29. "Book Review: Key Ray Chong, Americans and Chinese Reform and Revolution, 1898-1922: The Role of Private Citizens in Diplomacy," *Pacific Historical Review* (May 1986), pp. 328-329.

30. "Book Review: Michael Hunt, The Making of a Special Relationship: The United States and China to 1914" *China Quarterly* 98 (1984), pp. 367-368.
31. "Book Review: Pat Howard, Breaking the Iron Rice Bowl: Prospect for Socialism in China's Countryside," *Asian Thought and Society: An International Review* XV.44 (May 1990), pp. 333-334.
32. "Liuqiu Islands," in David Pong (ed.) *Encyclopedia of Modern China*, Vol. 2 (New York: Charles Scribner's Sons, 2009), p. 522.
33. "Transition from De-ethnicization to Re-ethnicization: The Re-emergence of Chinese Ethnic Identity and the Birth of a New Culture in Macao since the Handover," in Heong Iok Lei (ed.) *Macao's Ten Years since the Handover*. Vol. III (Macao: Macao Polytechnic Institute, 2009), pp. 267-274.

II. Publications in Chinese (中文著作):

A. Books / Monographs (書籍) :

1. 《正義的天使張純如》 (武漢 ： 湖北人民出版社, 2010 年)
2. 《全球化下中西文化的交流: 回顧與前瞻》 (澳門：澳門理工學院, 2008 年)
3. 《近代中國在世界的崛起》 (武漢 ： 武漢大學出版社, 2006 年)
4. 《近代中國外交的巨變—外交制度與中外關係變化的研究》 (香港 ： 商務印書館, 1990 年)
5. 《近代中國外交的巨變—外交制度與中外關係的研究》 (台灣版) (台北 ： 台灣商務印書館, 1991 年)
6. 《抗戰勝利五十週年國際研討會論文集》 (合編) (台北 ： 國史館, 1997 年)
7. 《複製成功的魔法》 (香港 ： 匯訊出版有限公司, 2003 年)
8. 《順逆境自強》 (合著) (香港 ： 天地圖書有限公司, 2000 年)
9. 《中大人在紐約—香港中文大學美東校友會千禧文集》 (合編) (香港 ： 天地圖書有限公司, 2001 年)
10. 《美國大學升學指南》 (香港 ： 中華書局, 1996 年)
11. 《美國大學升學指南》 (中國大陸版) (成都 ： 四川大學出版社, 1997 年)
12. 《美國大學升學指南》 (台灣版) (台北 ： 書林出版有限公司, 1997 年)
13. 《美國大學獎助學金手冊》 (香港 ： 中華書局, 1998 年)
14. 《美國大學獎助學金手冊》 (中國大陸版) (成都 ： 西南財經大學出版社, 1998 年)

15. 《經濟環境》 (浙江大學—香港理工大學國際企業培訓中心企業管理學高級文憑教材) (香港 ： 香港理工大學, 1998 年)
16. 《國際商業貿易》 (浙江大學—香港理工大學國際企業培訓中心企業管理學高級文憑教材) (香港 ： 香港理工大學, 1999 年)

B. Articles (論文) :

1. "華人的全球意識—中西文化整合的反思", 《人文論叢》 (武漢大學) 2002 年卷, 頁 125 – 129
2. "台灣事件的真相與中日琉球爭端的反案", 李金強等編 ： 《我武維揚 ： 近代中國海軍史新編》 (香港 ： 香港海防博物館, 2004 年), 頁 222 – 231
3. "李鴻章和琉球爭端, 1871 – 1881 年", 劉廣京及朱昌峪合編, 陳絳譯校 ： 《李鴻章評傳》 (上海 ： 古籍出版社, 1995 年), 頁 198 – 214
4. "台灣事件與琉球問題的關係", 黃康顯主編 ： 《近代台灣的社會發展與民族意識》 (香港 ： 香港大學校外課程部, 1987 年), 頁 237 – 251
5. "容閎的西學與洋務", 《中國文化研究所學報》 (香港中文大學) 第十六卷 (1985 年), 頁 43 – 52
6. "中外學者對 [留美幼童] 研究的成果", 《六十年來中國近代史研究》 (下冊) (台北南港 ： 中央研究院近代史研究所, 1989 年), 頁 719 - 729
7. "歐美學者對容閎與留美幼童研究的成果", 《社會科學動態》 (湖北省社會科學院圖書情報中心) (1989 年 10 月號), 頁 39– 41

8. "中國首批官費留學生：廣東的 [留美幼童]", 鄭良樹主編：《潮州學國際研討會論文集》 (下冊) (廣州：暨南大學出版社, 1994 年), 頁 763 – 774
9. "容閎的西學與中國的現代化", 吳文萊主編：《容閎與中國近代化》 (珠海：珠海出版社, 1999 年), 頁 307 – 322
10. "學人專訪—郭穎頤教授", (合著) 《漢學研究通訊》 卷七第三期 (1988 年九月), 頁 148 – 152
11. "王德昭教授與近代中國史研究", 《中報月刊》 總第 40 期 (1983 年 五 月), 頁 88 – 89
12. "悼念德昭師", 《史潮》 (香港中文大學聯合書院歷史學會) 新刊號 第 八 期 (1982 年 11 月), 頁 4
13. "歷史論文的寫作" (整理王德昭教授演講), 《王德昭教授史學論集》 (香港：《王德昭教授史學論集》 編輯委員會, 1985 年), 頁 52 – 58
14. "論中國的傳統政體—中外學者對中國傳統政體是否專制的論爭",《史潮》 (香港中文大學聯合書院歷史學會) 第 五、六 期合刊 (1970 年 八 月), 頁 16 – 21, 35
15. "洋務運動期間滿清外交政策轉變的審榷" 《史潮》 (香港中文大學聯合書院歷史學會) 第 七 期 (1971 年 10 月), 頁 7 – 24
16. "辛亥革命與新軍—關於革命份子獲取軍力的途徑與辛亥革命成敗之關係", 《史潮》 (香港中文大學聯合書院歷史學會) 第 八 期 (1973 年 1 月), 頁 1 – 3
17. "追求中國現代化—談近代中國知識份子的思想傾向", 《聯合學生報》 (香港中文大學聯合書院) 第 55 期 (1971 年 6 月), 頁 1

18. "書評 : Michael Gasster, Chinese Intellectuals and The Revolution of 1911: The Birth of Modern Chinese Radicalism", 《歷史學報》 (香港中文大學 聯合書院歷史學會) 第 二 期 (1973 年 5 月), 頁 25 – 28
19. "學術大觀園隨想", 梁伯華等主編 : 《中大人在紐約》 (香港 : 天地圖書 有限公司, 2001 年), 頁 1 - 6
20. "九一一的文明衝突震撼", 《中大校友》 (香港中文大學) 第 28 期 (2001 年 12 月), 頁 8 – 9
21. "教授夢 · 我的夢", 《中大美東校友通訊》 創刊號 (1994 年 11 月), 頁 7
22. "一個香港人在北京—北大講學隨想", 《海外香港協會會刊》 (2002 年), 頁 22
23. "璀璨多姿的中國多元文化", 《李文斯頓中文學校二十週年校慶特刊》 (2003 年), 頁 7
24. "李帆的世界" (序言), 李帆編著 : 《紐約華僑奮鬥成功錄》 (紐約 : 李帆工作室, 1995 年), 頁 3
25. "申請大學獎助學金的書籍 . 軟件 . 網址及諮詢熱線", 《漢新月刊》 (美國新澤西州) 第 77 期 (1998 年 1 月), 頁 22 – 23
26. "社會與人際關係的網絡", 《美華專業人士協會會刊》 (1997 年), 頁 5
27. "複製一個成功的你", 《戰國策商業月刊》 (香港) 第一期 (2002 年 8 月), 頁 100 – 104
28. "柯維的企業領導成功術", 《戰國策商業月刊》 第二 期 (2002 年 9 月), 頁 106 – 109
29. "柯維的 [時間管理] 成功術", 《戰國策商業月刊》 第三期 (2002 年 10 月), 頁 104 – 107

30. "希爾的創富成功學", 《戰國策商業月刊》 第四期 (2002 年 11 月), 頁 108 – 111
31. "希爾的成功致富術", 《戰國策商業月刊》 第五期 (2002 年 12 月), 頁 108 – 111
32. "希爾的積極心態成功學", 《戰國策商業月刊》 第六期 (2003 年 1 月), 頁 108 – 111
33. "激發心靈潛力成功術", 《戰國策商業月刊》 第七期 (2003 年 2 月), 頁 102 – 105
34. "卡耐基走向成功的心理致勝術", 《戰國策商業月刊》 第八期 (2003 年 3 月), 頁 108 – 111
35. "卓巴的成功心靈魔法", 《戰國策商業月刊》 第九期 (2003 年 4 月), 頁 102 – 105
36. "贏家致勝的談吐成功術", 《戰國策商業月刊》 第十期 (2003 年 5 月), 頁 110 – 113
37. "人際關係與社會網絡的致勝成功術", 《戰國策商業月刊》 第十一期 (2003 年 6 月), 頁 114 – 117
38. "複製成功的魔法", 《戰國策商業月刊》 第十二期 (2003 年 7 月), 頁 114 –117

(附註: 梁伯華教授另撰有逾百篇各類文章, 散見於各大報章, 期刊及雜誌。)

Sources of Articles That Appeared in This Book

By Edwin Pak-wah Leung

I. Diplomacy and Territorial Integrity

1. "The Quasi-war in East Asia: Japan's Expedition to Taiwan and the Ryukyu Controversy," *Modern Asian Studies*, 17.2 (April 1983), 257-281.
2. "Li Hung-chang and the Liu-ch'iu (Ryukyu) Controversy, 1871-1881," in Samuel C. Chu and Kwang-ching Liu, eds., *Li Hung-chang and China's Modernization* (Armonk, NY: M. E. Sharpe, 1994), 162-175.
3. "General Ulysses S. Grant and the Sino-Japanese Dispute over the Liu-ch'iu (Ryukyu) Islands," *Proceedings of the First International Symposium on Asian Studies*, Vol. II (1979), 421-449.
4. "From Prohibition to Protection: Ch'ing Government's Changing Policy toward Chinese Emigration," *Asian Profile*, 14.6 (December 1986), 485-491.

II. Politics and Leadership

5. "The Characteristics of Political Leaders in Modern China," Introduction of Edwin Pak-wah Leung, ed., *Political Leaders of Modern China: A Biographical Dictionary* (Westport, CT: Greenwood Press, 2002).

6. "Chiang Kai-shek, 1887-1975," in *Read More About It: An Encyclopedia of Information Sources on Historical Figures and Events* (Ann Arbor: The Pierian Press, 1989), 111-113.
7. "The Politics of Chinese Communism during the Kiangsi Period, 1931- 1934," *Asian Profile*, 7.4 (August 1979), 389-393.
8. "The Chinese Civil War: Microscopic and Macroscopic Perspectives," Introduction of Edwin Pak-wah Leung, ed., *Historical Dictionary of the Chinese Civil War* (Lanham, MD: Scarecrow Press, 2002).

III. Education and Modernization

9. "China's Decision to Send Students to the West: the Making of a 'Revolutionary' Policy," in Edwin Pak-wah Leung, ed., *China and the West: Studies in Education, Nationalism and Diplomacy*, Special Volume of *Asian Profile*, 16.5 (October 1988), 391-400.
10. "The First Chinese College Graduate in America: Yung Wing and his Educational Experiences," *Asian Profile*, 16.5 (October 1988), 453-458.
11. "China's Quest from the West: the Chinese Educational Mission to the United States, 1872-1881," *Asian Profile*, 11.6 (December 1983), 527-534.
12. "The Making of the Chinese Yankees: School Life of the Chinese Educational Mission Students in New England," *Asian Profile*, 16.5 (October 1988), 401-412.
13. "The Quest for an Education in America: Chinese Students' Legal Battle and the Supreme Court's Decision," *The Courier: Journal of International Affairs* 11.2 (Spring 1983), 22-26.

IV. Ethnicity and National Integration

14. "Regional Autonomy versus Central Authority: The Inner Mongolian Autonomous Movement and the Chinese Response, 1925-1947," *Journal of Oriental Studies* XXV.1 (1987), 49-62.
15. "China's Minority Nationalities under Communism," *Endeavors* I.1 (Spring 1983), 19-20.
16. "Ethnic Compartmentalization and Regional Autonomy in the People's Republic of China," Introduction of Edwin Pak-wah Leung, ed., *Ethnic Compartmentalization and Regional Autonomy in the People's Republic of China*, Special Volume of *Chinese Law and Government* XIV.4 (Winter 1981-82).
17. "Educating China's Minority Nationalities: Integration through Ethnicization," *Proceedings of the 8th International Symposium on Asian Studies*, Vol. II (1986), 309-319.
18. "Transition from De-ethnicization to Re-ethnicization: the Reemergence of Chinese Ethnic Identity and the Birth of a New Culture in Macao since the Handover," in Heong Iok Lei (ed.) *Macao's Ten Years since the Handover*. Vol. III (Macao: Macao Polytechnic Institute, 2009), 267-274.

V. Book Reviews

19. "Jane Leonard, WEI YUAN AND CHINA'S REDISCOVERY OF THE MARITIME WORLD," *The China Quarterly* 108 (December 1986), 736-737.
20. "Key Ray Chong, AMERICANS AND CHINESE REFORM AND REVOLUTION, 1898-1922: THE ROLE OF PRIVATE

CITIZENS IN DIPLOMACY," *Pacific Historical Review* 55 (May 1986), 328-329.

21. "Michael H. Hunt, THE MAKING OF A SPECIAL RELATIONSHIP: THE UNITED STATES AND CHINA TO 1914," *The China Quarterly* 98 (1984), 367-368.
22. "Pat Howard, BREAKING THE IRON RICE BOWL: PROSPECTS FOR SOCIALISM IN CHINA'S COUNTRYSIDE," *Asian Thought and Society: An International Review* XV.44 (May 1990), 333-334.

INDEX

Homa & Sekey Books Titles on China

THE LEGEND OF HAIBAO SERIES
(Paperback, All color, Cartoon/Comics)
The Legend of Haibao 1: The Myth of the Crystal Palace, Order No 1067, ISBN: 9781931907637, 96p, $14.95
The Legend of Haibao 2: A Journey of the Gourmet, Order No 1068, ISBN: 9781931907644, 96p, $14.95
The Legend of Haibao 3: Meeting Friends from Afar, Order No 1069, ISBN: 9781931907651, 96p, $14.95
The Legend of Haibao 4: A Journey through Space, Order No 1070, ISBN: 9781931907668, 96p, $14.95

Folk Culture in China's Zhejiang Province: The Flowing Mother River by Tong Shaosu, trans. by Yu Jianqing and Shen Mingxia. Order No 1066, ISBN: 9781931907620, Paperback, 216p, Color illustrations throughout, $29.95, Culture/History

The History of Chinese Printing by Zhang Xiumin, revised by Dr. Han Qi, trans. by Chen Jiehua et al. Order No 1065, ISBN: 9781931907613, Paperback, 550p, Color illustrations throughout, Limited edition, History

EDUCATION IN CHINA SERIES (Hardcover)
Educational System in China by Ming Yang. Order No 1060, ISBN: 9781931907569, 410p
Educational Policies and Legislation in China by Xiaozhou Xu et al. Order No 1061, ISBN: 9781931907576, 275p
Basic Education in China by Libing Wang. Order No 1062, ISBN: 9781931907583, 147p
Higher Education in China by Jianmin Gu et al. Order No 1063, ISBN: 9781931907590, 227p
Technical and Vocational Education in China by Xueping Wu et al. Order No 1064, ISBN: 9781931907606, 283p

Seven Kinds of Mushrooms: A Novel of the Cultural Revolution by Zhang Wei, trans. by Terence Russell. Order No. 1059, ISBN: 9781931907552, Paperback, 214p, $16.95, Fiction

Homa & Sekey Books Titles on China

Two Lifetimes: A Novel by Joanne Guo. Order No. 1058, ISBN: 9781931907545, Paperback, 242p, $16.95, Fiction

The Art of Mogao Grottoes in Dunhuang: A Journey into China's Buddhist Shrine by Fan Jinshi & Zhao Shengliang. Order No. 1057, ISBN: 9781931907538, Paperback, 172p, Color illustrations throughout, $29.95, Art, Buddhism

Everything I Understand About America I Learned in Chinese Proverbs by Wendy Liu. Order No. 1056, ISBN: 9781931907521, Paperback, 173p, $16.95, Social Studies

From Ironing Board to Corporate Board: My Chinese Laundry Experience in America by Ginny Gong. Order No. 1054, ISBN: 9781931907507, Paperback, 151p, $12.95, Asian-American

September's Fable: A Novel by Zhang Wei, trans. by Terrence Russell & Shawn X. Ye. Order No 1050, ISBN: 9781931907460, Paperback, 495p, $29.95, Fiction

The Bitter Sea: "Morphing" and Other Stories by David Ke, PhD. Order No 1048, ISBN: 9781931907446, Paperback, 226p, $16.95, Fiction/Asian Studies

Journey across the Four Seas: A Chinese Woman's Search for Home by Veronica Li. Order No: 1047, ISBN: 9781931907439, Paperback, 298p, with b&w photo inserts, $14.95, Nonfiction/Memoir

The Holy Spark: Rogel and the Goddess of Liberty by Yu Li. Order No 1046, ISBN 9781931907422, Hardcover, 260p, b&w illustrations throughout, $16.99, Fiction/Children

Willow Leaf, Maple Leaf: A Novel of Immigration Blues by David Ke, PhD. Order No 1036, ISBN: 9781931907248, Paperback, 203p, $16.95, Fiction/Asian-American Studies

Homa & Sekey Books Titles on China

China's Generation Y: Understanding the Future Leaders of the World's Next Superpower (with b&w photo inserts) by Michael Stanat, United Nations International School.
Order No 1029, ISBN 9781931907255, Hardcover, 222p, $24.95;
Order No 1040, ISBN 9781931907323, Paperback, 222p, $17.95, Contemporary Affairs

Paintings by Xu Jin: Tradition and Innovation in Chinese Fine Brushwork, foreword by Prof. Robert E. Harrist, Jr., Columbia University. Order No 1028, ISBN 9781931907231, Hardcover, 128p, Color illustrations throughout, $39.50, Art

The Eleventh Son: A Novel of Martial Arts and Tangled Love by Gu Long, trans. by Rebecca S. Tai. Order No. 1020, ISBN: 9781931907163, Paperback, 320p, $19.95, Fiction/Martial Arts

Breaking Grounds: The Journal of a Top Chinese Woman Manager in Retail by Bingxin Hu, Foreword by Louis B. Barnes, Harvard Business School. Order No 1019, ISBN: 9781931907156, Hardcover, 256p, with b&w photo inserts, $24.95, Business

The Dream of the Red Chamber: An Allegory of Love
by Jeannie Jinsheng Yi, PhD.
Order No 1016, ISBN: 9780966542172, Hardcover, b&w illustrations throughout, $49.95, Asian Studies/Literary Criticism

The Haier Way: The Making of a Chinese Business Leader and a Global Brand by Jeannie J. Yi, PhD & Shawn X. Ye, MBA. Order No 1009, ISBN: 9781931907019, Hardcover, 280p, with b&w photo inserts, $24.95, Business

Splendor of Tibet: The Potala Palace, Jewel of the Himalayas by Phuntsok Namgyal. Order No 1008, ISBN: 9781931907026, Hardcover, 160p, $39.95, Art/Architecture

Ink Paintings by Gao Xingjian, the Nobel Prize Winner
Order No 1007, ISBN: 9781931907033, Hardcover, 92p, $34.95, Art

Homa & Sekey Books Titles on China

Musical Qigong: Ancient Chinese Healing Art from a Modern Master by Shen Wu. Order No 1006, ISBN: 9780966542158, Paperback, 160p, b&w photo and illustrations throughout, $14.95, Body-Mind, Self-help

Always Bright, Vol. II: Paintings by Chinese American Artists edited by Eugene Wang, Harvard Univ., et al. Order No 1005, ISBN: 9780966542165, Hardcover, 208p, $50.00, Art

Always Bright: Paintings by American Chinese Artists 1970-1999 edited by Xue Jian Xin et al. Order No 1004, ISBN: 9780966542134, Hardcover, 180p, $49.95, Art

Butterfly Lovers: A Tale of the Chinese Romeo and Juliet by Fan Dai, PhD. Order No 1003, ISBN: 9780966542141, Paperback, 256p, $16.95, Fiction

The Peony Pavilion: A Novel by Xiaoping Yen, PhD. Order No 1002, ISBN: 9780966542127, Paperback, 256p, $16.95, Fiction

Flower Terror: Suffocating Stories of China by Pu Ning, trans. by Richard Ferris, Jr. & Andrew Morton. Order No 1001, ISBN: 9780966542103, Paperback, 256p, $13.95, Fiction

www.homabooks.com

ORDERING INFORMATION: U.S.: $5.00 for the first item, $1.50 for each additional item. **Outside U.S.**: $14.00 for the first item, $7.00 for each additional item. All major credit cards accepted. You may also send a check or money order in U.S. fund (payable to Homa & Sekey Books) to: Orders Department, Homa & Sekey Books, P. O. Box 103, Dumont, NJ 07628 U.S.A. Tel: 800-870-HOMA; 201-261-8810. Fax: 201-384-6055; 201-261-8890. Email: info@homabooks.com